ISBN: 9781313630269

Published by:
HardPress Publishing
8345 NW 66TH ST #2561
MIAMI FL 33166-2626

Email: info@hardpress.net
Web: http://www.hardpress.net

IN PERIL OF CHANGE

IN PERIL OF CHANGE

ESSAYS WRITTEN IN TIME OF TRANQUILLITY

BY

C. F. G. MASTERMAN, M.A.

FELLOW OF CHRIST'S COLLEGE, CAMBRIDGE

"*We cannot but acknowledge that we are not yet at rest: nor can we believe we have yet enjoyed or seen enough to accomplish the ends of God.*"
THE PARLIAMENT TO THE PEOPLE OF ENGLAND, 1653

NEW YORK
B. W. HUEBSCH
150 NASSAU STREET

To

NOEL BUXTON

IN MEMORY OF TEN YEARS OF FRIENDSHIP

AND EFFORT IN A COMMON CAUSE.

PREFACE

THE essays in this book represent an effort made in a time of tranquillity, to estimate forces which are making for change. Some are attempts to examine the ideals of the age immediately past, as one by one the voices of the nineteenth century have sunk into silence. Some deal with the life of the present, endeavouring to reflect some immediate impression of the panorama of life as it passes by. And some are concerned with the future, seeking to interpret, in literature, in religion, in social ideals, those obscure beginnings which are to direct the progress of the years to come.

In every case I have been less interested in the manner of saying than in the thing said. Literature has only been called in to pronounce its verdict upon the business of life. It is this business of life, the experience of a hurrying present, which is the one absorbing question : the actual high effort, apathy or despair crowded into that interval when to-morrow is becoming yesterday. To some the procession passes as a pageant, to others as a masquerade, to others again as a funeral march with the sound of solemn music. But to all in that moment a world has perished, a world been born.

PREFACE

If the note is in general sombre, with the sadness of things more emphatic than their splendour, I can only plead an experience more than usually complex and baffling, spent in communication less with the triumphs of civilisation than with its failures.

Expectancy and surprise are the notes of the age. Expectancy belongs by nature to a time balanced uneasily between two great periods of change. On the one hand is a past still showing faint survivals of vitality; on the other is the future but hardly coming to birth. The years as they pass still appear as years of preparation, a time of waiting rather than a time of action. Surprise, again, is probably the first impression of all who look on, detached from the eager traffic of man. The spectator sees him performing the same antics in the same grave fashion as in all the past: heaping up wealth which another shall inherit, following pleasure which turns to dust in the mouth, and the end weariness: thinking, as always, that he will endure for ever, and calling after his own name the place which shall know him no more. But surprise passes into astonishment in confronting the particular and special features of the age. Here is a civilisation becoming ever more divorced from Nature and the ancient sanities, protesting through its literature a kind of cosmic weariness. Society which had started on its mechanical advance and the aggrandisement of material goods with the buoyancy of an impetuous life confronts a poverty which it can neither ameliorate nor destroy, and an organised discontent which may yet prove the end of the Western civilisation. Faith in the invisible seems dying, and faith in the visible is proving inadequate to the hunger of the soul. The city state, concentrated in such a centre as London,

PREFACE

remains as meaningless and as impossible to co-ordinate with any theory of spiritual purposes as the law of gravitation itself.

Experience in the heart of such a universe of necessity takes upon itself a character of bewilderment. Those whom I loved have died: and the miracle of their parting has seemed more strange than the miracle of their presence. I have seen so many sunsets, so many radiant dawns. This man has failed and that succeeded, and both have grown tired of it all. "What right have I to grieve," as Thoreau said, "who have not ceased to wonder?"

And I think that I am not alone in longing for a time when literature will once more be concerned with life, and politics with the welfare of the people: and religion fall back again upon reality: and pity and laughter return into the common ways of men.

CONTENTS

CONTENTS

AFTER THE REACTION

"Yea, if no morning must behold
Man, other than were they now cold,
    And other deeds than past deeds done,
    Nor any near or far-off sun
Salute him risen and sunlike-souled,
    Free, boundless, fearless, perfect, one,

Let man's world die like worlds of old,
    And here in heaven's sight only be
    The sole sun on the worldless sea."
                                —SWINBURNE.

AFTER THE REACTION

LITERATURE as detached as is the literature of to-day from the middle and working classes, the unconscious rulers of England, would appear to be independent of the actual processes of political and social change. A few vigorous story-tellers, a group of writers of pleasant verse, some young and clever journalists, will initiate a literary " movement "; which will take itself seriously, parade a pomp and circumstance, and continue until the respectabilities of advancing age, and often, alas! the revelations of a failing inspiration, have once again demonstrated the triumph of time and change. Yet this emphasis of aloofness is not the whole truth. Literature, indeed, has no direct concern with the dust of the party struggle, with bills of licensing or local government. But the larger transitions of the period, the spirit which underlies some definite upheaval, whose appearance in the world of action astonishes the un-thinking, is certain to find itself first articulate in the universe of art. Estimate in that universe a vital move-ment of revolt from some accepted tradition or ideal; you will be estimating a force which in no long time is destined to enter into the play of outward affairs and to mould the courses of the world.

No better example could be advanced than the history

3

of the Reaction in the later years of the nineteenth century. Weary of the long effort of reform, a little bored by the strenuousness of the appeal to disinterested causes, conscious of the possession of unparalleled means of enjoyment, and of great possessions, the nation was evidently prepared for a new spirit, a new inspiration. That spirit and inspiration came with the Reaction; whose literature some fifteen years ago revealed the only confident and secure proclamation of any kind of definite appeal. As the former enthusiasms subsided and the former systems were found unsatisfying; as, in a word, the new England disentangled itself from the old; so the message proclaimed by a few men of genius, and diffused through a thousand obscure channels in Press and platform, became suddenly arresting: and now stands crystallised as the product characteristic of those extraordinary years.

The contrast was glaring between the literature of the earlier Victorian era and the literature of the closing days. The old had been cosmopolitan. The new was Imperial. The old had proclaimed the glory of the "one imperishable cause," allied through all lands; the struggle for liberty against the accumulated atheisms of a dozen centuries. The new was frankly Tory; with the Tory scoffing at the futilities of freedom, described now as a squalid uprising of the discontented against their masters. The old had been "Liberal"; in that wide definition including such extremes as a Browning and a Tennyson. The new branded Liberalism as but a gigantic fraud by which the weak deluded the strong into an abnegation of their natural domination. The old had been humanitarian; preaching, if with a somewhat thick voice, yet with a sanguine air, the coming of the golden age. War would be abandoned as irrational.

AFTER THE REACTION

A free and universal trade would bind the nations into one brotherhood. The sweet reasonableness of the English character would shine forth its radiance through all the envious nations of the world. The new had no such hopes or dreams. It revolted always against the domination of the bourgeois. It estimated commerce as a means of conflict and a weapon of offence. It clamoured for the ancient Barbarism; and delighted in war; and would spread an English civilisation, not by the diffusion of its ideas but by the destruction of its enemies. It was a message of vigour and revolt congruous to a nation wearied of the drabness of its uniform successes; with the dissatisfaction and vague restlessness which come both to individuals and communities after long periods of order and tranquillity. To the friends of progress the dominance of such a spirit seemed of the elements of tragedy. Literature, after its long alliance with the party of reform, had deliberately deserted to the enemy. In the minds of the few faithful the dismay was somewhat similar to that aroused in the defenders of the inviolate city, when the Shekinah departed from the courts of the temple and passed over to the camp of its foes.

This new spirit of the Reaction gathered itself especially round two men, each possessing more than a touch of genius—Mr. W. E. Henley and Mr. Rudyard Kipling. Mr. Henley's denunciation of the accepted codes of life, the thirst for blood and violence of one physically debarred from adventure, became reflected in a hundred eager followers, who plied the axe and hammer of sneer and gibe round the humanitarian ideal and the house of the good citizen. Mr. Kipling's proclamation of the Imperial race co-operating with God in the bloody destruction of alien peoples was interpreted into the commonplaces of a journalism demanding above all things sensation. The toiler of the cities in his life of grey monotony, labouring for another's wealth, found existence suddenly slashed with crimson. And every morning the astonished clerk was exalted by the intelligence of his devastation of Afghanistan, or civilisation of Zanzibar, or slaughter of ten thousand fantastic Dervishes in a night and a day.

It was a literature of the security of a confident triumph; with that quality which distinguishes the work of a dawn from the work of a declining day. Its appeal was to enduring elements of human emotion. It proclaimed the supremacy of England, a mother, worth dying and living for; her children seeking danger as a bride, searching all the confines of the world; encountering and joyfully mastering enemies and natural forces, the winds and the seas and the terrors of elemental things. There were visions of ships steering through deep waters and harvests gathered from all seas; of the pioneers whose bones have marked the track for the advancing army that this might follow where these had trod; of the flag of England descried amid mist and cold or under the Southern sun as everywhere triumphant by the testimony of all the winds of heaven. It was a literature of intoxication; adequate to a nation which, having conquered the world in a fit of absence of mind, had suddenly become conscious of the splendour of its achievement. Small wonder that to the eyes of the men of the time there came with it something of the force of a gospel; as the boundaries of their thought lifted to disclose larger horizons than they had ever known.

It was a literature, on the other hand, of a rather forced ferocity; of an academic enthusiasm for the noise and trappings of war; the work of men who despised death because there was present in their minds, not death as a reality but only death as an idea. It preached a boastful insularity; with a whole-hearted contempt for disloyal Ireland or the cretins of the continent. The Briton was revealed to himself, a majestic figure, lord of the earth, who, with the approbation of God, but by the power of his own right arm, had gotten himself the victory. It presented a figure of the Imperial race, like Nietzsche's Overman, trampling over the ineffective, crushing opposing nations, boasting an iron supremacy, administering an iron justice. It thought scorn of all the ideals of philanthropy of the middle classes, with their timidities and reticence and dull routine; of the poor with the clumsiness of their ineffectual squalor. "More chops, bloody ones with gristle,"—so a critic has summed up in Mr. Kipling's own words, his demand from life. It neglected and despised the ancient pieties of an older England, the little isle set in its silver sea. Greatness became bigness; specific national feeling parochial. Imperial Destiny replaced national well-being; and men were no longer asked to pursue the "just" course, but to approve the "inevitable."

The thing lasted only so long as it could keep divorced from real things and confined to its world of illusion. While British wars consisted of battues of blacks, with the minimum of loss and pain to ourselves, the falsity of the atmosphere of Mr. Kipling's battle tales was undiscoverable. The blind and gibbering maniac at the end of "The Light that Failed," who shrieks, "Give 'em Hell, men, oh, give 'em Hell," from the security of an armoured train, while his companions annihilate their enemies by pressing the button of a machine gun, seemed not only a possible but even a reputable figure. The sport of such " good hunting " —" the lordliest life on earth "—was not recounted by the historian of the hunted, the tribes of the hills whose land was laid desolate and wells choked up and palm-trees cut down and villages destroyed, who were joyfully butchered to make an Imperial holiday. Their verdict upon such " hunting " might have been less exuberant. As Newman said in his defence of Catholics in England, " Lions would have fared better, had lions been the artists."

With the outbreak of real war and some apprehension of its meaning the spell snapped. Directly Mr. Kipling commenced to write of the actual conflict in South Africa, the note suddenly jarred and rang false. His judgment was found to be concerned not with war but with the idea of war ; the conception in the brain of a journalist. The jauntiness and cocksureness, the surface swagger, were suddenly confronted with realities ;— Death and Loss and Longing. " There was a good killing at Paardeberg ; the first satisfactory killing of the whole war " ;—this attitude immediately disclosed its essential vulgarity ; a grimace from the teeth out-wards ; war as viewed from Capel Court or Whitechapel, or any other place where men are noisy and impotent. Real war gave indeed a revelation of high sacrifice, the coming of the " fire of Prometheus " into the common ways of men ; flaming up under the stress of a vast upheaval in the conflict of life and of death. It was not given to the Apostles of the New Imperialism to estimate or even to understand those deeper tides of the human soul. Their conception was of war carried on in the spirit of the music-hall comedy ; the men at the close of the struggle wiping their hands which have successfully gouged out the eyes of their enemies, while they hum the latest popular song. It was left for another poet of a different spirit, Mr. Henry Newbolt, to voice the commonplace of an unchanging tragedy in the only memorable verse called forth by this three years' struggle.

With the coming of a war which it had so furiously demanded, the literature of the Reaction fell, first into shrillness, then into silence. Read to-day, the whole thing stands remote and fantastic, the child of a time infinitely far away. Of its authors, some are dead; and some continue a strange shadowy life in an alien time. Mr. Kipling compiles such mournful productions as "Traffics and Discoveries." But the pipe fails to awaken any responsive echoes. Even those who before had approved now turn away their heads. He appears like one dancing and grimacing in the midst of the set grave faces of a silent company. And so of the others. Mr. Street, one of the briskest of the disciples who once were young, contributes long letters on Tariff Reform to the columns of the *Times*. They suggest nothing so much as the return from beyond the grave of the tenuous phantoms of the Greek heroes. The spectacle is not without its pathos. *We* have not changed, these writers may complain. Here is the same music which you once approved, which once moved you clumsily to caper in the market place. What has caused the charm suddenly to cease? It has ceased—is the reply—because your world of phantasy has been judged and condemned by real things; because with that judgment a new Spirit is dawning in England.

This new Spirit should make its first appearance in

literature. And the question immediately arises: can we estimate to-day anything confident and vital which can be interpreted as the work of the pioneers, the Spring of a Summer to be?

We shall find, I think, on examination two classes of such writings. The first is of those who growing up under the spirit and dominance of the Reaction, have yet refused to give it their allegiance; a Literature of protest coloured by a sense of isolation from the ideals of its age. The second is of those developing when that dominance is passing away, and who exhibit therefore all the security and triumph which comes from the conviction of a winning cause.

Of the first, the most noteworthy name is of one who has always stood apart and alone, whose verse is everywhere conscious of a popular indifference and estrangement. The work of Mr. William Watson will be judged in the future with that of Mr. Rudyard Kipling as representing a conflict of ideas which go down to the basis of man's being. The very methods reflect the diversified ideals. The one is detached, elusive, cold; standing apart upon the height; content in a serenity and a fastidious taste in words. The other is coloured, barbaric, human; tumid and rhetorical; moving and rejoicing in the every-day world; vital, appealing and alive. The one "magnificently imperturbed," preaches always a vehement, if austere, virtue; judging the present by the ancient traditions of an older time, by a past consecration of effort and sympathy in disinterested service. The other beats with the emotion of a crowd; from the midst of which, and as its voice, he directs men's gaze towards an illimitable future.

And the changes of the time could be no better

illustrated than in the comparison of two appeals. In "The Purple East," contrasted with "The Seven Seas," the divergence is manifest between one who is speaking the mind of a nation and one obviously beyond its sympathies. Mr. Watson demanded with the violence of despair that England should accept the obligations of her deliberate responsibility, and embark in the spirit of the crusaders upon the vindication of an unchanging justice. And the note of a baffling indifference and defeat is over all the volume. Mr. Kipling sang of the glories and the greatness of an Empire swollen into one-eighth of the habitable world and splashed around the seven seas; and every line of his vigorous verse seems punctuated with the applause of invisible multitudes.

Ten years after appear two other volumes, almost contemporaneous. The time has changed. The wheel has come full circle. In "For England" there breathes through every page the consciousness of vindication, an appeal to a judgment which even now has proclaimed an honourable acquittal. In "The Five Nations" the rhetoric has passed into bombast; an audience slipping away or turning their backs is everywhere apparent. The sneers at indifference, the heaped-up insults upon "fools" and "oafs," the jibes and abuse hurled upon a nation which will not rise to the new gospel, stamp upon the whole mournful volume the consciousness of failure. In the one is the jealousy of the discarded favourite :—

"And ye vaunted your fathomless power and ye flaunted your iron pride,
Ere ye fawned on the younger nations for the men who could shoot and ride.

11

AFTER THE REACTION

Then ye returned to your trinkets; then ye contented
    your soul
With the flanneled fools at the wicket and the muddied
    oafs at the goal."

In the other is the dignity of confidence secure in an ultimate verdict which is independent of man's applause :—

"Friend, call me what you will: no jot care I:
I that shall stand for England till I die.
    *   *   *   *
The England from whose side I have not swerved;
The immortal England whom I, too, have served,
Accounting her all living lands above,
In Justice, and in Mercy, and in Love."

With the passing of the bitter days we may hope for an increased consciousness of sympathy with an England immortal and secure, restored to sanity and desirable life after the fever of its dreams.

Next to the work of this isolated figure you may turn to the work of a school. One original inspiration has survived through all the clamorous days, in that particular literature of Ireland which has disdained the noise of the Reaction. That literature boasts many men and women of rare and delicate talent : one, Mr. George Russell, of a real if remote genius ; and one, Mr. W. B. Yeats, with the power of a universal appeal.

Mr. Yeats stands for the genius of the Celt; not unmixed, indeed, with a mysticism culled from other sources; but more than any other individual writer now representing the soul of a nation. He is the outstanding figure in a literary movement which is one of the few vital things in the world of to-day. The movement is the child of a Nationalism which is the antithesis of Imperialism, whose scene is set in one of the great tragic failures of the world. From the heart of that failure, from a race as it would seem visibly dying in its own land, Mr. Yeats and his comrades proclaimed their judgment of the forces to which has been given domination. This "progress," with its noise and bustle, its material opulence, its destruction of all old and beautiful and quiet things, stand everlastingly condemned by one whose first search is for the Rose of an undying beauty, whose concern is only with the ardours and hungers of the soul. He looks out upon the tumult and the shouting, the noise and splendour of passing things. He learns that Tenderness, Compassion, Humility, those white-winged angels of healing, find no place in this hot and heavy air. He stands aside, an apostle of defeat; of defeat yet triumphant in its fall; deliberately proclaiming allegiance to the vanquished cause. "They went out to battle but they always fell" is written over all this haunting and musical verse, this haunting and appealing prose. And into the old legends, mingled of dreams and shadows, from twilights and dim dawns, the mystery and the sadness of moving waters and hidden places, the wind among the reeds, the rose-leaves falling in the garden, he has woven, with something of the quality of magic, all the sorrow of an elegy over a doomed and passing race.

Beauty and the love of beauty, the old things, visions in the sunset, dreams by the fire light, are passing from the world. The note of that passing and of the judgment of the destructive forces enters into a kind of exultant rejection of a civilisation which carries even in its victory the seeds of decay; which has received its heart's desire and leanness. in the soul. Here is the defiance of one who notes that all the noise and triumph of his conquerors will one day also become ashes and a little dust.

So the dominant note of the work of his attractive, wayward genius is this sadness and appeal. All the soul's longing turns from the call of the wind and shadowy waters, from a world ravaged by change and time, to the "Land of the ever young," and the "Land of Heart's Desire." "It is time now to go into the glens," he can say with Don-nacha'Bàn, "for gloom is falling on the mountains and mists shroud the hills." "There is enough evil in the crying of wind"; "For the world's more full of weeping than you can understand" : so runs the record of ruin and pain :—

"We who still labour by the cromlech on the shore,
  The grey cairn on the hill when day sinks drowned in dew,
  Being weary of the world's Empires bow down to you.— "

Weariness of the world's Empires; the "vanity of Sleep, Hope, Dream, endless Desire"; a defiant estrangement from all the courses of the world, become visibly flat, stale and unprofitable, are written over all this literature of protest and sorrow. Beauty passes as a dream; and "we and the labouring world are passing by"; and the consolation chiefly rests in the knowledge that one day all will have gone, good and evil, man's laughter and his tears, the yearning which can never be satisfied. "God's wars" will end, not in victory, but in silence.

    "And when at last defeated in His wars,
      They have gone down under the same white stars,
      We shall no longer hear the little cry
      Of our sad hearts, that may not live nor die."

AFTER THE REACTION

In his later work, indeed, Mr. Yeats has proclaimed a real Eastern Nihilism. He sings the triumph of Death and nothingness. Du Bellay's "Le Grandeur du Rien" is set up as the consummation of all things. And the soul rejoices that even "Le Grand tout" into which "all other things pass and lose themselves" is "some time itself to perish and pass away." In that remarkable play, "Where there is Nothing," which perplexed the inhabitants of Kensington on its performance and provided food for the humours of the dramatic critics, there is an almost passionate expression of this hatred of "making things," this hunger for the primitive abyss and void. Paul Ruttledge, the hero, is a kind of wild Tolstoy preaching the return, not to nature, but to nothingness. He seeks satisfaction first in the escape from the artificiality of society to life with the tinkers on the open road; later in the asceticism of the monastery; and then again to the simplicities of the ruined abbey and bare subsistence from day to day. His followers who have been attracted by his preaching totally misunderstand this new gospel of despair, and are found planning to build up again all which he has destroyed. In the passage, which forms the climax of the play, the apostle of Nihilism proclaims his faith :—

"Oh! yes, I understand, you would weave them together like this (*weaves the osiers in and out*), you would add one thing to another, laws and money and Church and bells, till you had got everything back again that you had escaped from. But it is my business to tear things asunder like this (*tears pieces from the basket*), and this, and this— "

"At last," he cries, in the crypt of the church, "we must put out the light of the Sun and of the Moon, and all the light of the World and the World itself. We

15

must destroy the World; we must destroy everything that has Law and Number, for where there is nothing, there is God."

Yet at other times this assertion of the ultimate triumph of cold and darkness gives place to a hope that the weak things of the world may even at the end overcome the strong; and Beauty and Romance and the old Desires of the heart and the Vision of far spiritual horizons return again into the ways of men. "The movement of thought," Mr. Yeats proclaims, "which has made the good citizen, or has been made by him, has surrounded us with comfort and safety and with vulgarity and insincerity. One finds alike its energy and its weariness in churches which have substituted a system of morals for spiritual ardour, in pictures which have substituted conventionally pretty faces for the disquieting revelations of sincerity, in poets who have set the praises of those things good citizens think praiseworthy above a dangerous delight in beauty for the sake of beauty."

But while the old is crumbling the new is building. Sometimes the hope is triumphant that "the golden age is to come again and men's hearts and the weather to grow gentle, as time fades into eternity"; and at times a confidence awakens in the coming of "a change, which, begun in our time or not for centuries, will one day make all lands holy lands again."

Mr. Yeats, in part as the expression of a national movement, more, perhaps, through the compelling force of his talent, has attained even under the uncongenial skies of the Reaction some recognition of his sincerity and power. An English author, Mr. H. W. Nevinson, no less individual and arresting, and far less remote from ideals definitely English, has waited longer for acceptance. Like Mr. Yeats, he belongs to a period of protest—protest against a dominant spirit whose departure seemed far distant. This protest has taken varied forms. He has translated into literature the appeal of the poor against the cruel indifference and, perhaps, more cruel "charity" of the rich. He has voiced the protest of the little nations with their particular civilisations against an Imperialism which rolls as a Juggernaut car, guided by sightless eyes, not deliberately but clumsily, over all their variegated lives. He has set up for judgment by the ancient, wayward things of man's existence, its high ardours, its delight in the charged spirit of emotion, love and battle and the open road, a civilisation spreading its by-laws and decencies over all the broken lands, and estimating its progress by its expenditure upon sanitation and the dimensions of its public lavatories. Against such "progress" he has appealed always for those elements of transfiguring flame by which alone man apprehends something of life and its purposes. Behind "the set grey life and apathetic end," he has discerned the flare of the fires of Prometheus. Beneath the noise of the cities he can hear the pipe of Pan among the reeds. In the midst of experience, set in custom and routine, he can exalt the moments, rare and imperishable, in which the "pent-up spirit" breaks through into Eternity.

Mr. Nevinson is a child of Shrewsbury and Oxford, of both of which he has written with that love for particular places which is the essence of the spirit of patriotism. He has lived in a block-dwelling; and from that life came the writing of "Neighbours of Ours," the best volume of tales which ever took as their theatre of

C

action the desolate and fascinating region of the "East End." The contrast between the Reaction and the newer spirit is conspicuous in the comparison of Mr. Nevinson's stories of the life of the poor with the fruitful crop of pictures of slum life—the mean street, the Jago, "Badalia Herodsfoot" or "'Liza of Lambeth"—which developed under the inspiration of that insistent tyranny. The cleverness, the essential ignorance of the journalist who prowls through the streets of poverty as he would prowl through the interior of China seeking copy;—with the same eye for picturesque effect and the same contempt for its peoples, splashing on the canvas his hard yellows and purples—is revealed in its insolence by the work of one who has lived in sympathy and comradeship with those who have failed. Mr. Nevinson's stories—notably the "St. George of Rochester" and "Father Christmas"—may be commended to all who would understand the meaning of tenderness and a man's compassion for the men and women and children who are trampled under in the modern struggle, the crowd whose acquiescence is more tragical than its despair.

From the homes of poverty Mr. Nevinson passed into the larger world; to see cities and men; and everywhere the strong triumphant and the weak suffering. He was present at the pitiful comedy of the thirty days' war in Greece; present also at the more pitiful tragedy of the destruction of two free nations in South Africa amid the heroism of the one side and the other. From these and the lessons learnt in them, from the "things seen" in the great moments of life and the quiet interludes "Between the Acts," he has collected those volumes of impression and appeal which have revealed his power in literature.

AFTER THE REACTION

Two elements mingle in all his work. The one is pagan, the plea of Pan, the protest of the "Savage Soul." It is life passion protesting against the cramping boundaries of convention and dead things. The other is Pity, learnt by the older gods in the watching of the human tragedy through so many hurrying centuries ; pity for all who find themselves with the few against the many, crushed by the clumsiness and violence of the world. The one thing which appears to him intolerable is the rotting at ease. The one tragedy is the burning out of high emotion into a little heap of ashes. "To grow fat and foul in clubs and country-houses," is the nightmare of one of his characters, "till I slime away in the funeral of an elderly country gentleman who had been in the army once." Against this vision of the faint-hearted he exalts the company of the warrior saints. "Life piled on life were all too little for the unquenchable passion of my eyes." The praises of a mechanical civilisation leave him cold. "To set two bulging, flat-footed gentlemen," is his verdict, "to stand on a flagstone instead of one, seems an unworthy aim for Evolution after all its labours."

Pan is not dead. He but waits, a little contemptuous of it all till the tyranny be overpast. Even in the heart of tranquillity and rational order he can still be found disguised : a wanderer : abiding his time and sure of his ultimate triumph.

He appears in Greece, his old home, with all the pageant of an unchallenged beauty, hill and heather, and violet sea. He is found again by the ancient wall across Britain marking the boundaries of another Empire which once thought itself immortal. His laughter startles the Cathedral close as he mocks the anger of the Canon against his servant, Elizabeth, for

19

her transgression with her soldier-lover. He is present with the new knowledge of pity upon the war-scarred slopes of Waggon Hill above Ladysmith in the clear night after the storm of men and elements, watching over the bodies of the dead.

The contrast between this vision on the hillside, the mingled sorrow and rejoicing over the body of a dead peasant, with any of Mr. Kipling's latest tales, "The Captive," or, "Private Capper," will reveal the meaning of a change. All the music-hall song and cleverness have vanished from the horizon of this poor sightless body. Not in this lies its greatness: but in that Divine Fire which entered into the heart of him as he moved through the slow routine of his toil, and drove him out here from his dear home into the battle in passionate response to the call of the Fatherland: and has left him here at evening, with all the story told; the dust gathering on his lips, silent in the summer rain.

The author will re-echo the protest of Pan against the plaint of the priest at man's seeming wickedness. Surveying the long course of history, he will testify with something approaching awe to an endurance and indomitable will which raises him above the level of the older gods. There is a passage in this testimony not unworthy to be placed with Lamennais's "Hymn of the Dead," or Stevenson's awful vision in "Pulvis et Umbra":—

"They appear and are gone. Like shipwrecked boys they are cast upon the shoals of time, and drop off into darkness. No research of history, no deciphering of village tombs can ever recover them. We think that somewhere they may still lie nestled up, with all their age about them; but even darkness holds them no more.

They stood on this flying earth, we see their footsteps, we hear the thin ghost of their voices, and on the stones lies the touch of their dead hands, but they are nowhere to be found at all. They knew how short their dear life was, yet they filled it with labour and unrecorded toil. Morning and night, through their little space of minutes, they struggled and agonised to keep on living and feed their children for the struggle and agony of a few minutes more. The sun blasted them, ice devoured their flesh, their mouths were mad with thirst, hunger twisted them with cramps, plague consumed them, they rotted as they stood, bolts of torture drove through their brains, their bodies were clamped into hoops; in battle, in child-bed they died with extremity of pain. Yet they endured, and into the chinks and loopholes of their misery they crammed laughter and beauty and a passion transfiguring them beyond the semblance of the gods."

'Tis a sombre picture; yet not without its triumph. "Let us leave it to the priests to marvel at men's wickedness," he cries at the end. "Over any such thing as love or laughter in the heart of man I could stand astonished with admiration throughout the life-time of a god."

The work of these writers is written, in Mr. Watson's phrase, "in estrangement." Over all is the consciousness of battle upon a losing side. They have kept the faith in a dark hour when all the world seemed against them. The tumult swept past them. They stood alone, alien in spirit from the company : from the noisy rout, which seemed the procession of an unending day. With the visible passing of all this clamour has come the growth of a newer spirit, with an ardour and buoyancy lacking in those who suffered from its domination. Such is the spirit of those younger writers who first have apprehended that the Reaction, instead of being living and dominant, was become at heart dead and sterile. Of such, two of the most vigorous to-day are Mr. Hilaire Belloc and Mr. Gilbert Chesterton.

Mr. Belloc has produced work which is excellent in itself and more excellent in its promise of better things to come. He exhibits especially two qualities always rare in English writing—the quality of rhetoric and the quality of irony. His earlier works, studies of the Revolution, Danton and Robespierre, are full of the triumph of human personality over the influences of outward things. His work, like the architecture of that Middle Age which he loves so ardently, reveals the union of this spirit of romance with the spirit of laughter. The high roofs and spires are mingled with the gargoyles and grotesques, and all the humour and aspiration which gave its life to the greatest century which the world has ever seen. He will pass from the record of romance to the roaring satire of "Dr. Caliban," or collaboration with Mr. Chesterton in the ridiculing of the Tariff Reform Commission. High spirits and a kind of elemental energy are characteristic of all his work. No present-day writing conveys so much the impression of a huge enjoyment in its preparation. Much of Mr. Belloc's humour is indeed recondite, written to please himself and for the few who will understand ; the decent citizen but becomes conscious that some one is laughing at him as indignant he hurries by.

In " The Path to Rome," the most popular of all his books, this vitality is everywhere present. Youth, its sincerity, its self-sufficiency, its vigour and hope and enormous dreams, is present in all this record of pilgrimage. As the traveller swings out from Toul in the sunset by the Nancy gate and strikes in a bee-line across the backbone of Europe to the goal of his wandering, he pours out all his experience of outer and inner things. He makes up songs, and sings them as he journeys, in dispraise of heretics or praise of God. He finds companionship in the common people, the people of the road, the people of the villages, away from the dust of the cities. He apprehends "the solid form of Europe under him like a rock"; unchanged and permanent, beside which all the noise of progress appears but vaporous and transitory.

In the story of "Emmanuel Burden," Mr. Belloc's ironical method has attained its clearest expression. The elaborate satire penetrates every page; from the pompous parody of the title, through the nonsense of the preface, to the Burden genealogies designed in the futile exactitude of the three-volume biography. To nine out of ten, reading, as they think, a dull and straightforward narrative, all this will appear very tedious. But in the underlying spirit there is a marked and momentous change from the spirit of the social satire of fifteen years ago. The literature of the Reaction found the subject of all its humours in the middle-class tradesman. It was never tired of mocking at his outlook, his contempt for art and literature and all ideas, his confinement within the grooves of sectarianism and the making of money. To these clever young men Mr. Grundy, the husband of the dictator of the suburbs, was the subject of an unfailing ridicule. They pelted him with epigram. They caricatured his decencies and devotions. They rolled the poor old gentleman in the gutter and departed laughing hugely at their own smartness and his bleats of indignation.

AFTER THE REACTION

With Mr. Belloc the process is reversed. Satire has come over to the other side. Over against the new wits, the cleverness engaged in the intervals of self-indulgence in running (or ruining) an Empire; with its surface sparkle and its inner emptiness and frivolity, Mr. Grundy with his tenacity, his simplicity, his austere devotion to duty, appears as an entirely reputable figure. Mr. Burden is Mr. Grundy, the "honest man and good citizen," ironmonger of Thames Street. In his side whiskers and frock-coat, as depicted by Mr. Chesterton, with his impossible mid-Victorian residence at Avonmore, Alexandrovna Road, Upper Norwood, with his forty years' daily devotion to his trade, "his home, manner and habit of life seemed to me who knew him to be always England, England." "To see him open his umbrella was to comprehend England from the Reform Bill to Home Rule."

Against this old and passing England, the England which had built up the great heritage of Empire, Mr. Belloc exhibits the dismal crowd who have entered into that goodwill and seems determined upon its destruction. Here are the children of the old, mocking at the limitations of their fathers; cosmopolitan financiers of Semitic origin, exploiting, ostensibly, remote marshes, in reality the British public, under the sonorous claptrap of "Empire Expansion"; broken down relics of the feudal system compelled to re-establish their shattered fortunes; the new yellow journalism; and the rank and file of greedy persons of all classes who rushed into the flotation, as clergymen and society ladies and respectable country gentlemen rushed into the gigantic gambling in South Africans which preceded the Jameson Raid. These are the figures which fill the foreground of the flotation of the M'Korio Delta

24

Development Co. Experience of the bitter food of those astonishing nineties in England, the Hooley scandals, the Liberator, the Chartered Company, Whitaker Wright, are woven into a satire in which the restraint of the irony scarcely veils the passionate protest against all this new corruption of a nation marching down calamitous ways.

In such a morass of foulness Mr. Burden is engulfed. He finds himself immediately in the toils, surrounded by vague forces of evil. There is nothing definite. The outline moves. As soon as he strikes out, the walls, which seemed to be closing around him, part aside and elude his blows. The business is of a kind to which he is unaccustomed. The suavity and plausibility of his confederates are equal to all his approaches. There is a spirit in the air, in the public Press, around the office of the company, a miasma which poisons the blood and turns the balance of the brain. Although the shares still stand high and there is outward prosperity, the conviction deepens that he is in the grasp of unclean forces. He is troubled in the daytime with a haunting sense of shame, at night by monstrous dreams. The attempt of his colleagues to "freeze out" his friend, Mr. Abbott (another absurd, early-Victorian figure), who had refused to "come in," produces a climax. The poor, bewildered mind breaks under the strain. Mr. Burden, feeling actually in the presence of a crowd, "the massed forces of this new world surging against him," in one great scene of fury denounces all his fellow-directors as rogues and thieves and scum, and reels home to Upper Norwood to die. The death scene is not inadequate to life's perpetual irony. On the one hand is the outward, pitiful and grotesque incident : a stout old man, muttering gibberish, being put to bed by the knife-boy and the cook. On the other is the inward grandeur, Death and his armies and majesty visibly present in this suburban villa, and present also the three great Angels, " the Design and the Justice and the Mercy of God."

The M'Korio flourishes. Mr. I. Z. Barnett, who is chief promoter, becomes Lord Lambeth. The shares rise. But away in a remote suburb they have buried Emmanuel Burden, Merchant, of Thames Street and Upper Norwood (for whom, one is relieved to hear, Mr. Belloc " has no fears at the Judgment seat ") ; and with him they have buried the older England.

This remarkable work in some sense gathers up all the threads of remonstrance into one deliberate impeachment of the spirit of the Reaction ; the fine fruits of that " Imperialism " which ran like a species of fluid madness through the veins of England during the late disastrous years. Memorable in itself, it is more memorable as a kind of pioneer of the revolt which is essaying a return to sanity, and the broken tradition of reform.

The rise of Mr. Chesterton in the public estimate has exhibited the most sudden growth of all recent reputations. While still on the right side of thirty, he leapt into a position of which older men might well be envious. His early work, " Greybeards at Play," a volume of fantastic verse, " The Wild Knight," serious poetry of remarkable originality and power, " The Defendant," a collection of paradoxical essays, revealed only to the few the presence of a new writer and a new method. His life of " Browning," however, both in its merit and its definite challenge, evoked a universal testimony that here was something which, whether you liked it or not, was henceforth to be reckoned with in literature. Since then have followed " Twelve Types," and " Watts," and a novel, once again of daring originality, " The Napoleon of Notting Hill "—a parable of the perpetual survival of the spirit of patriotism, however mystical and irrational, against all the forces of ridicule and common sense. The output continues of an astonishing fertility in daily and weekly and monthly magazines. It is these outpourings of himself, stripped of all reticence, which have earned for Mr. Chesterton the bulk of his fame. He loves the very breath of controversy. Open any newspaper interested in the things for which he cares : you will have a good chance of finding Mr. Chesterton in the midst of a lively argument against a host of opponents, with a calm confidence in his rightness, an unfailing good temper, a boisterous delight in the shrewd blows given and taken. You will find him simultaneously protesting against Dr. Clifford conducting a campaign against Romanism under the guise of an attack upon the Education Acts ; explaining to Mr. Blatchford and Mr. McCabe the impossibility of Agnosticism, and his envy of their simple belief ; or expounding to an audience inarticulate with wrath the necessity of desiring Russia's success in the war against Japan.

Beneath all there is no mere love of paradox or intellectual agility, but a very definite philosophy of life. As the attitude of Mr. Yeats was one of protest, so that of Mr. Chesterton is one of acceptance. The denial of life, the longing of a fatigued age for nothingness and the great Void, is to him a fundamental atheism and blasphemy. Not "where there is nothing," but " where there is anything," there " is God." He is a mystic and an optimist, entirely satisfied, as he swaggers down Fleet Street, that all things are very good. With Whitman he can protest, "No array of terms can express how much at peace I am about God." To many this boisterous content appears as an offence and irreverence. To such he appears of those who are too readily at ease in Zion. To others this revolt from the denials of life has come with something of the nature of an inspiration.

He is all for acceptance of the things that are, and the revelation through these of the things that endure. In all experience the present becomes a transfigured past; to the few only, as to this writer, that transfiguration has been immediately accomplished. He has no controversy with the results of modern progress, the city, in slum or suburb. As wild and flaming meanings call to him from beneath that dull surface as any appeal in ancient forest or the voices of the mountains and the sea. The great city he finds as something "wild and obvious." The "casual omnibus" wears "the primal colours of a fairy ship." The lights in the dark "begin to glow like innumerable goblin eyes." Bermondsey is decked with fairy bubbles for gas-lamps and haunted with Presences of good and evil. The door-knockers of Clapham, as he gazes at them, writhe into strange shapes, the fat, red, polished pillar-boxes shout their mystical meaning to the skies. Hardly a hair's breadth below the cellars of Kensington flare the ancient elemental fires. He is intoxicated by the "towering and tropical visions of things as they are," the "gigantic daisies, the heaven-consuming dandelions, the great Odyssey of strange-coloured oceans and strange-shaped trees, of dust like the wreck of temples, and thistledown like the ruin of stars." Day by day the seeing eye beholds God renewing his ancient rapture. The wild Knight in his quest, hearing " the crumbling creeds, like cliffs washed down by water, change and pass," finds " all these things as nothing "; confident that the turn of the road will reveal the goal of all his wandering.

> " So with the wan waste grasses on my spear,
> I ride for ever seeking after God.
> My hair grows whiter than my thistle plume,
> And all my limbs are loose; but in my eyes
> The star of an unconquerable praise ;
> For in my soul one hope for ever sings,
> That at the next white corner of a road
> My eyes may look on Him."

To one inspired by such visions all the spirit of the Reaction is summed up in the tremendous picture of Watts's " Mammon." The vision is not Mammon or Commerce, but " something intangible behind," a ruling element in modern life. Here is " the blind and asinine appetite for mere power "; symbolised in " the all-destroying God and king adorned with the ears of an ass, declaring that he was royal, imperial, irresistible, and, when all is said, imbecile."

" This is something which in spirit and in essence I have seen before," he proclaims, " something which in spirit and in essence I have seen everywhere. That bloated, unconscious face, so heavy, so violent, so wicked, so innocent, have I not seen it at street corners, in billiard rooms, in saloon bars, laying down the law about Chartered shares, or gaping at jokes about women ? Those huge and smashing limbs, so weighty, so silly, so powerless, and yet so powerful, have I not seen them in the pompous movements, the morbid health of the prosperous in the great cities ? The hard, straight pillars of that throne, have I not seen them in the hard, straight, hideous tiers of modern warehouses and factories ? That tawny and sulky smoke, have I not seen it going up to heaven from all the cities of the coming world ? This is no trifling with argosies and Greek drapery. This is commerce. This is the home of the god himself. This is why men hate him, and why men fear him, and why men endure him."

Let all who are satisfied with the courses of modern England during the past decade consider if there be not at the last some warning of judgment in this verdict upon an evil thing.

What is there common, it may be asked, to these different writers, what spirit which may form the key to the movement of the immediate years to come ? There is much evidently divergent; a continuous transition indeed from the complete denials of Mr. Yeats to the complete assertions of Mr. Chesterton. But in all may be traced one element; the assertion of a passionate Nationalism against both the cosmopolitan ideals of the Victorian period at its beginning and the Imperial ideals at its close. In the vision of the earlier age all national differences were to smooth themselves out by the advance of knowledge and reasonableness. Common sense, commerce, a universal peace were to create a homogeneous civilisation, secure in comfort and tranquillity and a vague, undogmatic religion. In the preaching of this ideal, undoubtedly some of its advocates came perilously near the abnegation of any special national affection, any particular pride in, or devotion to, their land; and gave a handle to the dreary chatter of a Press which branded them as the friends of every country but their own. Against this came the reaction. Imperialism asserted, indeed, the devotion of the individual to his own land ; but crudely denied the right to others of a similar affection. It was convinced in pathetically sanguine fashion of the Divine mission of England to elevate each separate and subject race to the level of Mayfair or Brixton. So the Irish, the Dutch of South Africa, the natives of India, or of Nyassa ("half devil and half child") for their own good were to be educated out of their own ways into English ways. They would be placed under the cold justice of the Imperial rule. They would be taught to forget their own language and deny their own religions and ancient pieties. They would learn to ascend the steep path of labour and virtue which would eventually turn them into some replica of that finished product of the universe, the Imperial Briton.

Such was the ideal at its best. At its worst it became a crude assertion of dominance, with a contempt as much for the old England which had not apprehended these Imperial ideals as for the foreigner who still obstinately resisted their sway.

Against both these movements is now being set a Nationalism which, on the one hand, passionately asserts a mystical and entire devotion to its own land ; on the other, a respect for the devotion of others. It brands the murder of a nation as a sin alike against man and God. One catches a note even of laughter in the defiant scorn with which the newer spirit confronts those who identify their own calamitous methods with the welfare of their country, and would brand all others as traitors. It is in the name of England, as Englishmen concerned primarily with the honour of their own land, as those to whom the very fields and flowers, and the breath of the particular soil speaks with an unchanging appeal, that these writers fling back the charges of disloyalty, made by those who have never been able to understand the meaning of the mystery of Patriotism.

This is common to all. Mr. Yeats is at the heart of that National revival in life and literature which, in the past few years, has made Ireland, on the remote boundaries of Europe, the centre of one of the few living and compelling movements of the age. All his devotion gathers towards the preservation of this individual spirit, the spirit "at the heart of the Celt in the moments he has grown to love through years of persecution, when, cushioning himself about with dreams and hearing fairy-songs in the twilight, he ponders on the soul and on the dead."

Mr. Watson laughs openly at "that odious charge of inconstancy to my beloved and worshipped motherland." "To one conscious of these noble origins, conscious, too, of having loved his country with the vigilant love that cannot brook a shadow upon her honour, the charge of being against her because he deplores her temporary attitude and action, brings a kind of amazement that has in it something akin to despair."

Mr. Nevinson has devoted his days to appeals for the struggle of martyred nations to maintain their own life,—in Ireland, in Macedonia, in South Africa. But all his affection centres upon the very soil of his own homeland.

"The seas gulf and fall around her promontories," is his testimony, "or lie brooding there in green and purple lines. Her mountains are low, like blue waves they run along the horizon, and the wind flows over them. It is a country of deep pasture and quiet downs and earthy fields, whore the furrows run straight from hedge to hedge. There is moorland too, and lakes with wild names, and every village is full of ancient story. The houses are clustered round old castle walls, and across the breezy distance of fen and common the grey cathedrals rise like ships in full sail."

Mr. Belloc is perhaps the most entirely Nationalist. He is all for the smaller community against the larger. He sings the praise of the South country whose "great hills stand along the sea," and of the men of the South country against the remoter regions of England. When he drinks the home-brewed ale he drinks (in his own absurd and happy phrase) "Nelson and all the Victories." He will even protest in great language patriotism for a Europe encompassed with alien forces, a world outside which can never understand devotions beaten into her soil by the passion of a thousand years ;—

" She will certainly remain.

" Her component peoples have merged and have remerged. Her particular, famous cities have fallen down. Her soldiers have believed the world to have lost all, because a battle turned against them. Her best has at times grown poor and her worst rich. Her colonies have seemed dangerous for a moment from the insolence of their power, and then again (for a moment) from the contamination of their decline. She has suffered invasion of every sort; the East has wounded her in arms and corrupted her with ideas ; her vigorous blood has healed the wounds at once, and her permanent sanity has turned such corruptions into innocuous follies. She will certainly remain."

And Mr. Chesterton has made himself the very apostle of a new Nationalism which proclaims this variegated development as an essential for the preservation of the sanity of the world. "There is a spirit abroad among the nations of the earth," he cries, " which drives men incessantly on to destroy what they cannot understand, and to capture what they cannot enjoy." This is the spirit which all these men find in the faction which has been dominant in politics and literature. Its final and desperate rally is now gathering in the forces enlisting with Mr. Chamberlain, under the appeal both to cupidity and Imperial dominance, in a last effort to maintain a departing supremacy. And this is the spirit against which the new movement has declared uncompromising war.

If literature be any guide, therefore, one can prophesy certain notes of the spirit of the coming time.

First, this spirit will be National; with no appearance of balanced affection and an equal approval and sympathy for all men, a universal benevolence. It will proclaim always a particular concern in the well-being of England and the English people ; a pride in its ancient history, its ancient traditions, the very language of its grey skies and rocky shore.

Second, it will, I think, dissever itself entirely from those former rallies of a national spirit which have immediately identified a nation with a small and limited class, throwing up boundaries round its privileges against a hungry and raging crowd. There will be none of the follies of the " young England," or attempts to revive a feudalism which had vigour in its day, but now has ceased to be. The assertion will be of a spiritual democracy, with a claim for every Englishman and woman and child to some share in the great inheritance which England has won.

And third, therefore, you will note a bedrock demand

in the thrusting forward of those problems of social discontent and social reform, which are destined ultimately to brush aside the futilities of the present party strife. Against those who protest their devotion to their country, but who have done nothing to make that country more desirable for the masses of its millions, and more secure in the devotion of free and satisfied peoples, will be set up a determination at all costs and through all changes to create an England more worthy of the land of our desire. The repatriation of a rural population with free men strong in the tenacity which only security and contact with the land can give, the grappling with the problems of our restless cities, the more even spread of the national wealth, the wider distribution of the good things which have flowed so plentifully into our store, the assertion of a minimum standard of life for each citizen of such a land—these are the things which will become more and more insistent through the spirit that is arising after the Reaction.

No gleam of such radiant visions penetrates through the dusty atmosphere of contemporary politics. The observer, limited to so dreary an outlook, might well claim exoneration for despair of his country. Government and Parliament are to-day seen mouthing and mumbling over dead things with a kind of pompous futility which would be ridiculous if it were not so entirely tragical.

Such verses as those of Shelley in 1819 seem alone adequate to the present; with their vision of a "Senate" with "Time's worst statute unrepealed"; religion as "a closed book"; "rulers who neither see nor feel nor know."

But now, as then, there can be hope of the presence

also within these graves of that " glorious Phantom ' which may " burst to illumine our tempestuous day." And those who have been watching all the long night for the signs of its passing can even now see the darkness lightened with the coming of the dawn.

DE MORTUIS

"*Ils ont aussi passé sur cette terre, ils ont descendu le fleuve du temps : on entendit leurs voix sur ses bords, et puis on n'entendit plus rien. . . .*

"*Il y en avait qui disaient : Qu'est-ce que ces flots qui nous emportent ?   Y a-t-il quelque chose après ce voyage rapide ? Nous ne le savons pas, nul ne le sait.   Et comme ils disaient cela, les rives s'évanouissaient. . . .*

"*Il y en avait aussi qui semblaient dans un recueillement profond écouter une parore secrète, et puis l'œil fixé sur le couchant, tout à coup ils chantaient une aurore invisible et un jour qui ne finit jamais. . . .*

"*Ou sont-ils ?   Qui nous le dira ?   Heureux les morts qui meurent dans le Seigneur.*"

—LAMENNAIS.

WILLIAM ERNEST HENLEY

YOU can count on the fingers of one hand the original and formative minds in English letters; and there is one fewer to-day than yesterday. The advent of W. E. Henley marked the coming of a new spirit. His career coincided with its riotous supremacy. It was dead before he died. Its followers gathered round him as disciples round a master. It found expression in the short-lived journals which he edited so brilliantly. It stamped its seal upon a whole generation of young authors who became infected with its scorns and its devotions, and spread its faith through the English-speaking world. For the first time since the days of "Young England," literature was whole-heartedly on the side of the reaction. Barbarism and the joy of existence was one side of it, with a craving for the sharp and bitter rind of life. Imperialism and love of adventure was another—the assertion of the right of the strong man to rule, to trample on the weak, to crush under and destroy for his pleasure. These were combined with the hunger for the raw and primitive and elemental; the sloughing off of an ancient civilisation, the calling up of the beast and the savage to arise from their long sleep. No body of blameless citizens ever wallowed in blood so fearfully as Henley's young men. No man ever hated any cause more untiringly than

DE MORTUIS

Henley hated all that is meant by modern Liberalism. Democracy and the rule of the many; the protection of the weak against the strong and the poor against the powerful; the decencies and respectabilities of ordered life; the sentiment which dislikes pain and shrinks from the brutalities of war; all attempts to find a sanctity in the rights of the common people, the cry of the oppressed—these causes were involved in one universal condemnation. It was a spirit and a cult not without pose and affectation. But it was alive, fervent, consuming while it lasted much dead refuse. We who are emerging from its tyranny to the saner realities need not grudge an acknowledgment of the strength of the thundercloud and the fiery splendour of the storm.

What a feast of good things was represented by the old *National Observer* ! For a Saturday's sixpence one could obtain the first work of a dozen original and daring minds. There would be ferocious political leaders, sarcastic, bitter, striking to kill. These might be followed by a poem from an unknown author, just becoming talked about, a Mr. Rudyard Kipling. For "Middles" you might read one of that series of "Modern Men," the most incisive and dramatic character sketches in modern journalism; or one of Henley's appreciations, as whole-hearted as his hatreds; or Mr. Kenneth Graham's "Golden Age" tales; or Mr. Marriott Watson's sketches (he has never done better work); or, perhaps, the table-talk of Mr. Street's inimitable "boy," or Mr. Harold Frederic's Uncle. And in the reviews you would find something equally unexpected, a distinctive note behind the summary of contents, a sifting and judgment of ephemeral literature by the light of the fixed stars of criticism. Financially, it was a failure. The cleverness and originality were too naked and unashamed. Men reeled back into the sobriety of *The Spectator* and similar safe periodicals. But for the few of that age who had received the great gift of youth all this noise and sparkle and glitter represented an adventure into fairyland.

And the man who was at the centre of it all, the heart of this exuberant and boisterous activity, was the man who has died after a life of pain. The figure suggested was of a great laughing giant, full of the open air and physical well-being and personal response to the zest of the battle of existence. The reality was a tortured body, the experience of enormous suffering, life creeping ever on broken wing in a maimed and restless discomfort. With his life-long friend, Stevenson, he has gone down singing into the darkness. History will see these two optimists always in a clear white light of afternoon. While stout burgesses with ample means wept or squeaked over the miseries of existence and demonstrated their dolors to an admiring world, these two great sufferers from their beds of pain were proclaiming the triumph of things. Coughing his life out in his darkened room, Stevenson sang carols in praise of God; so insistent that the innocent like Mr. Archer could reproach him for his too complacent exultation, and praise of this " brave gymnasium." In hospital, stricken by poverty and perpetual pain, with nerves on the rack and the things he loved for ever beyond his grasp, Henley responded with thanks for his " unconquerable soul." Undoubtedly, when all transitory disputes have vanished, the world will deem itself the richer for so bracing an example.

More even than in most men of genius the child

survived in Henley. As a child he was wayward, capricious, vain; never reconciled to the limitations of life; difficult to satisfy. He had all the child's passionate loves and hatreds, the sudden transitions of temper, the almost fierce affection; with the occasional inexplicable impulses to injure those he loved. The attack on Stevenson, which caused the scandal of a day, was but an example. It was one of the great friendships of history with depth and intimacy not yet fully revealed. The lines to Baxter—"How good it sounds, Lewis and you and I"—the dedications of "A child curious and innocent," and "Time and Change," the collaborated plays, show one side; the figure of Burly in Stevenson's "Talk and Talkers," the unforgettable tribute at the end of the Christmas Sermon, the other. But he saw a lay figure set up for worship. He struck fiercely and blindly: at the figure and his dead friend. The world was scandalised and delighted. "Lewis" would have understood.

It is for the child elements that he will stand in literature. He possessed a child's quick apprehension of the sensuous aspect of things—the dying year and the coming of spring, night and the sea in storm, and all the magical world of out-of-doors. He loved with a child's delight the pageantry of war, the sword's "high, irresistible" song, the bright flash of steel, and the tramp of armed men. He had a childlike, unreserved love of England, expressing in a few magnificent ballads the mystery and sacredness of a Patriotism rare in these latter days. And in the most appealing and universal of all his poems, it is the child shrinking from the Unknown and the Future: the child that has suffered so much wistfully asking the meaning of it all: the simple, pitiful note of fear and surprise at

WILLIAM ERNEST HENLEY

"The terror of Time and Change and Death
That wastes the floating, transitory world."

There is little spontaneity in these songs. The
experiments in rhymeless metre are not altogether
successful. Even in the voice of triumph and exultation there is always the background of doubt and
menace. The chill of the coming cold is in the songs
of Summer: "in the sun, among the leaves, upon the
flowers," creeps the shadow of the approach of Death.
For all the indomitable spirit, the proclamation that life
is worth living, and the refusal to whine and whimper,
it is the sombre side of life which Henley paints in his
poems. The Hospital Rhymes are mere jagged cries of
agony. "Into the night go one and all," "fatuous,
ineffectual yesterdays," "the menace of the irreclaim-
able sea "—of such stuff are his verses woven. Perhaps
they will be remembered in the future more for their
occasional magnificence of phrase than for any natural
inevitableness and charm. "The past's enormous
disarray"; "the unanswering generations of the
dead"; "the immortal, incommunicable dream";
"the high austere, unpitying grave"; "night with
her train of stars, And her great gift of sleep "—these
are as elemental and memorable as the great summaries
of Whitman. His is the poetry read by poets, the
quarry from which others will mine the marble and
fashion it into a thing of beauty.

As a great spirit unbreakable by time and fate,
Henley will go down to the future. To this man were
given many of the world's good things, varied interests,
a power of passionate appreciation of the best in
literature and common life, high and generous friendships, love which was the inspiration of all the most

43

triumphant of his songs. To him also were given failure and pain : a perpetual ill-success in every enterprise : such suffering of body and spirit as seemed to make him the sport of mischievous powers. All his literary schemes collapsed : he lacked money and the little satisfactions of a sheltered and tranquil existence. The craving for a life of action perpetually fretted him, the " home sickness " of " those detained at home unwillingly." He had one child whom he adored. She was torn from him ; and in one poem which sounds the uttermost depth of tears he pictures " the little exquisite Ghost" calling back across the grave to her Father and Mother in those home kingdoms left desolate by Death. Sometimes he was irritable and indignant, and struck at the friends who loved him. But for the most part there was a resignation, a determination to make the best of things, a resolute refusal to give up and acknowledge the triumph of the powers of darkness, which lifts the whole tragic record out of the region of sorrow, and transfigures it with a kind of glory.

> "So be my passing!
> My task accomplished and the long day done,
> My wages taken, and in my heart
> Some late lark singing.
> Let me be gathered to the quiet west,
> The sundown splendid and serene,
> Death."

The spirit of one of the most appealing of his earlier poems is the spirit in which most who knew and loved him will wish to bid him farewell.

J. HENRY SHORTHOUSE

TWO writers are most responsible for whatever popular success has been attained by the movement termed a little grandiloquently "the Anglo-Catholic revival in England." The one, Christina Rossetti, wrote a few poems ; the other, J. Henry Shorthouse, one novel. A woman and a layman of the middle classes thus strangely provided the particular atmosphere of mysticism and aspiration which softened the often hard, dogmatic teaching and the fantastic ritual of the younger clergy. The enormous popularity of " John Inglesant," described upon its first appearance as " having taken the world by storm " and enduring until to-day, is a little difficult fully to explain. It is written in a rare and delicate prose, revealing a rare and refined personality ; but this, if anything, would militate against a wide acceptance. It advertises itself as a " Romance," but readers anticipating " Tushery " of the familiar type are dismayed by an immediate plunge into Platonic discussions upon the nature of the soul. It possesses little sense of unity, and violates every law that should govern the successful novel. Yet it has never ceased to attract a varied array of champions. Its reception, indeed, is largely a matter of temperament. Mr. Birrell, with all his eclectic taste, has confessed that he cannot away with it. And many

45

others less candid have probably in silence endorsed this condemnation.

The secret of this acceptance lies, I think, in an appeal to a type, widely spread, desirous of accepting a certain view of life. The world of Shorthouse in all his novels is a world viewed under a particular aspect. Existence is pictured as a perplexing and disturbed dream. Guidance is doubtful. The good is often at cross purposes with the good. Human life assumes the aspect now of a brilliant phantasia, now of a masquerade. The later renaissance in Italy, as shown in these pages, is progressing in an intoxicating atmosphere and under a vague sense of oppression. Men and women move through an enchanted landscape charged with emotion. It is a vision above all of sudden transitions, of the irony of Change and Death everywhere crashing in upon the players. The transition is immediate from masques and revelry and unbridled license to the "*Memento, homo, quia pulvis es,*" in which the lights suddenly wax dim and all the music changes into terror and tears. Through this strange pageant—the strange pageant of life in all time viewed from the towers of Eternity—John Inglesant "walked often as in a dream."

But the appeal which caught the imagination of men living in an equally perplexing age rests in the conviction of the author that there is a clue to the mystery. As was said of Dante, "he believed, and in spite of all affirmed the high harmony of the world."

This he was enabled to do by his spiritual interpretation both of the inward voice and the outward pageant of things. In the latter he definitely accepted the sacramental view of Nature. We are back in the Middle Age. "All redness becomes blood, all water tears." The natural is but the thin veil of the super-natural, for ever almost bursting through. God is visibly acting in His world ; the most trivial events are charged with a spiritual significance. Other Presences are watching the little decisions of the little life of man. This view tolerates immediately, and without any sense of disturbance, the incursions into the story of mystery and miracle, the appearance of the ghost of Strafford, or the crystal vision of the death of Eustace. It is an attitude towards things which finds a satisfaction in the dramatic symbolism of an external ceremony, in music and light and ritual, which to the ordinary man may be but irritating. Others have shared the discovery of John Inglesant, in that most touching description of his visit to little Gidding, that "the gracious figure over the altar and the bowed and kneeling figures," are essentially con-gruous with "the misty autumn sunlight and the driving autumn rain."

And the other clue to life's mazes Mr. Shorthouse found in that doctrine of the Inner Light which he received with his Quaker upbringing, and unfolded with so winning an appeal. The Platonic doctrine of the Divine guidance, of the direct call of God within the soul of man, is the belief which leads John Inglesant through the confused and troublous life of the seven-teenth century. It is heard in the three great crises of the book, to which all the lesser events lead, but which, when they come, come suddenly. The first is the temp-tation of the world, when De Cressy, the Benedictine, at Paris, offers him the more excellent way. The second is the temptation of the flesh, in the damp mists and breathless air in the flight with Laurétte from Florence to Pistoia. The third is the temptation of the devil, in that most wonderful scene in the mountains of Umbria, when John Inglesant lays his sword on the altar of the little hillside chapel, and delivers his brother's murderer to the judgment of God. Through these and all other incidents of this play of tired children, amid the troublous clash of war, in strange ways, with love and loss, to the final serene sadness of old age, he has ever the apprehension of this unseen hand. The promise was to his eager boyhood. "I think you may find this doctrine," said his teacher, "a light which will guide your feet in dark places; and it would seem that this habit of mind is very likely to lead to the blessedness of the beatific vision of God." That promise survived through all the vanity and terror of existence tost amid the whirlpools of divergent spiritual tides. And after it is all over he can assert with the confidence of a direct experience that "we may not only know the truth, but we may live even in this life in the very household and courts of God."

Shorthouse only wrote one book. For twenty years he put into these pages all his philosophy of existence. He had said his say, and there was nothing more to be said. Like Olive Schreiner, an author with whom, despite superficial incongruities, he has much in common, he revealed his heart's secret in one supreme emotional utterance. Pressed by his friends, he did indeed essay further efforts. In the tranquil life of the little German Court of the eighteenth century, he could almost retain the atmosphere of large issues and spiritual meanings, and in consequence the story of little Mark nearly approaches success. But in the comfortable existence of nineteenth-century England, grave and sane and without fear, in the life of the ordered city concerned with sanitation and the Poor Law, the particular spiritual ardour which he loved to portray appears forced and artificial. So Lady Falaise failed, and Sir Percival, his hero warrior, modelled after Gordon's pattern, whose actual description perhaps almost justified Barry Pain's cruel parody of the conversation under the Tulip Tree. The writer who has most nearly approached the spirit and success of Shorthouse's hero in the modern world is John Oliver Hobbes in her "Robert Orange." The record of the fashioning in Vanity Fair through great bitterness in the School for Saints of a Weapon keen and pliant to the will of God, is a record of one moving amongst the phantom society of the nineteenth century, as Inglesant moved through the phantom courts of Italy three hundred years ago. But the book most revealing the same inner spirit, with something of the delicacy and charm of style, is the "Road Mender," the work of an author also indebted to a Quaker upbringing for keen insight into the things of the spirit, and a capacity for the estimating, at true value, of the Temporal and the Eternal.

The style of Shorthouse at its best stands almost without rival in the literature of the past twenty years for a particular refinement and delicacy. The inevitable comparison is with Newman: not that "John Inglesant" achieves even a momentary rivalry with that supreme perfection of English prose, but that in each case there is an altogether personal secret and appeal which defies analysis. Passage after passage reads like music. Who is ever likely to forget the concluding scene of this great spiritual record: the sunset over the city: and after the storm, in the quiet air of England, far from the confused and passionate life of Italy, John Inglesant's farewell?

"We are like children, or men in a tennis-court, and

before our conquest is half won the dim twilight comes and stops the game ; nevertheless, let us keep our places, and, above all things, hold fast by the law of life we feel within. Let us follow in His steps, and we shall attain to the ideal life ; and, without waiting for our 'mortal passage,' tread the free and spacious streets of that Jerusalem which is above.

"He spoke more to himself than to me. The sun, which was just setting behind the distant hills, shone with dazzling splendour for a moment upon the towers and spires of the city across the placid water. Behind this fair vision were dark rain-clouds, before which gloomy background it stood in fairy radiance and light. For a moment it seemed a glorious city, bathed in life and hope, full of happy people who thronged its streets and bridge, and the margin of its gentle stream. But it was ' *breve gaudium.*' Then the sunset faded, and the ethereal vision vanished and the landscape lay dark and chill.

" ' The sun is set,' Mr. Inglesant said cheerfully, ' but it will rise again. Let us go home.' "

Only to those secure in such a serenity, amid all the terror of passing things, can come, in the splendour of sunset, so tranquil an acceptance of the ending of the day.

HENRY SIDGWICK

"THE year 1851," was said when Turner died, "will in the future be remembered less for what it has displayed than for what it has withdrawn." The same prophecy may surely be made of the year which took from us, scarcely noticed amid the clamour of disastrous war, John Ruskin and Henry Sidgwick.

Each was in many respects typical of the University he served so well. Ruskin was a child of Oxford. Eloquent, famous, dogmatic, no worshipper of consistency, he lived before the world, taking all men into the confidence of his changing opinion. Sidgwick, retired, restrained, almost unknown to the crowd, advanced with cautious steps, weighing each sentence before giving it utterance, putting his life-force into work for his University. The one attracted crowded audiences to his lectures, which were subsequently read wherever the English language was spoken. The other at Cambridge addressed twelve or twenty students, and only appealed in his writings to a few serious minds. The death of the one, even in the most perilous period of the war, was marked by the lamentation of the multitude. The death of the other passed almost unnoticed by the Press and the busy world. Future ages, I think, will find a difficulty in deciding to which of these two thinkers the world owes the profounder debt of gratitude.

DE MORTUIS

Clarity of thought and unwavering fairness towards opponents are characteristic of Sidgwick's philosophical writings. Only once did he appear to approach the limits of legitimate criticism : in his half-contemptuous dismissal of Herbert Spencer's philosophy as a serious advance in the progress of thought. For the rest his expositions of other men's systems were astonishingly clear and generous. He sometimes humorously complained that he had never been able to found a school at Cambridge : that no body of students acknowledged him as their master. How could he found a school of followers, who so temptingly placed before us the claims of so many different philosophies : who would expound another's creed with the same enthusiasm as his own ? The school he founded was a school of those who attained divergent positions, but who all acknowledged the lessons learnt from him:—fairness to opponents, ardent search for enlightenment, devotion to truth wherever it might lead them.

He had resigned his fellowship in early life as incompatible with his beliefs. He never faltered in his conviction of the impossibility of the old tests and articles. Yet all must have noted in his controversy with Dr. Rashdall on the limits of religious conformity, how anxious he was not to draw these limits tightly round others. He would allow for all possibilities before branding any fellow-man as guilty of the moral laxity which with him always ranked amongst the deadly sins. And yet with all this was no mistiness, no vagueness in which all distinction vanishes. The limit may be made as comprehensive as possible. But it is drawn at the last with no faltering hand. Beyond this line, as he can see it, there is a region to which no man may go without peril to his soul.

HENRY SIDGWICK

His "Ethics" is his greatest work. As a moralist he will first be remembered. They are right who say that he possessed a mind essentially analytical. They are wrong who assert that he confined himself to criticism and presented no constructive system. He broke up the old Utilitarianism, with its illogical confusion of the claims of self and others. He attempted to resolve all the social duties into the primary virtue of benevolence. And he acknowledged that the impulse to seek the happiness of others owns its origin to an intuition which no purely human outlook can justify or explain. So in his famous concluding chapter he protested the insufficiency of all the popular naturalistic systems, and the inadequacy of the moral sanction without the postulates of God and Immortality.

His work was greater than his writing. The University of Cambridge in its present constitution is largely his creation. For twenty years he was the acknowledged leader of the party of reform which effected the transition from the old age to the new. All through the struggle he was working for the expansion of the University beyond its ancient limitations, for the increasing of its capacity of national service. In the efforts for the abolition of sinecures, the abandonment of theological tests, the growth of the University beyond the limits of the Colleges, above all in the opening of its teaching to women students, he played a prominent part. He lived to see the quiet induction of changes which a former time would have contemplated with forebodings of ruin. Only at the close of his long term of service was the outlook clouded by the reaction inevitable after far-reaching reform. During his later years there came the triumph of a conservatism once impotent. All the special movements he had

DE MORTUIS

advanced were suddenly checked in their progress. The recognition of external students was refused by the rejection of their appeal for the diploma. The struggle for religious liberty was checked by the refusal to sanction St. Edmund's Hostel for Roman Catholic students. Above all, the long effort for the education of women was disastrously closed by the defeat of the appeal for the titular degree. He could not be indifferent to this change in the University he loved so well. He recognised the inevitable, resigned his position on the Council, and withdrew himself from the arena of conflict. Here was no feeling of pique or transitory despondence. But he acknowledged that his own work was done ; that the future belonged to a newer generation, inspired by different ideals.

So he noted a similar change in the wider questions of his time. He had thrown himself with ardour into the struggle for religious liberty which ennobled the middle years of the century. " Absorbed," he described the company to which he belonged, " in struggling for freedom of thought in the trammels of an historical religion." He had lived to see the triumph of his cause. Now a new age had dawned and new dangers threatened the health of society. He turned to confront the problems of the newer time. "Freedom is won," he said, "and what does Freedom bring us to ? It brings us face to face with atheistic science : the faith in God and Immortality, which we had been struggling to clear from superstition, suddenly seems to be *in the air :* and in seeking for a firm basis for the fight we find ourselves in the midst of the ' fight with death.' "

The Metaphysical Society of which he had been a member had represented the older struggle : the conflict of widely disordered faiths and denials. It had seen the triumph of its aims—the practical toleration of all forms of belief and negation. Now the time for reconstruction had come the survivors should gather together after the great conflict. So the newer Synthetic Society was formed: endeavouring to unite all those to whom the word "God" bore some intelligible meaning. He himself had laid down the first principles of union in his admirable clear essays. And in all the further work of reconstruction it is difficult to over-estimate the loss of his penetrating criticism, unflinching expression of truth, and eager search for faith adequate to save mankind from advancing indifference and decay.

His active work for the Psychical Research Society was but an application of the principle which guided all his progress. Here was no credulous search after a spirit of divination, or hunger for marvels in an age staled by custom. But he was ever the seeker for all knowledge which could throw light upon the things of life. He advanced as readily along new and unpopular paths as on the beaten tracks of progress. He ever waged unceasing war against the spirit of condemnation without judgment, of rejection of evidence because undesired, whether manifested in the older theology or the newer sciences. So he gave his great name and critical powers to the study of the mysterious phenomena of the border world. He was once the dupe of clever schemers, and often the subject of tho mockery of the Press. But he continued to support the work until the end. The evidence convinced him of the presence of dim, undefined forces, of something operating in the world of human consciousness which the ordinary man had failed to recognise and science had hitherto ignored: and he was determined in the necessity for the continuance of the study and the wresting of the control of obscure mental phenomena from the hands of the quack and the charlatan. But it failed to yield him, as it seemed to yield to some, clear and indubitable proof of the life beyond death. Neither here nor in any past time could he find satisfactory evidence of the penetration of the inscrutable secret of the grave.

The philosophical proofs of Theism he was unable to accept as satisfactory. "The more sceptical attitude," he said, "has remained mine through life." But he was convinced that belief in God and in Immortality are vital to human well-being. "Humanity" —this was his unshakable conviction—"humanity will not and cannot acquiesce in a godless world." He was eager to recognise the complete relativity of our knowledge : the vast sea of ignorance that surrounds us. One of his favourite theses rested on the possibility of another great religious inspiration. He could hope for the return of a period of unclouded faith after the age of disintegration had passed away. He re-echoes the famous lines of his friend, which he says he "could never read without tears " : the protest of the heart against the " freezing reason " and the sound of "an ever-breaking shore that tumbles in the godless deep " : the spirit that feels as "a child that cries but crying knows his Father near." *Wir heissen euch hoffen*—the sad yet not entirely mournful refuge of so many of the great men of his time—was his final message. "The revealing visions come and go : when they come we feel that we know : but in the intervals we must pass through states in which all is dark, and in which we can only struggle to hold the conviction that—

HENRY SIDGWICK

" Power is with us in the night
Which made the darkness and the light
And dwells not in the light alone."

Beyond the work, greater far than the creed, was the personality of the teacher we knew and loved. To the younger of us at Cambridge, seeing in him a figure who had "drunk delight of battle with his peers " in the controversies of the age, he seemed indeed the " Man of Wisdom " of the Greek dreamer ; the philosopher whom the people, were they not blind, would drag forth and crown king. To us he stood for "philosophy " at its highest. Here was the spirit which showed the power of the student of all time ând all existence. We noted in him the capacity for weighing evidence, the detached judgment, the multifarious interests in all the thought and progress of the world. His lectures were attended by a scanty few. Men complained that they were of little utility for the schools. In metaphysic he would spend the course of a term in defining the words used and laying down the first principles. The more impatient fled away. In ethic he would trace the course of his own spiritual development : from the Utilitarianism of Mill through the influence of Butler : a progress always directed to one end through the troubled waters of controversy. To those pursuing a difficult voyage through the same unquiet sea, the lectures proved unique and fascinating. When we came to know him personally, our respect and admiration deepened. His hospitality at Newnham was long to be remembered. Without the asceticism he repudiated or the luxury he deplored in the newer generation, he proved a host to whom we would readily have given all our evenings. He was a brilliant talker, and we would gladly have listened to him in silence. This he would never allow. He would draw out the retiring, tolerate the absurd, welcome even the dull and commonplace. Our most fatuous remarks would be accepted and discussed. We left feeling that we were worth more than we had thought before : humbled indeed by comparison with an almost impossible standard of attainment : but saved from utter self-distrust by the recognition that even to the mediocre and ignorant there was the possibility of an occasional inspiration.

Nor will his assistance be forgotten in deeper matters. More and more his advice was sought on questions of perplexity and honour. It came to be accepted that any course meeting with the approval of his high ideal of life could be pursued with clear conscience. Those alone who were accustomed to turn to him in the difficult problems of practical life could adequately understand the dreary, almost incredible blank created by the knowledge of his death.

The end was worthy of the life. A paper read before the Synthetic Society marked the beginning of the end. "Everybody was struck by the power of the paper," wrote one who was present, "but they were even more impressed by the animation and brilliance with which the reader took part in the subsequent debate. A few days later his hearers learnt that their guest had gone through the evening with the prospect of almost imminent death before him." The command had suddenly come to set his house in order. He prepared for death by a rapid and terrible disease as one going on a journey. One after the other he detached himself from the multifarious accumulated interests of a busy life. He resigned the professorship to which he had added such distinction, only anxious that the work should be carried forward by the most competent hands. He enforced secrecy as to the nature of his illness. He would leave the place in which he had played so high a part without any needless demonstration of ceremony or of pity. He set himself in the last few months of suffering, with no complaining against the inscrutable decree, to await the end : still willing, as far as in him lay, to perform the duties of life, still interested in the activities of the scene he was so soon to leave for ever.

Although all knew the end was inevitable and the most speedy was the most kindly, the news came with no ordinary wonder that Henry Sidgwick had joined the "unanswering generations of the dead." His writing represents the philosophy of a transitional time, and may not be destined long to endure. His reputation, always confined to the few, will soon vanish from the memory of man. But the character which shone so brightly through those closing scenes, greater far than his thought or his work, cannot but survive the inexorable years. *Wir heissen euch hoffen.* We bid you to hope. Is there anything more to say ?

FREDERIC MYERS

TOWARDS the end of Myers's life, inspired by that shining energy which only seemed to increase as the sun dropped to the horizon, the Psychical Research Society initiated an inquiry into the attitude of modern man towards the promise of immortal life. The investigation was, I believe, abandoned in England, where reticence still forbids an eager sincerity about ultimate questions. But it flourished mightily in America, where a new child race will discuss its own spiritual anatomy with all the candour of interested children. I am not sure if the complete results have ever been published. I know some of the replies to the printed questions were of extraordinary interest. The inquiry was of belief in immortality and of hope for immortality. The main revelation was of the latter. The attestation of man's belief is irrelevant. Few know what they believe at all. Belief changes from day to day, and in various atmospheres, like a guttering flame. Belief over the breakfast-table is something different from belief in time of the soul's upheaval, or confronting the piteous silence of the dead. And in any case belief or disbelief in life beyond the grave can have no effect upon that life's reality or illusion. But hope is more vital. A man is more at home with his desires. And the hope itself may be a

60

factor in that hope's fruition; in a universe where, as a matter of experience, each hungry soul receives its heart's desire; life more and fuller for those who demand it, for those who demand it also the sleep of an eternal night.

The answers exhibited a large and sincere body of opinion joyfully accepting this second alternative. The note of some was contentment with life well spent, slowly rounding off the long day's work into the tranquillity of evening. The cry of others was the old cry of startled fear at the unknown. "In that sleep of death what dreams may come" seems to become a question even more haunting with the advance of the years. They feared to take the chance. Visions of a future menace have been intensified by the spectral discoveries of the sciences. The rolling up of the curtain of space and time has revealed a boundless universe of night and terrors, flaring fires of sun and star, an abyss without purpose or plan. The perplexity of Tennyson in old age before the vision of Vastness, the pathetic cry of Spencer as he confronts an unintelligible evolution and dissolution with, beyond, an emptiness or reality all unknown, has bitten deep into the minds of the more serious men of the age.

But with most the desire for an end was built neither upon contentment with the present nor fear of an incalculable future. The proclamation of life-weariness was the dominant assertion. The shrinking was not from life's suffering and confusion, but from life itself. The assertion has come from a civilisation tired alike of so much—and so little—that the effort of hope and change is itself an evil; in a universe the fit consummation of whose courses will be rest and quietness.

Against such acquiescence all the life of this man

was one passionate protest. He was filled with a fury of aspiration similar to that of Tennyson after life's unending day. Better life in all the circles of the mediæval inferno, both of these life-worshippers asserted, than life vanishing like the vapour or the candle-flame when the tale is told. The triumph of death was the one unendurable consummation. The acceptance of such a belief, while it lasted, in his own experience emptied the zest from human action, stole all the colours from the flowers. Life under such a domination of greyness became a mere gnawing of dead bones, a mumbling in the darkness ; told by an idiot ; signifying nothing. Myers refused to accept such a negation until some voice which rendered doubt impossible proclaimed the death of man, and no hope in dust. In the midst of an age and civilisation stamped with life-weariness, literature everywhere finding a sombre satisfaction in the end of it all, he appears as a figure from another, more ardent, age. He belongs in spirit to that earlier time when life piled on life appeared all too little for the hungry heart of man ; or to the new outburst of human energies in the birth of modern days, when man flung himself with a kind of heroic fury upon the boundaries of his tiny world.

It is in this nursing of the unconquerable hope through an age too much inclined to abandon the quest in despair, that Myers remained as a figure of unfading interest ; far more than in any definite discovery which he thought himself to have made of that hope's vindication. Given life, he was entirely content with anything that life might bring. He never had any fear of the possibilities of evil dreams. He demanded no paradise of jewels and gold. He feared no clumsy or malignant forces. He asked merely " the glory of going on and still to be."

FREDERIC MYERS

His attitude to the last was one of a large curiosity ;
"a little disappointed," he once wrote to me after
illness, at not "passing over." It was a re-echo of
Kingsley's "Beautiful, kind Death, when will you come
and tell me what I want to know?" Something was
there of Whitman's brave spirit as the shadow crept
ever nearer over the hills—

> " The untold want—by life and land ne'er granted
> Now voyager, sail thou forth to seek and find."

The fragment of autobiography, published after his
death, so perfect in form, so resonant, to those of us
privileged to know its author, of that triumph of certainty
which filled all its later years, so tantalisingly brief and
broken to some who knew how much he had to say of
life's spiritual voyages, exhibited in every line this concern in the one absorbing question. Early religion
which never gripped the heart yielded immediately to
the fascinations of the Hellenic ideal. It was a species
of intoxication ; fostering evil as well as good ; aiding
in his own words " imaginative impulse and detachment
from sordid interests " ; but providing " no check for
pride." It rose in a night as a revelation of a world of
unfading beauty. It fell in a day with the realisation that
nothing remained of it all but ruins and a dream. In a
vision, gazing from the summit of Syra on Delos and the
Cyclades, and those straits and channels of purple sea,
he apprehended that all this was dead and gone for ever.
And he turned, "with a passion of regret," from a world
which suddenly had crumbled to a little dust.

Afterwards, through the influence of Josephine Butler,
"Christian conversation came in a potent form." He
was introduced by an inner door, "not to its encum-

bering forms and dogmas, but to its heart of fire."
That "heart of fire" breathes through every line of
"St. Paul," the one great Evangelical poem of the
century :—

> " Yea through life, death, thro' sorrow and thro' sinning
> He shall suffice me, for He hath sufficed;
> Christ is the end, for Christ was the beginning,
> Christ the beginning, for the end is Christ."

Alas! the vision faded, and the ardour. "I, even I,"
at first he could write to a friend, "wretched and half-
hearted beginner as I am, can almost say already that I
know the thing is true." "Gradual disillusion" came
from increased knowledge of history and of science, from
wider outlook on the world. That Christ, as in the
vision of a whole age, now appeared as "dead in that
lone Syrian town." The manger is found, filled with
mouldy hay; the rain pours through the broken roof;
the wind moans outside unheeded :—

> " The ancient stars are tired and dim,
> And no new star announces Him."

"Insensibly the celestial vision faded"; and "left
me to ' pale despair and cold tranquillity.' "

" It was the hope of the whole world that was
vanishing," he wrote, "not more alone." The effect
of agnosticism upon him was wholly evil. "During
this phase only can I remember anything of dreariness
and bitterness—of scorn of human life, of anger at
destiny, of deliberate preference of the pleasures of the
passing hour."

An entry in the diary, "H.S. on Ghosts," marked the
first line of light on the horizon. The thought came
to him of turning the weapons of negation against itself
and utilising in the work of rebuilding the very forces

64

which had destroyed the cloud-capped palaces. Life's continuance should no longer be guaranteed by dreams and visions, wild, unsupported hopes, à priori philosophy, or the shadowy remembrance of things belonging to an ever remoter past. But the evidence of the empirical method itself, the severest tests which reason could desire of manifestations now actually in the world, should certify existence beyond the grave. Science should itself rebuild what science had destroyed.

Varied motives drew first together that little band of adventurers who were prepared to explore and to occupy regions of experience, avoided by the common man as poisonous and unclean. With some it was the demand for rescue of such mysterious kingdoms from the dominion of the criminal and the charlatan. With others it was the conviction, an inheritance from the ardour of the Renaissance, that no element in this unintelligible world should be ruled out of investigation. With a third was a faint, if never entirely articulate, hope that here might be given the very key of the unopened door, which every generation of man had sought to find in vain. Myers, then, as in all his days, made no secret of his motive. It was less to investigate dispassionately with a scientific detachment than with a kind of furious determination to tear from Nature herself the secret she had hidden for so long that he undertook this exploration of the rubbish-heaps of life. He confesses his first reluctance to "re-entering by the scullery window the heavenly mansion out of which I had been kicked by the back door." But he wrestled with this mysterious spirit behind the world's outward show, as Jacob wrestled with his mysterious visitant till the breaking of the day. "'I will not let thee go until thou bless me'—so cried I in spirit to that unanswering shade."

F

DE MORTUIS

In that heroic struggle he consumed the remainder of his days. From near the beginning he held himself to have obtained the evidence he desired. That hope sustained him to the end. The results can be studied in innumerable green volumes, *The Transactions of the "Psychical Research Society,"* and in the great work issued after his death, in which he sets out at length the evidence and the theories he had built upon it. It was not an opinion, but a conviction. It transfigured all his later life. I had the privilege of working some slight degree with him in the last years. I shall never forget the eagerness with which he essayed the work of investigation, the welcome to all obscure and remote testimony, the sense almost of awe with which he would announce some fresh fragment of evidence, however grotesque or ridiculous. No devotee of the older religion hunted for souls more eagerly than Myers hunted for news of ghost stories and telepathy and roaming personalities and inexplicable tricks of hypnotism and magic. I remember in sorting evidence with him noting how his spirits would rise as the record of some particular incident would deepen in mystery and horror. It was a lifelong disappointment to him that, although he pursued ghosts with the ardour of the youthful Shelley, the actual vision was never vouchsafed to him. No evidence of fraud deterred him. No ridicule in the least affected him. After the detection of deliberate cheating in one notorious " medium " at Cambridge, his companions (perhaps wisely) refused to have any further communication with her. Myers was undeterred He was summoned to fresh *séances* at Paris ; and I well remember being called to meet him on his return and finding him triumphantly convinced that in this particular case phenomena had occurred beyond the possibilities of human trickery to devise.

66

FREDERIC MYERS

The generations of undergraduates who passed so quickly by him regarded all this with perplexity. He was a magnificent lecturer upon literature and much in demand for literary societies. He always charged his discussion of his subject—Swinburne, Morris, and the rest—with the expression of the one hope which burned like a flame at his heart. He would gather small bands of students, attracted somewhat fearfully, to listen to his occult revelations. One meeting especially I recollect, in which, after Myers had told a succession of ever more blood-curdling ghost stories, in the breathless silence a late arrival suddenly crashed against the door outside. The effect was somewhat similar to the knocking at the gate after the murder of Macbeth, an immediate galvanic shock in the " startled air."

His own life and vitality seemed more convincing evidence of immortality than all these testimonies of strange forces. It was impossible to conceive that strong soul passing into nothingness, the triumphant energy meekly bowing before the supremacy of death. His purpose was ever to sail beyond the sunset. Exultation was in all his doing. It is upon a note of exultation he closes his brief testimony of a life given to high causes. Exultation remains in the great line which is carved upon the tablet erected to his memory beyond the walls of Rome, in that most sacred spot of English ground outside the boundaries of England. Above the tomb where lies all that is mortal of Shelley, stands the self-chosen summary of his life's devotion—

Ἀρνύμενος ἥντε ψυχήν καὶ νόστον ἑταίρων,

" Striving to save my own soul, and my comrades homeward way."

GEORGE GISSING

OF all the losses which literature has lately endured, the death of Gissing stands out as most exhibiting the ragged edge of tragedy. That Death should come just at the wrong moment was indeed entirely congruous with a life which seemed all through the sport of the gods. The irony of some malign or malicious power seemed to be laid upon the course of this troubled existence. It was almost with a clutch of some frantic laughter—a laughter more desolate than tears—that there came to his friends, at the moment when life at last seemed beginning, the news that life was at an end.

One's whole being revolted against such a bitter bludgeoning of fate. Readers of "Mark Rutherford" will remember the restrained but passionate irony of the close. After the unendurable years are over, when life has emerged into afternoon, with a prospect of light at eventide, a few dispassionate sentences tell of a sudden chance chill, a few days' struggle, and then—another of earth's unimportant millions lies quiet for ever. So it was with George Gissing. A long struggle against heavy odds, the experience of the worst, public neglect and private tragedies, had at last given place to something like hopefulness and fame. Recognition, long deserved, had arrived. The crudest of life's cruelties had vanished. A benigner outlook, a softer, kindlier vision of the "farcical melodrama" of man's existence had been apparent in these later months. The words of the last of his books he saw published sound strangely prophetic. "We hoped"—so he wrote of "Henry Ryecroft"—"we hoped it would all last for many a year ; it seemed, indeed, as though Ryecroft had only need of rest and calm to become a hale man." "It had always been his wish to die suddenly. . . . He lay down upon the sofa in his study, and there—as his calm face declared—passed from slumber into the great silence."

This is not the time to tell the details of that troubled life, of the tragedy which lay behind that arduous literary toil and coloured all the outlook with indignation and pain. Some day, for the edification or the warning of the children of the future, the full story will be told. All that it is necessary to know at the present is contained in those books in which the author, under the thin veil of fiction, is protesting out of his own heart's bitterness against the existence to which he has been committed. "For twenty years he had lived by the pen. He was a struggling man beset by poverty and other circumstances very unpropitious to work." "He did a great deal of mere hack-work : he reviewed, he translated, he wrote articles. There were times, I have no doubt, when bitterness took hold upon him ; not seldom he suffered in health, and probably as much from moral as from physical overstrain." The tyranny of this nineteenth-century Grub Street drove his genius into a hard and narrow groove. He might have developed into a great critic—witness the promise of his essay on Dickens. There was humour in him all unsuspected by the public till the appearance of "The Town Traveller."

And a keen eye for natural beauty, and a power of description of the charm and fascination of places, and a passionate love of nature and of home were only made manifest in "By the Ionian Sea," and the last and most kindly volume.

All this was sacrificed: in part to a perverted sense of "Mission," the burden, as he thought, laid upon him to proclaim the desolation of modern life : partly to a determination to make manifest to all the world his repugnance and disgust. He remains, and will remain, in literature as the creator of one particular picture. Gissing is the painter, with a cold and mordant accuracy, of certain phases of city life, especially of the life of London, in its cheerlessness and bleakness and futility, during the years of rejoicing at the end of the nineteenth century. If ever in the future the long promise of the Ages be fulfilled, and life becomes beautiful and passionate once again, it is to his dolorous pictures that men will turn for a vision of the ancient tragedies in a City of Dreadful Night.

Gissing rarely if ever described the actual life of the slum. He left to others the natural history of the denizens of "John Street" and the "Jago." The enterprise, variety, and adventurous energy of those who led the existence of the beast would have disturbed with a human vitality the picture of his dead world. It was the classes above these enemies of society, in their ambitions and pitiful successes, which he made the subject of his genius. He analyses into its constituent atoms the matrix of which is composed the characteristic city population. With artistic power and detachment he constructs his sombre picture, till a sense of almost physical oppression comes upon the reader, as in some strange and disordered dream.

70

GEORGE GISSING

There are but occasional vivid incidents; the vitriol-throwing in "The Nether World"; the struggle of the Socialists in "Demos," as if against the tentacles of some slimy and unclean monster; the particular note of revolt sounded in "New Grub Street," when the fog descends not merely upon the multitude who acquiesce, but upon the few who resist. But in general the picture is merely of the changes of time hurrying the individuals through birth, marriage, and death, but leaving the general resultant impression unchanged. *Vanitas vanitatum* is written large over an existence which has "never known the sunshine nor the glory that is brighter than the sun." Human life apprehends nothing of its possibilities of sweetness and gentleness and high passion. The energies, rude or tired, flaming into pitiful revolt or accepting from the beginning the lesson of inevitable defeat, end all alike in dust and ashes.

The Islington of "Demos," the Camberwell of "The Year of Jubilee," the Lambeth of "Thyrza": how the whole violent soul of the man revolted against existence set in these! The outward obsession of the grey labyrinth seemed to reflect the spirit of a race of tragic ineptitude. Comfort has been attained, and some security. But beauty has fled from the heart, and the hunger for it passed into a vague discontent. Religion has lost its high aspiration. Passion has become choked in that heavy air. The men toil—the decent and the ignobly decent—without ever a sense of illumination in the dusty ways, or the light of a large purpose in it all. The women—what an awful picture-gallery of women appears in Gissing's tales of suburban existence!—nag and hate, are restless with boredom and weariness, pursue ignoble, unattainable social

71

aspirations, desire without being satisfied. The whole offers a vision more disquieting and raucous than any vision of the squalor of material failure. Here, the Showman seems to announce at intervals, always with an ironic smile, here is the meaning of culture, civilisation, religion—in the forefront of your noisy "progress," in the city of your heart's desire.

"Her object," said Mr. Hutton, of George Eliot's "Middlemarch," "is to paint not the grand defeat, but the helpless entanglement and miscarriage of noble aims, to make us see the eager stream of high purpose, not leaping destructively from the rock, but more or less silted up in the dreary sands of modern life." I have often thought this might serve for a verdict upon all Gissing's characteristic work. To produce this result he had, indeed, to cut out great sections of human activity. The physical satisfaction in food and the greater physical satisfaction in drink ; the delight in the excitement of betting, an election, an occasional holiday ; the illumination which comes to a few, at least, from a spiritual faith or an ideal cause ; even the commonest joy of all, " the only wage," according to the poet, which " love ever asked " :

"A child's white face to kiss at night,
A woman's smile by candlelight " :

—all these, if introduced at all, appear merely to relieve for a moment the picture of the desolation of London's incalculable, bewildered millions. Gissing set himself a legitimate artistic effort : the representation of modern life in a certain aspect, seen under a certain mood. It is London, not in the glories of starlight or sunset, but under the leaden sky of a cold November afternoon. The third of Henley's "London Voluntaries" is the characteristic outward scene of Mr. Gissing's gaunt picture ; in which the " afflicted city "

> " seems
> A nightmare labyrinthine, dim and drifting,
> With wavering gulfs and antic heights, and shifting,
> Rent in the stuff of a material dark,
> Wherein the lamplight, scattered and sick and pale,
> Shows like the leper's living blotch of bale."

The vision does not even possess the sense of magic and mystery of twilight and gathering night. The universe is simply raw and wretched, with a wind scattering the refuse of the gutter, and, too hideous and grotesque even to evoke compassion, a few old tramps and forlorn children shivering in the cold.

It was because we saw in Gissing's later works an escape from this insistent and hideous dream, a promise of a warmer, saner outlook upon human development and desire, that we felt as a kind of personal outrage the news of his early death. For skilled, artistic craftsmanship he held the first place in the ranks of the younger authors of to-day. He was only forty-six years old. The later books seemed to open possibilities of brilliant promise. The bitterness had become softened. The general protest against the sorry scheme of human things seemed to be passing into a kind of pity for all that suffers, and an acceptance with thankfulness of life's little pleasures. The older indignation had yielded to perplexity as of a suffering child. With something of that perplexity—with a new note of wistfulness, the sudden breaking of the springs of compassion—George Gissing passes from a world of shadows which he found full of uncertainty and pain.

SPENCER AND CARLYLE

A COMPARISON

HERBERT SPENCER tells, in his autobiography, how shortly after his migration to London George Henry Lewes took him to see a writer whose work he had already examined with interest. "My visits numbered three," he notes, "or at the outside four, always in company with Lewes, and then I ceased to go. I found that I must either listen to his absurd dogmas in silence, which it was not in my nature to do, or get into fierce arguments with him, which ended in our glaring at one another. As the one alternative was impracticable and the other disagreeable, it resulted that I dropped the acquaintanceship." And Spencer goes on to complain of Carlyle that "he thought in a passion" (and, hence, could not be regarded as a philosopher, who, above all others, thinks calmly) ; that the "old Norse ferocity" was strong within him ; that he "lacked co-ordination alike intellectually and morally." "He had a daily secretion of curses which he had to vent on somebody or something."

A verbatim report of these three or four meetings would prove to-day inimitable reading. For when Carlyle and Spencer came together there was an encounter not only of two personalities but of two civilisations.

74

SPENCER AND CARLYLE

Spencer exhibited a life, for perhaps the first time in history, entirely organised on a rational and scientific basis. Each separate action was referred to general laws. Guidance was sought in the complicated tangle of life not in any "venture of faith," still less in the commands of human emotion; but in a codified system of evolutionary ethics, with a deliberate search for such elements of pleasure as could be obtained without interference with the pleasure of others. In places this system of natural morality became as casuistical and exacting as any of the rules and systems of venial and mortal sins of the Catholic moralists. Spencer turned back upon past action directed towards a certain end to examine with an almost pathetic refinement whether as a matter of fact the end has been attained; whether, for example, he had derived more happiness from billiards than might have been derived from other alternative occupation; whether he was justified in the use of opium; whether in his final examination of his whole life history he could pronounce, with some anticipation of an ultimate verdict of a Day of Judgment, that he had chosen aright in determining to devote his life to the cause of Evolution. He acknowledged a continuous tradition of Nonconformist upbringing and ancestry, with no crossing of the pure stock—so that by inheritance he became the very incarnation of the "Dissidence of Dissent." This, overlaid with the inheritance of the "acquired characters" of three generations of schoolmasters, explained sufficiently to himself the prevalence of those unamiable characteristics which he confessed with such naïve simplicity. An aggressive disagreement with persons and accepted traditions, refusal always to brook contradiction, that inability to tolerate error in others which compelled him always to set them right when wrong, combined to make him a difficult person in society. "No one will deny," he said, "that I am much given to criticism. Along with exposition of my own views, there has always gone a pointing out of defects in the views of others." The "tendency to fault-finding is dominant—disagreeably dominant." Such fault-finding, he dismally announced, had brought into his life a double loss—on the one hand leading " to more or less disagreeableness in social intercourse "; on the other "it has partially debarred me from the pleasures of admiration by making me too much awake to mistakes and shortcomings."

Carlyle's dissent from current opinion was, indeed, as intolerant and even louder-voiced; but it was passionate instead of rational, and hence far easier to endure. All his opponents were consigned in storm to the nether pit. The extravagant ferocity of denunciation was streaked with gleams of wild humour revealing a human being, an inspired, wilful, petulant child. There was nothing of the child in Spencer. The fault-finding was thin-lipped, rational, probably in every case justified, and hence intolerable. Each of these men was the product of inherited traditions of belief and conduct : of traditions which regarded happiness as outside the legitimate objects of man's endeavour. When Spencer attempted to organise his life upon an hedonistic basis all these traditions, which had become part of the very fibre of his being, leapt upwards in protest and rendered the experiment a failure. He was ever asking himself, "what have been the motives prompting my career—how much have they been egoistic and how much altruistic?" Caught in such cobwebs he painfully laboured through the whole catalogue; examining in detail how far in controversy "the wish for personal success has gone along with the wish to establish the truth," and how far the one has predominated over the other ; or, whether he would have done better to marry ; or explaining how " in the kind of beneficence distinguishable as positive," the incentives " have been commonly neutralised by dislike to taking the requisite trouble." And every day as it passed became a subject of critical study and regret because it had gone charged with less positive pleasure than might have been.

In the " reflections " at the end of the autobiography Spencer told of a chance incident of travel " in the days of my difficulties when compelled to travel in third-class carriages." " Opposite to me," he says, " sat a man who, at the time I first observed him, was occupied in eating food he had brought with him—I should rather say devouring it, for his mode of eating was so brutish as to attract my attention and fill me with disgust, a disgust which verged into anger. Some time after, when he had finished his meal and become quiescent, I was struck by the woebegone expression of his face. Years of suffering were registered on it, and while I gazed on the sad eyes and deeply-marked lines I began to realise the life of misery through which he had passed. As I continued to contemplate the face, and to understand all which its expressions of distress implied, the pity excited in me went to the extent of causing that constriction of the throat which strong feeling sometimes produces."

This extract might serve as a sample of the whole life history. The dispassionate pomposity of language, the dispassionate contemplation of his own emotions, the absorption first in the nature of the resonances and reactions produced by external events in the mind of the individual Herbert Spencer, accompanied by a detachment and cold criticism which frees such absorption from any charge of selfishness—such elements combined made of those thousand pages one of the most extraordinary of all human records. It would appear not impossible, indeed, that the author may be remembered for the personal history taken up in old age, and mainly to break the tedium of enforced idleness, long after the laborious constructions of the synthetic philosophy have become not only buried, but forgotten.

Much of the life reads like frank caricature, the kind of rather cruel satire that used to be written by Mr. Mallock in his younger days. The reference of each chance action to large principles, the humourless judgment of events, the laborious justification of fishing or billiards—all these produce an effect which would be inexpressibly ludicrous but for the pathos of the whole affair. In the author's earlier years "there was no sign of marked liking for children," he says in his quaint, impersonal fashion. "My feeling was of a tepid kind." Late in life, in an existence "passed chiefly in bed and on the sofa, I one day, while thinking over modes of killing time, bethought me that the society of children might be a desirable distraction." Children were demanded and children supplied. The result was "to awaken, in a quite unanticipated way, the philoprogenitive instinct," and the society of two little girls "afforded me a great deal of positive gratification." Henceforward "the presence of a pair of children, now from this family of the clan, and now from that, has formed a leading gratification—I may say the chief gratification—during each summer's sojourn in the country." Criticism is struck dumb by such entries as these. It is life organised on the system of the Data of Ethics and the millennium there preached; a man moving through the rich and passionate experience of to-day with complete obedience to a reasonable appeal : a kind of nightmare of an entirely rational world.

One possible variation from such frantic sanity was rejected as soon as it was understood. Spencer describes his early friendship with George Eliot, "the most admirable woman, mentally, I ever met." He took her to the opera and the theatre, where he had free admissions—more used " because I had frequently— indeed, nearly always—the pleasure of her companionship, in addition to the pleasure afforded by the performance." He was then but thirty-two, and the philosophy had scarcely been projected. There were out-of-door walks, discussions on the terrace outside Somerset House. "People drew inferences." "Quite definite statements became current." "There were reports that I was in love with her, and that we were about to be married. But neither of these reports was true." In the reflections at the end, forty years afterwards, some indication of the reason was revealed. He had described in painful detail her actual physical appearance. "Usually heads have here and there either flat places or slight hollows : but her head was everywhere convex." He had once criticised a great beauty, alike in face and figure, " I do not quite like the shape of her head." "This abnormal tendency to criticise has been a chief factor," he sadly acknowledged, "in the continuance of my celibate life." "Physical beauty is a *sine quâ non* for me; as was once unhappily proved where the intellectual traits and the emotional traits were of the highest."

Spencer's sturdy individualism produced a complete

disregard of authority, and that contempt or indifference for accepted opinion which was perhaps necessary for the elaboration of a new and unpopular philosophy. The extraordinary judgments on books and men scattered through the life are examples both of this waywardness and of that complete absence of moral fear which the author also recognised in himself. Of Plato, "time after time I have attempted to read," he said, "and have put it down in a state of impatience with the indefiniteness of the thinking and the mistaking of words for things." "To call that a 'dialogue,'" he added, with that disordered common-sense which was the curse of his existence, "which is an interchange of speeches between the thinker and his 'dummy,' who says just what it is convenient to have said, is absurd." For Ballads with recurring burdens he felt "a kind of vicarious shame, at their inane repetition of an idea." Commencing Homer, "for the purpose of studying the superstitions of the early Greeks," after reading some six books he "felt what a task it would be to go on—felt that I would rather give a large sum than read to the end." He found "the tedious enumerations of details of dresses and sums," the "boyish practice of repeating descriptive names," "the many absurdities, such as giving the genealogy of a horse while in the midst of battle," the "ceaseless repetition of battles and speeches" intolerable. Delighted with the "Modern Painters," he opened the "Stones of Venice" with raised expectations. "On looking at the illustrations, however, and reading the adjacent text, I presently found myself called upon to admire a piece of work which seemed to me sheer barbarism. My faith in Mr. Ruskin's judgment was at once destroyed, and thereafter I paid no further attention to his writings than was implied by reading portions quoted in reviews or elsewhere."

Such vigorous dismissal became more serious when the work was a piece of essential criticism in his own subject. Commencing the reading of Kant's critique, Spencer fell upon the proposition that "Time and space are nothing but subjective forms." This "I rejected at once and absolutely; and having done so went no further." "It has always been out of the question for me to go on reading a book the fundamental principle of which I entirely dissent from," owing to the "utter incredulity of the proposition itself" and "the want of confidence in the reasonings, if any, of one who could accept a proposition so incredible." Kant was flung aside. "Whenever in later years I have taken up Kant's critique I have similarly stopped short after rejecting its primary proposition." It is interesting to remember that two of the most influential minds of the nineteenth century, who, if not exactly philosophers, at least dealt largely with the subject-matter of philosophy—the one from the side of theology, the other from that of the natural sciences—had thus failed to read the work which has laid the foundation of all future speculation. If Newman had read Kant earlier in life or Spencer's impatience of absurdity had not prevented him from persevering in its study, both the theological and scientific progress, the "Oxford Movement" and the "New Reformation," might have been profoundly modified.

The actual effort demanded in the construction of the synthetic philosophy was nothing short of heroic. The struggle through so many years of neglect and failure, the persistence, through failing health, in poverty, at the cost of final nervous collapse, is an achievement for which the world is richer, which should go down to the future as one of the great triumphs of human resolution over circumstance. After the early years spent in engineering invention and wanderings, Spencer felt the call to his life work. Intense mental strain at the age of thirty-five upon a constitution naturally neurotic—he was the only surviving child of parents both of whom exhibited marked and painful mental derangement—produced insomnia and mental disturbance, which lasted the remainder of his life. All excitement had to be avoided, correspondence declined, the working parts of life jealously guarded for the great undertaking. Many of the chapters were dictated at intervals of racquets or rowing, the only practicable method—a quarter of an hour's exercise, then ten minutes' dictation, then exercise again.

No less heroic was the long struggle for persistence against poverty. There is a letter written to John Stuart Mill inquiring concerning the possibility of a post at the India Office, which is almost elemental in its simplicity and dignity. "Unhappily my books have at present no adequate sale," writes the author. "Not only have they entailed upon me the negative loss of years spent without remuneration, but also a heavy positive loss in unrepaid expenses of publication. What little property I had has been thus nearly all dissipated. And now that I am more anxious than ever to persevere, it seems likely that I shall be unable to do so. My health does not permit me to spend leisure hours in these higher pursuits, after a day spent in remunerative occupation. And thus there appears no alternative but to desist."

After an attempt to issue the books by subscription,

the failure of adequate support again threatened abandonment. To prevent this Mill offered to guarantee the expenses of future publication and past losses—"a simple proposition," as he termed it, " of co-operation for an important public purpose, for which you give your labour and have given your health." The letters in which this offer—" a manifestation of feeling between authors that has rarely been paralleled "—was made by Mill and declined by Spencer are permanent assets in the honourable record of literature.

Eventually, partly through liberal support in America, partly through small inherited legacies, the work went on. " I am quite content to give my labour for nothing. I am content even to lose something by unrepaid costs of authorship. But it is clear that I shall not be able to bear the loss that now appears likely." Such were the efforts by which a philosophy not remote and difficult, but perhaps the most widely popular of all nineteenth-century expositions, could alone become articulate.

The cost to its originator in vital power was irreparable. At the end he discussed whether he had chosen well. Financially, " it was almost a miracle that I did not sink before success was reached." " One who devotes himself to grave literature must be content to remain celibate." " Adequate appreciation of works not adapted to satisfy popular desires is long in coming, if it ever comes." Against such tardy recognition he set the exasperation of misstatement and the anger of threatened interests and offended prejudice. " Do I regret that I was not stopped by such dissuasions ? " he mournfully asked. " I cannot say yes." So great was the impulse to proclaim the truth that any resistance would merely have produced " chronic irritation hardly to be borne." "Once having become possessed by the conception of evolution in its comprehensive form, the desire to elaborate and set it forth was so strong that to have passed life in doing something else would, I think, have been almost intolerable."

To some, and especially to those hailing the synthetic philosophy as immortal, the triumph of the achievement may seem amply to compensate the ruin of its cost. I must confess a different impression. An enormous sadness broods over Spencer's life history. At the beginning are the shadowy recollections of ancestors, of hard, joyless lives, whose ultimate impression is one of futility and failure. One grandfather appears as a gaunt, pitiful figure, whose mental decay "took the form of supposing that he had matters of business to look after, and led to rambles through the town with a vain desire to fulfil them." The other is "the image of a melancholy-looking old man sitting by the fireside, rarely saying anything and rarely showing any signs of pleasure." The substitution of a conscious creed of hedonism for the stern Puritan survey of life seemed to bring but little benefit to their descendant. All through happiness proves elusive : the secret of well-being is not apprehended ; the sense of failure and baffled purposes is written large over the whole story. At one period all his friends urged him to marry as a remedy for his nervous affections. "Ever since I was a boy," he sorrowfully writes, "I have been longing to have my affections called out. I have been in the habit of considering myself but half alive, and have often said that I hoped to begin to live some day."

That "some day" never arrived. To the end existence was woven in a kind of bloodless scheme of moral principle, with the changes rung on egoistic and altruistic impulse ; as divorced from the life of men who love and hunger and desire, as the vision of the under-world of the Greek hereafter to those who shivered at its advent. In the later years the fame of Herbert Spencer has gone out through all lands. Him-self, an old man, wearied, and much concerned with his maladies, is passing to his grave amid mournful memories. For a few minutes in the morning he can dictate perhaps half a page of his biography. "Through the rest of the day the process of killing time has to be carried on as best it may." Walking has to be re-stricted to a few hundred yards ; reading of the lightest kind proves as injurious as working ; conversation has to be kept within narrow bounds ; recreation is im-possible, " two games of backgammon " having " caused a serious relapse." At night, in spite of the use of opium, there is never a full, continuous sleep. "No ingenuity," was his pathetic summary, " can prevent weariness."

All outside the tangible, material universe had been rejected at the beginning, and rejected almost without a pang ; relegated to the region of the Unknowable and seemingly left there without any further interest or con-cern. Religion never left him because it never came to him. "Memory does not tell me the extent of my divergence from current beliefs," he here confesses. "The 'creed of Christendom' was evidently alien to my nature, both emotional and intellectual. The ex-pressions of adoration of a personal being, the utterance of laudations, and the humble professions of obedience, never found in me any echoes." Early he wrote, "We cannot know" over all the ultimate questions of the Universe ; and, with his entirely reasonable mind, de-clined any further to trouble himself about them.

DE MORTUIS

Occasionally, as when after his only game of golf with Huxley, he sees some boys bathing and wonders how such a creature as man has attained such dominance over the beasts of the field, some of the disordered and inexplicable things of life strike his fancy. But for the most part that sense of incongruity which is the foundation of humour was absent; wanting not only in the pleasant fancies of verbal play but in the large and fundamental ironies of things which form the soul of tragedy. To a mind so entirely synthetic the universe came to arrange itself in relations, cubes, and parallels, an orderly framework; and the elements which would not fit into this definite scheme of cause and effect were quietly dropped out of sight. Even the great bereavements common to the lot of man awaken no sense of deeper meanings or clamorous, unanswered questionings. After the death of his mother—the loss which he seemed to have felt most deeply—he laments, with sorrow but with a reasoned outlook, a life " of monotonous routine, very little relieved by positive pleasure." The utmost he will allow is regret for " the dull sense of filial obligations which exist at the time when it is possible to discharge them, contrasted with the keen sense of them which arises when such discharge is no longer possible." Some natural tears he shed, but dried them soon ; convincing himself, with more success than the philosopher in " Rasselas," of the folly of grieving over irrevocable things.

Only at the end, when he is suddenly confronted with the brooding menace of death, does he realise the fact that beyond the evolutionary scheme were strange unfathomed possibilities, that the reason of man was but a tiny rushlight in an immense solitude, a plumb-line swung into the midst of an unbounded deep.

SPENCER AND CARLYLE

With Tennyson, he trembles before a vision of Vastness, the abysm strewn with stars and the great cold beyond their transitory flames. He gazes back into a waste of time, forward into a future like a shoreless sea. He can make no meaning of the world itself, the strange life spreading in the depths of ocean, the thousand types which have for ever gone. The insistent query haunts him, "To what end?" Along with this is the paralysing thought, "What if of all this thus incomprehensible to us there exists no comprehension anywhere." Suddenly he finds a new sympathy awakened within him towards the adherents of the religions which he had formerly despised ; seeing these, as it were, the gathering of men together for warmth and companionship in the darkness of space, and the silence. "Religious creeds"—so he concludes his astonishing narrative—"I have come to regard with a sympathy based on community of need ; feeling that dissent from them results from inability to accept the solutions offered, joined with the wish that solutions could be found."

In the life of Carlyle we are breathing an entirely different atmosphere. The contrast cuts deep into the basis of being. Spencer is devoted above all things to liberty as an end. "As if it were a sin to control, or coerce into better methods human swine in any way," is Carlyle's scornful comment upon reading Mill's defence of the same position. Spencer again is at the heart of the scientific movement, the "New Reformation," which was to create new heavens and a new earth. "Can you really turn a ray of light on its axis by magnetism?" Carlyle shouts scornfully ; "and if you could, what should I care?" Beyond

these questions of opinion is the fundamental divergence
in the outlook upon experience and its meaning. If
Spencer's life was maimed by a too complete limitation
to the things which are seen, Carlyle's was troubled by
too insistent apprehension of the Unseen Universe. In
an entry in his journal he describes how "I have been
at Mrs. Austin's, heard Sydney Smith for the first time
guffawing, other persons prating, jargoning. To me,
through these thin cobwebs, Death and Eternity sate
glaring." And the Vision of Death and Eternity,
glaring through all that travail of eighty years, was
not conducive to tranquillity.

In one of his letters Carlyle tells how, after a period
of severe mental strain, he rode down solitary into
Sussex : through "the Norman Conqueror's country,"
the "green chalk hills, pleasant villages, good people,
and yellow corn." "It is all, in my preternatural
sleepless mood," he writes, "like a country of miracle
to me. I feel it strange that it is there, that I am here."
The sentence might stand for the secret of that
violent life. The record is of one moving through
a drowsy world in a "preternatural sleepless mood";
and the nineteenth century, however to the dulled
eye mechanical and grey, is to this man always "a
country of miracle." The sense of magic, of enchantment, hangs over the whole history. The present,
so mean as it appears and so commonplace, has become
transfigured with something of a glory only in general
realised when that present has become the past and to-
day has consented to be yesterday. The world of Nature
is everywhere charged with glamour, silences and
appeals which awaken emotion beyond the power of
words. The world of man, the turmoil of politics
and society chatter, is stricken through with the

sense of great issues and a purpose beyond time. The humble society of peasants living obscurely in remote regions, the deaths and births and affections which form the common lot of common humanity, are illuminated with colours which are the stuff of dreams, and set in a background of all the Eternities.

It is this transformation of the drab things of to-day which gives this man his power of fascination and wonder. In the letters is the real Carlyle: the man in his true self: " a wild man," as he describes himself, " a man disunited from the fellowship of the world he lives in." It is a life lived at a furnace heat of emotion, extravagant in laughter, in affection, in denunciation. He passes from a ferocity of contempt or an uncontrolled, shaggy humour, to outbreaks of appealing and mournful beauty. He beholds always good and evil visibly at death grips in the lives of men. Like his own favourite hero, he has enough fire within him to burn up the sins of the whole world. Consumed with a continuous restlessness, he is ever seeking quiet. " Learn to sit still, I tell you : how often must I tell you," he breaks out. " I persist in my old determination to be at rest," he declares again and again. " God help us all ! " " God be merciful ! " " As God lives I am weary ! "—these are his constant burden. " Solitude is indeed sad as Golgotha ; but it is not mad like Bedlam ! " The world of wild warfare came more and more to be contrasted with a future beyond the storms of time. " We have hope through our Maker's goodness," he writes to his mother, " of a time that shall be always calm weather." " The soul that has been devoutly loyal to the Highest," he cries again, " that soul has the eternal privilege to *hope*. For good is appointed it, and not evil, as God liveth." The best good for one so fire-tost and tormented is rest ; " such rest as God's holy will has appointed, and as no man knows."

Such thoughts were the only consolation after each outburst of astonished anger at the madness of men. "Poor Protectionists," he flared forth after the Disraeli Budget of 1851, " there never were men so ' sold ' since Judas concluded his trade." " *This* Jew, however, will not hang himself ; no, I calculate he has a great deal more of evil work to do in the world yet, if he lives." " Whatever British infatuation has money in its purse, votes in its pocket, and no tongue in its head, here is the man to be a tongue for it." Immediately he turns from such a ravening spectacle to that eternity which was ever his " strong tower." " The day is drawing down (with the generation I belong to), and the tired labourers one by one are going *home*. There is rest *there*, I believe, for those who could never find any before. God is great. God is good."

All his letters are crowded with those verdicts on men which read so ferociously, whose first publication scared the company of Carlyle worshippers, and tumbled to pieces the monstrous image they had erected of the Apostle of Silence. Beneath the Carlyle charged with a cold, intellectual restraint, weighing his words, preaching endurance and an austere, ethical creed—a lath-and-plaster figure—the real man is emerging ; infinitely more human, infinitely more lovable ; lacking, above all things, restraint, seeing the better course, but unable to follow it, violent, with fierce affection, drawing deep and fiercely the outlines and shadows of things. The prim moralist is offended at the reckless scattering of contemptuous and fiery judgments. Only those who have some similarity of temperament, who are accustomed to speak and think in superlatives, will understand the spirit in which these verdicts are cast forth; understanding, they will refuse to condemn.

There is a wild humour about him, a mingling of denunciation with a kind of elemental laughter, in which the bitterness is dissolved. After reading a *Quarterly* attack on Kingsley and Maurice, "very beggarly Crokerism," "no viler mortal," Carlyle suddenly ejaculated, "calls himself man than old Croker at this time." "One Merivale" attacked him in a review. "He is a slight, impertinent man," was Carlyle's comment, "with good Furnival's Inn faculty, with several dictionaries and other succedanea about him—small *knowledge* of God's universe as yet, and small hope of now getting much." Of the theory of life of this economist " it struck me I had never seen in writing so entirely damnable a statement." "It is to me not a sorrowful prognostic," he concluded, "that the day of that class of politicians does in all ways draw towards its close."

Others who had not thus the temerity deliberately to draw upon themselves the lightning of the gods were not spared. Of Jowett, "a poor little good-humoured owlet of a body " was the verdict, "'Oxford Liberal,' and very conscious of being so : not knowing right hand from left otherwise. Ach Gott ! " Of Palmerston, "a tall man, with some air of greediness and cunning," was the unflattering description, "and a curious fixed *smile* as if lying not at the top, but at the bottom of his physiognomy." The worthy philanthropists of the forties became "scraggy critics of the 'benevolent' school." Louis Philippe was dismissed with contemptuous pity : "I begin to be really sorry for him, poor old scoundrel." "An old man now, and has not learned to be an honest man—he learns, or may learn, that the cunningest knavery will not serve one's turn either." The "Bentham Radical Sect" were treated to a crescendo of vituperation till they were finally dismissed as "wretched, unsympathetic, scraggy Atheism and Egoism," which Nature will never make "fruitful in her world." "Enough, thou scraggy Atheism; go thy ways, wilt thou!"

But there were enthusiasms for famous men no less superlative; in addition to that continual flow of unclouded family affection, the love of the clan, of the peasant for the peasant family; above all the wholehearted elemental devotion of the son for the mother who bore him, which illuminates all the violent and passionate correspondence of nearly fifty years. In a memorable letter to Browning, "You seem to possess a rare spiritual gift," is the generous tribute, "poetical, pictorial, intellectual, by whatever name we may prefer calling it." "Persist in God's name, as you best see and can, and understand always that my true prayer for you is, good speed in the name of God." There was often a touching gratitude for favours given, a surprise at the toleration extended by "people in the highest degree zealous to accommodate the surprising monster who has been stranded among them." "Kindness is frequent in this world," he declared in a sudden quietude, "if we reckon upward from zero (as were fair), not downwards from infinity; and always very precious, the more so the rarer."

Carlyle saw with the eye of the mystic, the eye of the prophet. Common things lost their hard outlines. The world appeared as a procession of spectres and shadows. Again and again he cried

that man is of the substance of dreams, and his little
life is rounded with a sleep. " The dead seem as
much my companions as the living," he asserted in
one letter. " Death as much present with me as
life." Sometimes the effect was ridiculous. The Devil
visibly walks in Cheyne Row, Chelsea, inspiring the
unspeakable fowls of his neighbours to crow lustily in
the morning, or stimulating the thirst for gin of the
harassed domestics. More frequently, however, the
vision closes in splendour. The things of the present
are charged with the sense of mystery. The homely
virtues and affections of the Carlyle clan are carried
into a region of high emotion. The chatter and gossip
of society are seen but as a flickering candle flame in
the great red glare of sunrise. And in each successive
bereavement Carlyle is caught up into regions of mystic
sorrow and rejoicing, " a sacredness that led one beyond
tears."

Each obscure human life was for him a matter of
infinite import. London, as he looked down on it from
the Surrey hills, " its smoke rising like a great dusky-
coloured mountain, melting into the infinite clear sky,"
became a meeting-place of Eternities in the " ever-
flowing stream of life and death." In the graveyard
of the dead, where " they all lay so still and dumb,
those that were once so blithe and quick at sight of us ;
gathered to their sleep under the long grass," the old
man " could not forbear a kind of sob, like a child's,
out of my old worn heart, at first sight of all this."
Read if you can without emotion the letter, magnificent
in its simplicity, in which Carlyle describes to his
brother in Canada the last days and death of his
mother. It is the end of an obscure life, full of toils
and sorrows ; the dust returning to the earth, as it was,

through that last indignity which is the common lot of man. But to the eyes of one watching with a love unconquered by the fretfulness of time, the voyage of this humble soul " through the gloomy clouds of death " was charged with a solemn splendour and triumph. All the mystery of the greatness of human existence gathered round the moment of the passing into eternity of the spirit, returning to the God who gave it.

The man to whom each solitary life was thus so sacred had the faith at bottom which alone can consecrate all human progress. He had, indeed, no certain solution of ultimate mysteries. But he refused to put them aside. " God is great ! God is good ! " is his continual burden; " there remaineth a rest," his perpetual prayer. " The ruins of time build the mansions of Eternity " is the one sustaining hope with the passing of the years. And all his longing goes out towards a meeting with those whom he loved, now so quiet, in " the Silent Kingdoms " where all that troubled the lot of man " shall there be without the walls for evermore."

In such a contrast between the mystic and the man of science is summed up much of the hunger and disturbance of an age. Spencer's story of his existence is like the even passage of a still and cloudy day. The hours pass with scarcely perceptible change. There is a light in the sky, dull, if cold and clear, slowly fading with the coming of the night. Carlyle's life-history is like a day of perpetual unrest. There is the flare of the dawn with sunshine succeeding; and thunder-clouds roll up in tempest with lightning and storm ; and the clouds are torn apart for a moment, revealing the blue sky beyond; and the sun sets in crimson and yellow light, with a menace of disquietude still on the horizon, rain and moaning wind, when darkness suddenly blots out the whole troubled scene.

The one story ends in a vision of desolation. An irony worthy of an ancient and tragic fate compelled the man who, more than any previous thinker, had fashioned his action upon rational and consistent ends, most completely to acknowledge failure. The conscious search for the prize resulted in the cry that the prize had somehow eluded the seeker ; and the neglect of all irrational things — love and human comradeship, the larger emotions, patriotism, and the losing of self in an ideal cause—evolved but the old cry of weariness, and the failure of orderly life to satisfy man's desires and his dreams.

The other, from the heart of uncertainty and storm, under the purple sky and sunset, lifts up his hope triumphant above the things of time, sure in the consummation of the victory and the abiding rest beyond. " It was the Most High God that made mothers," he testifies, " and the sacred affection of children's hearts ; yes, it was He :—and shall it not, in the end, be *all well :* on this side of death, or beyond death ? We will pray once more from our inmost heart if we can, ' Our Father which art in Heaven, Thy *will* be done ' ! "

" Alas ! the inexorable years," he cries, " that cut away from us, one after another, the true souls whom we loved, who loved us truly, that is the real bitterness of life." " How could one live," he had before written, " if it were not for Death ? " " We ourselves, my friend "—this is his conclusion of the whole matter—"it is not long we have to stay behind ; we, too, shall find a shelter in the Silent Kingdoms ; and much Despicability that barked and snarled incessantly round us *here* shall there be without the walls for evermore.   Blessed are the Dead. . . . God is great, say the Moslems; to which we add only, God is Good; and have not, nor ever shall have, any more to say."

So in faith and perplexity, the one with an unanswered question on his lips, the other with the great longing in his heart still unsatisfied, these two men went down into darkness : and the grasses blow above their graves.

DISRAELI AND GLADSTONE

A CONTRAST

OF all the memorable comparisons in history, in which two men of supreme talent have been exhibited struggling through a lifetime for the triumph of conflicting ideals, none will stand in history more illuminating than that of Disraeli and Gladstone. The superficial contrast has been a thousand times emphasised. But the material is now for the first time available which can enable the reader to penetrate beneath the surface show. All the accidents of birth, fortune, and education vanish ; and we enter those innermost recesses of man's being which all men hide from the multitude, in which the soul, stripped of the illusions of market-place and arena, is confronted only with itself and with Eternity.

I

The careers of Disraeli and Napoleon III. are the two great romances of the nineteenth century. Each seemed for all the earlier time "impossible." Each at the beginning absurdly failed. Disraeli became the laughing-stock of England, Napoleon the laughing-stock of Europe. The grotesque invasions at Strasburg and Boulogne seemed to certify an enduring collapse to the one.   Sydney Smith has described the first appearance of the other at Taunton, and how he was called the Old Clothes Man by the children and pelted with slippers, and finally driven out in contempt.   But each, confident in his genius and his star, pressed right onward, and each attained such dazzling success as must have excelled even his wildest dreams.   The career of both was closed in eclipse and ruin.   Both were assailed with such ferocity of vituperation as only falls to the few really great.   And both, when all is over, have secured disciples essaying to erect an image of benevolence and moral earnestness—images which would have astonished the men who, however self deceived at the last, would never have mistaken these ungainly creations for portraits of themselves.

Disraeli's career was " a romance of the will that defies circumstance, and moulds the soil where ideas are to flourish."   In the strange figure at the end as depicted by one of his admirers could be read all the history of the past.   " Few who gazed on that drawn countenance," says Mr. Sichel, " could have discerned in it the poetry and enthusiasm of his prime : only the unworn eyes preserved their piercing fires, and the sunken jaw was still masterful.   A long discipline of iron self-control, much disillusion, growing disappointments with crowning triumphs, and latterly a great desolation, had subdued the fiercer force and the elastic buoyancy of his heyday.   Yet the intellectual charm, and the spell of mind and spirit had deepened their outward traces. Fastidious discernment, dispassionate will, penetrating insight, courage, patience, a certain winning gentleness underneath the scorn of shams, stamp every lineament."

" He was truly unselfish, and he was never known to

blame a subordinate." "In two things only he was profuse—books and light." Unlike his great rival in this as in so many other characteristics, he was "utterly careless of money." "Like childless men in general, he was devoted to children." " He was a firm friend : loyalty he always extolled as a sovereign virtue." "If he was always 'the man of destiny,' he was also ever ' faithful unto death.' " "Of music and art he was a devotee." " In matters of courtesy he was old-fashioned and punctilious." "The common and the uncommon people fascinated him, for in them he found ideas: the middling charmed him less."

In the world outside also, that austere, pitiless, sentimental England of the mid-century, he was ever on the side of kindness and compassion. He possessed strong sympathy with labour and the sufferings of the poor. "He foresaw the overcrowding of huge cities through the waste of the soil with all its attendant miseries." With Ruskin he asserted that the English poor " compared with the privileged of their own land are in a lower state than any other population compared with its privileged classes." He was " prouder of his many social reforms than of his Berlin Treaty." "What he specially sought to mitigate was irresponsible Plutocracy."

The verdict of history will probably endorse Lord Acton's judgment upon Disraeli. " The man was more reputable than his party." He led them first by gratifying their hatreds, later by stimulating their hopes. He led them through strange ways, but ultimately into the promised land.

The attempt, indeed, to prove that he was " consistent " throughout all his political career, that he was not " an adventurer," that his only motive was the advancement of high moral causes, is an attempt compared to which the rehabilitations of Richard Crookback and John Lackland were but trifles. No one doubts Disraeli's greatness ; no one seriously imagines this greatness to be in the region of morality. His career is a study for the admirer of a great enterprise conducted through a lifetime with extraordinary tenacity and courage. It is an asset for the cynic, the historian, the detached observer of the absurd comedy of human life ; not, surely, for the moralist. The attitude of his admirers is more likely to be that of Mr. Swinburne in his protest against the whitewashing of Mary Queen of Scots. "Surely you were something better than innocent ?" Disraeli knew his world, "the islanders," as one of his biographers pleasantly terms them ; and he knew himself. He had the power of those who have stripped themselves of all illusions, swallowed all formulas. He posed, and every one laughed at him ; but step by step he succeeded in deceiving first his party, then his country, finally himself.

In such a survey, the superficial inconsistencies are negligible. Whether at first he appeared as a Tory or a Radical seems entirely irrelevant. Both opinions were quite reconcilable with his after-life. He hated the Whigs and the great houses who were excluding such as he from politics. He hated the middle classes, the Nonconformists. Above all, he hated that strenuous assertion of moral ideals which always seemed to him cant, which was to gather under the leadership of his great opponent and overthrow him at the last. He knew mid-century England as few others knew it. His novels, despite their absurdity and their bizarre, fantastic language, remain the most illuminating commentaries upon the changes which this England was undergoing, to which the many were so blind. Against these middle classes he apprehended, with the insight of genius and the detachment of the alien, there could be united the old English families from above and the populace from below. The Reform Act of '67, denounced as a betrayal, was merely an attempt practically to realise this conviction.

His policy was justified by its success. The force of moral earnestness and enthusiasm was the one force he could never understand. " I have been induced to analyse what ' moral ' means are," he once said ; " first, enormous lying ; second, inexhaustible boasting ; third, intense selfishness." This solitary mistake ended his career in apparent ruin. Undoubtedly had he made an adequate estimate of the power of moral enthusiasm, he would have adjusted his policy to its demands, and used it for his own aims.

But his success was never more apparent than after his death. He became a cult and a great memory. The romance of his marvellous career became magnified by time. His policy of uniting the gentlemen of England and the democracy which loves a lord against the manufacturers and middle classes prospered exceedingly. Other men entered into the heritage he bequeathed to them ; and England settled down with satisfaction at the end of the century under the Tory reaction for which he had worked with such unparalleled ardour and patience.

In this he was true to his own ideas, and true to the interests of the class who cried out that he had betrayed them. The most vehement opponents of the Franchise Bill of '67, such as the late Lord Salisbury, were those who lived to reap the great reward of the policy which they had denounced. Without this alliance the Conservative party were doomed to an everlasting sterility. With it they ruled England for seventeen out of the last twenty-five years of the nineteenth century. For such a transformation they have to thank this " alien adventurer " whom they never entirely trusted.

They might, indeed, have remained in power for decades to come if they could have learnt the lesson he had tried to teach them : to press forward Social Reforms, to demonstrate aristocracy as the true and disinterested leaders of the people : in ruling, to give all that the people would themselves demand if they themselves were in power. In Ireland he would have effected by English legislation all the reforms that an Irish Parliament could have effected for herself. At home, he would have pushed forward his " policy of sewage," persistently striven for better houses, better wages, shorter hours, a humaner life for the working population. He would have given everything except liberty : for he was shrewd enough to know that when everything which liberty demands is given, the demand for liberty itself becomes suddenly silent.

Secure in the triumph achieved by his policy the Conservative party have repudiated the principles by which that triumph was attained. If the coming collapse of the Tory Government in England will mark the end not only of a party but of an epoch, the future will but justify Disraeli's prophecies alike of success and failure. And if once more the party which calls itself " Liberal " enters upon power, it will be because in adversity that party has learnt on the one hand to forget many of the ideas whose inherent weakness Disraeli descried ; on the other, to remember that forces more vital than the middle-class individualism of the mid-Victorian period are necessary for the healing of the diseases of a newer England.

In face of so magnificent a spectacle as Disraeli's success, why arouse needless controversy, we may ask, by attempting to drag in something so irrelevant as questions of political morality? "I confess to be unrecognised at this moment by you," Disraeli writes to Sir Robert Peel in 1841—" appears to me to be overwhelming, and I appeal to your own heart—to that justice and that magnanimity which I feel are your characteristics —to save me from an intolerable humiliation." " Do not destroy all his hopes," Mrs. Disraeli added, "and make him feel his life has been a mistake." Five years after, when reminded of this by Sir Robert Peel, " I can say I never asked a favour of the Government," he calmly informed the House of Commons, " not even one of those mechanical things which persons are obliged to ask : yet these assertions were always made in that way, though I never asked a favour ; and as regards myself, I never, directly or indirectly, solicited office."

Biographers have been concerned to explain this incident in a thousand impossible apologies. It is warmly asserted that Disraeli's bitter attacks upon Sir Robert Peel were not directed by personal revenge for the rejection of his application. No one now imagines such an explanation. Disraeli was after too high stakes to be turned aside by anything so petty as personal revenge. He attacked Peel because with the eye of genius he saw that Peel's desertion of the country party gave him the opportunity for which he had waited half a lifetime. It was the direct way to the hearts of the " gentlemen of England " bursting with inarticulate fury, and welcoming with eagerness their spokesman as their leader. One can regard with admiration the imperturbable courage and audacity with which he threw down this challenge to Peel. "In the small hours of the morning following the debate," Peel "was fishing in a sea of papers for Disraeli's letter," which he could not find. Perhaps had he found it the history of England might have been changed. There is no need to attempt elaborate explanation of forgotten memory or momentary madness in this particular incident of a career which never pretended to acknowledge the impeding limitations of the accepted moral standards.

To any detached observer of an imaginary Gerolstein the career is one prolonged miracle. Even with a consciousness of the ruin effected, it is almost impossible not to cheer the onward advance. At the beginning, "looking like Gulliver among the Liliputians" suffering from chronic dyspepsia, he appears on the political arena "devoured by ambition I did not see any means of gratifying." He was an alien, without money, without friends ; obviously to the great families of England an adventurer ; impossible. At the end he has broken the charmed circle, penetrated to the centre, bent the great families of England to his will. He drives them unresisting along roads they dread, towards ends they cannot foresee. He has become the idol of the aristocracy. He is the intimate friend of the Queen. Finally, for one intoxicating moment, he stands in the full gaze of the world, Dictator of Europe.

One half of the mind refuses to acquiesce. It sees the lowering of public life, the unscrupulous manipulation of ideal causes to forward one individual ambition; the flattery, the adroitness, the despising of men. Estimated now as if a long time ago and far away the playing upon pettiness and silly ambition appears the work of one who, in Mr. Bryce's words, "watched English life and politics as a student of natural history might watch the habits of bees or ants." The critic apprehends the dire consequences of this theatrical display. Modern Jingoism is one of them, which has poisoned the springs. Another is the ruin of the Christians of the East. Here is a heavy price to pay for the set limelight scene of "Peace with honour."

But the other half of the mind is with him through it all. We applaud in whole-hearted fashion the spirit, the pluck, the unconquerable will and determination. We rejoice with almost a personal triumph as the long, seemingly so hopeless, efforts of thirty years terminate in the attainment of the desired goal.

And, indeed, something more reputable remains. Outside the "game" of politics there was much altogether admirable. He was a dutiful son, an affectionate brother. He showed a real kindness to friends ; a certain magnanimity. The never-wavering gratitude to his wife for her whole-hearted devotion illuminates this strange character with tenderness and emotion. Above all, we owe him a certain cynical sincerity very useful for "islanders," one of whose characteristics is an unparalleled power of self-deception. "Lying is a crime only where it is a cruelty." "When I meet a man whose name I have utterly forgotten, I say, 'And how is the old complaint?'" "No dogmas, no Deans." In country houses "their table talk is stable talk." "They think it the battle of Armageddon : let us go to lunch." "I am never well save in action, and then I feel immortal." These and similar sayings have become part of the current coin of England's worldly wisdom.

"Every one knows the steps of a lawyer's career—he

tries in turn to get on, to get honours, to get honest. This one (of a certain Lord Chancellor) edits hymns instead of briefs, and beginning by cozening juries he compounds with heaven by cramming children in a Sunday school."

There is a real pathos about the end, the pathos which shrouds the end of all great actors. The play is nearly played. The harsh world of reality can no longer be kept out of the kingdom of fantasy and illusion. Like another great actor, Chateaubriand, he has "seen so many phantoms defile through the dream of life." "Yes, but it has come too late," was the reply to congratulation on the great triumph. "I am so blind; I come here: I look round: I see no one: I go away." "Never defend me," was his last request.

His definition of the most desirable life as "a continued grand procession from manhood to the tomb" had been abundantly realised. "He faced the facts of life," said one who loved him, "psychological and spiritual, gravely, I had almost said sorrowfully: he faced them compassionately." "I had rather live," he asserted at the end; "but I am not afraid to die." His verdict upon one of the characters of his creation is perhaps the last word upon his own intimate soul, the self which withdrew so securely from the madness of life's fitful fever :—"What they called reality appeared to him more vain and nebulous than the scenes and sights of sleep."

II

Mr. Morley's great life and the Acton letters have revealed now for the judgment of the sympathiser and the cynic the springs of action of Gladstone's vast and complex character. Behind all the panorama of the outward show, the concern which for most men is all the world and its desires, stands that " heart of fire " whose history forms one of the most fascinating chapters in the story of men of renown.

" Not for two centuries," says his biographer, " since the historic strife of Anglican and Puritan, had our island produced a ruler in whom the religious motive was paramount to a like degree." Later, as earlier, there is the revelation of the inner life : an inner life " maintained in all its absorbing exaltation day after day, year after year, amid the ever-swelling rush of urgent secular affairs."

" Not a devotional child," this " great Christian ' described himself. " The planks between me and all the sins were so very thin." " The inner life has been with me extraordinarily dubious, vacillating, and, above all, complex," is his confession at the end. All the early years were spent in that rigorous, narrow, evangelical piety which fashioned the characters of most of the great men of nineteenth-century England. At Oxford he is organising prayer-meetings. When twenty-three years old he is refusing race-meetings and theatres as involving an encouragement of sin. In the early years of London life he is leading the limited and austere life of this bleak tradition. At first he cannot believe in liberty, and is bitterly hostile to atheists. As late as 1836 he is tormented with doubts as to whether a Unitarian can be saved. There is one characteristic scene in his biography, in which " I had my servant to prayers " before breakfast, and Wordsworth, who has come as a guest, obligingly makes a third. He is a member of a brotherhood formed by

Acland, with rules for systematic exercises of devotion and works of mercy. Amidst much that is inspiring there is much also that is tortuous and almost morbid in these earlier self-examinations and prim rules of conduct. "My inherited and bigoted misconceptions," he afterwards came to call them. He has not yet escaped from the stifling conception of a very limited salvation to the larger and freer atmosphere of a Catholic Church.

The change, when it came, seems to have been entirely independent of the great spiritual upheaval at Oxford. Quite suddenly, upon his first visit to Rome, the sight of St. Peter's aroused a longing for a visible unity of the Church. "The figure of the Church rose before me as a teacher," in addition to the Bible, hitherto the sole guide. The old cramping barriers gave way. A world vision of a vast society and fellowship, divinely ordered and guided for the salvation of the world, never afterwards left his mind. Henceforth, amid "the sublime and sombre anarchy of human history," he beheld, says Mr. Morley, a Church Catholic and Apostolic, with "its ineffable and mysterious graces" and its "incommeasurable spiritual force"—an immense mystery. "This is the enigma, and this the solution in faith and spirit, in which Gladstone lived and moved. In him it gave to the energies of life their meaning, and to duty its foundation."

But a principle which Oxford failed to teach her children was already commencing to work. "The value of liberty as an essential condition of excellence in human things" was to unite with this passionate devotion to a Catholic Church, and prove the thread to that labyrinth of policy which made Gladstone

through all his career the most perplexing of statesmen to his generation. It was to undermine and
cast aside all those frameworks of compulsions of
which in the early days he was so determined an
advocate. It led him into the tearing down of an
Anglican Establishment, the abolition of Church rates
and Church tests, and all the policy of liberality and
liberation with which his name will be associated
through all future time. Everything had changed at
the end but his religious ideas. His earlier dogmatisms
and disquietudes crumbled into dust as the years went
by. But the deep bedrock beliefs of his nature in God
and the soul and an immortal life remained always
abiding and secure. "The fundamentals of the
Christian dogma," says Mr. Morley, "are the only
regions in which Mr. Gladstone's opinions have no
history."

The early period is full of the movement of the
Church revival, with all its revolutionary consequences.
Dissuaded from his original desire for the Christian
ministry, Gladstone threw himself into the world of
affairs deliberately as a servant of the Church. "I
contemplate secular affairs," he says, "chiefly as a
means of being useful in Church affairs." "Political
life," says Mr. Morley, "was only part of his religious
life." This crusading energy made him a strange
figure in the realm of early Victorian politics, amongst
that particular section of English life which has never
learnt to take religion seriously. Continually and from
the beginning he is protesting against the infected
atmosphere of Parliament. Of public life, he confesses, "every year shows me more and more that the
ideal of Christian politics cannot be realised in the
State according to present conditions of existence."

DE MORTUIS

He was ever desiring a kind of monastic seclusion. "The tumult of business follows and whirls me day and night," he cries. He finds no time for tranquil collection of himself or the cultivation of the things of the spirit. He "anticipates a time" when he may "breathe other air."

But to the party and ideas he stood for his position was of supreme importance. The High Church School consisted mainly of theologians hidden from the world, of women, of amiable country gentlemen, endeavouring to maintain feudal ideas in an atmosphere removed from the new, energetic England. Here was a man adequate to all occasions, with a miraculous physical vitality, a frame of steel, toil "his native element." He stood as the one man of deep religious conviction endowed with capacity to direct the whirlwind and control the storm. For the first time a statesman of unparalleled energy and intellect was to confess himself before the world an ardent adherent of these new doctrines. He was to become the idol of a middle class utterly alien to the Catholic faith and tradition. He was to manipulate national finance, to encounter and to master, at their own poor game, the children of this world. Through all the crowd of cross purposes and shabby and pitiful ambitions which make up the universe of party politics he was to press forward as one on a journey, passing to a sure end.

Confusion and perplexity were produced in the minds of his contemporaries by this apparition of a man with convictions and an ideal amid the shadows and phantoms of the time. During the first sixteen years of his political life in close association with his two greatest friends, Manning and James Hope, he was daily planning efforts for the restoration of the Church.

DISRAELI AND GLADSTONE

The London movement advanced independently of the Oxford movement, although along parallel lines. "I stagger to and fro like a drunken man" was Gladstone's comment when he saw the great leader passing to a hostile communion. He was never quite in sympathy with Newman. His thought was too objective for free communion with that subtle mind. The motive was never, as in Newman, ardour for a personal salvation, but shame at "the laying waste of the heritage of the Lord." The six years that followed were years of a tense anxiety. Then, in 1851, came the great disruption and separation which changed the whole vision of the future. "Fully believing that the death of the Church of England is among the alternate issues of the Gorham case," he yet clung to the cause to which his life had been dedicated. But Manning and Hope passed over to the other side. "Their going," he records in his diary, "may be to me a sign that my work is gone with them." "Nothing like it can ever happen to me again." It was the close of an epoch.

Ten years were spent in unsatisfactory hesitations. In 1859 he could still be branded as "the Jesuit of the closet—really devout," and the "Simeon Stylites of his time." But the principle of liberty was steadily working. The change from Oxford to South Lancashire meant an escape from· shadows into the strong if cold light of day. In 1863 he commenced relationships with Protestant Nonconformists. Their whole point of view was alien to his own. Often, as in the education controversy, he strained their loyalty to the breaking-point. They were "attracted by his personal piety, though repelled by its ecclesiastical apparel." While his own Church regarded with distrust or hatred the greatest layman it has ever possessed, the Nonconformists followed him with a splendid devotion. "We believe in no man's infallibility," said Spurgeon; "but it is restful to be sure of one man's integrity." Only at the last, when he advocated a scheme for granting self-government to a Roman Catholic nation containing a Protestant minority, many with sorrow turned aside and walked no more with him.

And through all the gigantic endeavour of these later years the interior life continued its progress. Gladstone will appear in history as the "practical mystic"; one of those apparitions which exercise amid a world of cloudy purpose so miraculous a power. The consciousness of personal responsibility, the sense of a Divine call and election for service, the apprehension of a particular Providence, the increasing recognition of the necessity for some definite preparation for the hour of death and the day of judgment; these great commonplaces of the religious life are continually with him. Of a particular speech at the outset of his career:—"A poor performance," he writes, "but would have been poorer had *He* never been in my thoughts, a present and powerful aid." "On most occasions of very sharp pressure or trial," he testifies, "some word of Scripture has come home to me as if borne on angels' wings." In election contests or Budget speeches he is strengthened by verses of the Psalms. On his rejection by Oxford University the first lesson in church supplies his need:—"And they shall fight against thee, but they shall not prevail against thee, for I am with thee, saith the Lord of Hosts." Successive birthdays always drove him back in meditation to the basic principles of his faith. On his sixtieth birthday "The Almighty seems to sustain and spare me for some good purpose of His own, utterly unworthy as I know myself to be. Glory be to His name." Ten years afterwards, at the close of the intoxicating triumphs of the Midlothian campaign, he "professes to believe" that the battle has been fought for justice, humanity, freedom, law.

"If I really believe this," he writes, "then I should regard my having been morally forced into this work as a high election of God. And certainly I cannot but believe that He has given me special gifts of strength on the late occasion, especially in Scotland. Three things I would ask of God over and above all the bounty which surrounds me. This first, that I may escape into retirement. This second, that I may speedily be enabled to divest myself of everything resembling wealth. And the third—if I may—that when God calls me He may call me speedily."

There was to be given him another great decade of life, a struggle against doubt, cowardice, and the accumulated wrongs of time, which in its large energies and enthusiasms already seems the record of some combat of giants in a half fabulous past. And at the end there was given him also that gift which he had desired so eagerly and so patiently, the interval of tranquillity and preparation "between Parliament and the grave."

Two sentences adequately sum up the inner life of Gladstone. The objective result is recorded in the magnificent phrase addressed to him by an unknown correspondent :—" You have so lived and wrought as to have kept the soul alive in England." The inner springs of action are revealed in the line from the 3rd Canto of the *Paradiso*, which he accepted as possessing an "inexpressible majesty of truth"—as if spoken by the very mouth of God : "*In la sua volontade è nostra pace*": In His Will is our Peace. To the obedience of that Will he dedicated all the ardour of a soul beyond all men's impetuous and impatient. "The final state which we are to contemplate with hope and seek by discipline," he wrote, "is that in which we shall be one with the will of God."

The effort demanded a continual examination and struggle. He "achieved self-control," is the testimony of his wife, "by incessant watching and prayer." In all the Christian centuries no more splendid gifts have been offered with whole-hearted devotion and humility. The age has travelled beyond the special intellectual affirmations of Gladstone's belief. His principles were matured before the theory of evolution and modern research had created a new world. But the great ends and ideals of the passion of his soul, the "bright crystal laws of life," in Mr. Morley's fine phrase, "endure like pointing stars guiding a traveller's eye to the celestial pole by which he steers." A large benefaction remains to us and succeeding generations from so shining an example. He raised above the turmoil of the politics of a day a supreme moral ideal. He reconciled the large claims of a Catholic faith with the assertion of liberty as an essential condition of excellence in human things. He maintained always against the slow stain of the world's contagion the detachment and ardour of an inner life fixed in entire submission to the will of God. High efforts such as these are as essential to-day as in that vanished universe of Gladstone's first radiant dawn. To those amongst whom, in however limited a sphere, is offered a possibility of a similar enterprise, his life stands secure in the courses of Time; a challenge to all striving after transitory things, a message of victory in the troublous years to come.

THE CHURCH MILITANT

TEMPLE—WESTCOTT—CREIGHTON—DOLLING

THE ecclesiastical life is never a very cheering document. The atmosphere is often thin and rarefied, the interests divorced from the varied experience of the common thought of men. In so many success has meant the cautious pursuit of a well-trodden way. Who now remembers the name of the Archbishop of Canterbury of a hundred years ago or the penultimate Dean of Lichfield or Archdeacon of London? But where personality and strength are conspicuously present, the life of the priest or minister acquires an especial interest. Always there is the challenge, was it for that reason or for this, that he forsook the combats of the world and entered the service of a spiritual kingdom? And of late years interest has been intensified by the general break-up of the traditional theology. There are many to-day who are astonished that an honest man can still call himself a Christian, or assent to formularies historic and outworn. There are others perplexed to reconcile the Christian ethic with the modern economic organisation of society, and scorn God because the cry of the poor exercises so scanty a disturbance amid the apathy of the Sabbath congregation. The past few years have been heavy in the loss of those to whom these and other

115

questions were very pressing. Their lives are an attempt at answers. Temple was one of the strong men of the century. Creighton was the most agile and interested mind of his day. Westcott as a scholar and a thinker stands beyond the reach of challenge. Dolling was a personality who exercised a particular influence and attraction. The lives of these men should be fruitful in questions, if not in answers, to this problem of faith disturbed and uncertain guidance which broods over the future of England.

I

" We cannot understand how these opinions can be held consistently with an honest subscription to the formularies of our Church, with many of the fundamental doctrines of which they appear to us essentially at variance." So forty-two years ago, in scathing condemnation, two archbishops and twenty-five bishops publicly denounced seven writers who had united to issue a little volume of theological essays. Nine years afterwards the first of these writers was appointed by Gladstone Bishop of Exeter. A vast hubbub arose. Petitions poured in from Protestants and Ritualists, joining against the common enemy. The Chapter were urged to refuse to confirm the election. " I have letters from all parts of the country," said the Dean of Exeter, " about the sword of the Lord and Gideon, exhorting us to go to prison and promising us visits there." On the day of consecration bishop after bishop protested ; one (still living) " in the fear of God and the Church " ; others counselling delay or wringing their hands in despair. Time ultimately swept the clamour into silence. Thirty years after, this man who had been judged by his Church's leaders as dishonest, died one winter day amidst a universal tribute to a rugged honesty—Frederick, Lord Archbishop of Canterbury.

Few lives have been able to show so dramatic a revolution. Those who would understand the real nature of the man can be recommended to study the record of the long dead controversy over "Essays and Reviews." Entombed in the dusty immensity of Archbishop Tait's life is a chapter of Tait-Temple letters which for vigour and interest in ecclesiastical correspondence can only be paralleled by the Newman-Manning letters in Purcell's first edition. Tait, after promising to protect the writers, had yielded to the agitation and signed that scathing document of condemnation. Later he attempted to persuade Temple to desert the other essayists and leave them to their ruin. The replies ring true and tempered across the intervening years. It is strength against suavity. Here is the restrained, passionate protest of a man who feels himself wronged by the weakness and uncertainty of a friend cowering before a storm of public opinion. "If you do not wish to alienate your friends, do not treat them as you have treated me." "Nothing on earth will induce me to do what you propose. I do not judge for others, but in me it would be base and untrue." "You ought not to make it impossible for a friend to calculate on what you will do." "The greatest kindness you can now do me is to forget till all this is over that any friendship ever existed between us." "Your friends complain that they cannot count on you. Your enemies say they can." The sentences sear and burn after all the lapse of time. Not often do high dignitaries who attempt compromise thus learn the truth. The man is revealed in a moment of time. He is true as steel, honest as the day, with deep affection beneath the outward harshness. He scornfully refuses to exculpate himself at the expense of his comrades. He regards as, perhaps, the meanest act of which a public man could be guilty, the sacrifice of a cause or a friend to such an aimless, despicable thing as the clamour of the crowd.

These were the heroic days of Liberalism. This little book and these seven denounced men become the centre and rallying cry of the movement. Temple had not always been of this faith. At Oxford, with almost all others of his generation, he had been influenced by the Catholic revival. I once heard him describe the fascination exercised over the University by Newman from St. Mary's pulpit, with a voice, as he pictured it, like a silver bell; a pleading for righteousness and the judgment of God with the piercing simplicity of a child. In the break-up which followed he threw himself with energy into the liberal movement. The position of the "Essays and Reviews" has now become an accepted commonplace in the Church. As in the history of the dreaded five-point Charter in politics, men now only wonder at the consternation evoked by so mild a programme. But the spirit of these writers in religion as in politics is as necessary to-day as yesterday. The principle which underlay the definite position, the right of free inquiry, the acceptance of knowledge, indifference to accusations of dishonesty and the hostility of all that is comfortable and orthodox, were never more needed than now. From the grave the words of the great Archbishop come with a message of encouragement. " I joined in writing this book in the hope of breaking through that mischievous reticence which, go where I would, I perpetually found destroying the truthfulness of religion. I wished to encourage men to speak out." The study of theology and criticism, " so full of difficulties, imperatively demands freedom for its conditions. To tell a man to study, and yet bid him, under heavy penalties, come to the same conclusions with those who have have not studied, is to mock him. If the conclusions are prescribed the study is precluded."

And if his first legacy to modern Liberalism is a lesson of honesty and of progress, his second, no less needful, is a lesson of work. He was neither a great thinker, nor a great scholar, nor a great orator. He was in many respects typically English ; practical, not visionary, hating humbug and cant, sturdily pursuing his own business. There was work to do, and he set himself to do it. Plodding forward, shifting aside the faint and laggard, trampling down anything that opposed his progress, he drove along the machine : with creaking and protest, rusty joints and unoiled hinges : but still ever moving. A worker, he tested others by their work. Not Carlyle himself enforced more emphatically the Gospel of Labour. This was the key to all his ecclesiastical policy so little understood, so much debated. For millinery and sham he had no respect whatever. He disliked ritual, and where he found it hollow and lifeless, he ruthlessly condemned. Amidst endless apocryphal stories two may be accepted as authentic. He always, to the regret of High Churchmen, celebrated at the North side of the altar. At one advanced church at which he was to officiate the ingenious authorities had determined to force him to assume the Eastward position. The Bishop found the sides of the altar elaborately barricaded with flowers and greenery. At the proper moment, however, without any apparent emotion, he sturdily tramped through the palms and lilies, and standing amidst the flower-pots, to the astonishment of the congregation, concluded the ceremony with calmness. On another, in one of the dead "Catholic" churches of the West End, he entered at the tail of a long procession marching towards the brilliantly lighted altar. The procession entered the chancel, but without the Bishop. In the hush of surprise a stentorian command resounded from the end of the nave, "Put out those lights." These being hastily extinguished, the Bishop tramped his solitary way up the awestruck church. The vicar afterwards attempted remonstrance. "But at St. A——s, my lord (naming a church in a poor district), you allowed altar-lights." "They've got the kernel as well as the husk," was the discomforting response.

Yet, despite this habitual attitude, under his rule such developments of ritual were permitted as London had never before seen. So long as work was progressing —in the old language, so long as souls were being saved—he tolerated the widest divergence in non-essentials. In London's great welter of heathenism and crime he refused to persecute those whose fruits, however grown, were visibly good. Ritual seemed to him so unimportant, five or five hundred candles, marchings round the church, quaint or picturesque clothing. He would have permitted a procession to enter on their heads if it would have aided the great cause. The result of this toleration was a Church crisis, Mr. Kensit, Lady Wimborne, and a Protestant agitation which disturbed his successors but troubled him not at all. That a man should be in the least moved by popular clamour, or yield to a cause through the noise of its adherents, seemed to him not so much cowardly as absurd.

THE CHURCH MILITANT

To the last he remained strong in the principles for which he had fought with Gladstone in the old days. Yet he grew profoundly dissatisfied with the condition of English politics. A few months before his death, when we were discussing present-day questions, he suddenly burst in upon us with the conundrum : "But if you could call any living statesman to power, whom would you name?" The answer was impossible. Yet he always refused to attempt to read the future. In a collection of fatuous forecasts of well-known men, "What will the world be like at the end of the century?" his answer stands terse and characteristic : "I haven't the slightest idea." I remember an evening when we deliberately attempted to draw from him prophecies of the results of present-day movements. "I don't know," was his invariable reply. He had done his work. He belonged to a vanishing age. He knew his time was short, that a new England had arisen which must find its own leaders and work out its own salvation.

With others, however, he noted the transference of interest from political to economic questions. To the end he was a strenuous advocate of social reform. Two years before he died he unexpectedly appeared at the Brighton Church Congress in a lethargic discussion on the Housing Question, selecting this, as he said, from all the subjects, that he might emphasise the necessity for its consideration by the Church. It is no secret to state that he was no whole-hearted advocate of the Government's Education policy. The Bill as it stood was fashioned by other hands. Though giving a general assent he regarded it with misgiving. He had not the contempt for " undenominationalism " which is now fashionable. But he recognised the impossibility

121

of the present " religious " teaching in State schools.
" It may not be important," I heard him say a few
weeks before he died, " whether that or this dogma is
taught to children ; but *it is* important that whatever
religion is taught should be believed by the teacher."

" Some of those whom the gods love die young.
This man, because the gods loved him, lingered on to
be of immense, patriarchal age, till the sweetness it
had taken so long to secrete in him was found at last."
Pater's verdict on Michaelangelo naturally rises to
the mind in thinking of Temple's last days. To those
who only knew him at the close of his long career
the popular verdict of harshness seemed incredible.
Strength, simplicity, kindliness—these were the prevailing impressions. In the vastness of Lambeth
Palace he encamped as a temporary occupant and on
a journey. Here were the simple iron bedstead, the
bare equipment for work, simple furnishing, simple
meals, in which one was encouraged to consume barley
water—a deplorable drink. Messengers poured in and
out, an enormous correspondence flooded to the four
quarters of the earth. Around him surged armies of
courtiers and flatterers. In the midst was the simple,
family life, with, at the centre, the old warrior, with
eye dim but force unabated, having borne unscathed
through a strange and disordered time the heart of a
little child.

The end found him still at work. A month before it
came he was fulfilling his crowded round of engagements,
doing the work of ten with an iron constitution which
apparently nothing could disturb—rushing over England
in long night journeys, preaching, writing, advising, driving forward the machine. Suddenly, and in a moment,
the overwrought body collapsed ; he left the House of

Lords a dying man. Slowly, continuously, painlessly the life ebbed away. With tranquillity and a certain blitheness he waited for the end; leaving his work accomplished, carefully taking his farewell of all, apologising in historic words, for being such an unconscionable long time a-dying. (I like to think of him as seen in the evening service in Lambeth Chapel—amidst the memorials of innumerable transitory generations, in the broken lights and shadows, a strong and heroic figure reciting with unfaltering accents the creed of that faith which had sustained him for eighty years. An elemental force vanished with him, a great personality. *Requiem eternam dona ei Domine: et lux perpetua luceat ei.*

II

Westcott's life is the revelation of a character rather than a record of ecclesiastical history. Outwardly there is the career of usefulness: a fellowship at Trinity, a mastership at Harrow, canonries at Peterborough and Westminster, a Cambridge professorship; finally, the great Durham bishopric. But a similar course has been followed by many energetic and mediocre persons now reposing in unremembered graves. Behind all this, which in Westcott's case was accidental, is the life of thought in which he really lived. Like his comrade Hort in his country parsonage this man in the main was concerned with the things of the spirit.

It was a life of almost incredible toil combined with an ascetic simplicity. As an undergraduate, we hear of work from five in the morning until past twelve at night, with scanty intervals for meals and recreation, and a biscuit for lunch. Later, "when we came down to prayers in the morning," says his son, "we would find him writing away with a pile of finished letters before him, and when we went to bed he was working still." At Harrow he stood for extreme simplicity of living and a plea for the disciplined life. Here he elaborated the idea of the " Coenobium," a kind of community of families committed to three ends—the conquest of luxury, the disciplining of intellectual labour, religious exercises. The scheme was characteristic both of the splendour of the ideal and the inability to appreciate the littleness and vanities which make such an ideal impossible. " Whenever we children showed signs of greediness," says his son, " we were assured that such things would be unheard of in the Coenobium. We viewed the establishment of the Coenobium with gloomy apprehension." Even Harrow was unable to fasten upon him the usual intellectual sterility of the public-school mastership. Volumes of books on Christian philosophy and textual criticism were being issued all the seventeen years. This devoted intellectual labour was associated with a complete indifference to most things which men delight in. Every form of luxury was to him abhorrent. " When circumstances compelled him so to do, he practically went without a meal." He had an extreme disinclination to spend money on himself. " He would insist on pronouncing threadbare and green coats, condemned by the universal voice of the family, as ' excellent.' " In the enforced display of the bishopric he would sit huddled up with his back to the horses in his carriage, as a kind of mute protest against such outrageous luxury. The sense of life's intense seriousness was ever with him. " Holidays he could hardly take : he found no joy in them, and more especially so in later years. Expenditure on self was all but impossible."

124

The result of this ascetic toil was the accumulation of vast knowledge in varied fields. He was a scholar, in the exact sense, of European reputation. But with this detailed, textual research, which came to be the distinguishing feature of the Cambridge school of theology, he combined a wide acquaintance with other forms of science. He had dabbled in geology and botany, and was familiar with all those scientific discoveries which were filling the age in which he lived with noisy echoes. He had read deep in philosophy, ancient and modern. Comte, Browning, Baur, Mazzini, were the modern writers to whom he owed most. In the last years of life he commenced with all the ardour of youth the study of those social questions which he held were the real problems of the coming time. The novel was the only form of literature with which he was unfamiliar. " The Scarlet Letter," " Jane Eyre," " Villette," " Romola," " John Inglesant,"—this is the pathetic list of his library. His strange failures in reading men, the atmosphere of detachment which made so much of his work difficult for the man of the street, may be due to the dwelling in a universe of ideas alien to the world of modern fiction.

His name will always be associated with two main efforts : the elucidation of a text and the preaching of a philosophy. On the one side he is linked with Lightfoot and Hort in that critical and constructive examination of the New Testament canon which was the special work of the Cambridge school. The Westcott and Hort text, an epoch-making book, "probably the most important contribution to Biblical learning in our generation "; the great commentaries on St. John and the Epistle to the Hebrews, and the Revised Version of the Bible, are the permanent memorials of his life-work. On the other side, he stands by himself, rather pathetically alone. He elaborated a Christian philosophy which the student found mystical and the ordinary man perplexing. It was alien to the prevailing theology of the Oxford Movement, hard, clear-cut, dogmatic. It found no acceptance among the Evangelicals, with their demands for emotional satisfaction in a simple creed. It was distrusted by the new Broad Church divines, cheerfully iconoclastic and hating mystery. Occasionally the reader caught an illuminating sentence. Gleams of a splendour never felt before would disclose abysses of spiritual meaning behind the terms of a dead dogma. To a few, this teaching invested all things with a light that never was on sea or land. But, for the most part, there he walked alone. In the early days he had passed through a period of terrible doubt. He speaks of a wild storm of unbelief " from the midst of which he gazed on the hundreds who conform with a kind of awe and doubt—a mixture of wonder and suspicion." He emerged on to the height with a clear apprehension of spiritual things. All his later years he seemed to possess a spiritual vision, to walk amongst his companions in the cave with something of the bewilderment of those who had seen the light in Plato's allegory. One of his best-known works was at first suppressed, owing to the demand for modification made by the Society for the Propagation of Christian Knowledge. In the period of his first writings the orthodox were profoundly perplexed by his utterances.

It is difficult to summarise his teaching. It has been said that Westcott shifted the central fact of Christianity from the Atonement to the Incarnation. The vision of a humanity burdened with its sins and haunted by terrors of judgment became changed to the vision of a humanity inspired by hope and waiting expectant for a glory that shall be revealed. The concluding lines of Browning's " Karshish " sum up Westcott's creed. " The Bishop does not seem to believe in the Fall," it was complained of him. He scarcely realised the depth of degradation to which human nature could descend. When confronted with some particularly appalling case of clerical immorality he would frankly reject the overwhelming evidence adduced, upon the ground that his categories of being did not include the existence of such a monster. " Humanity," he was never tired of asserting, is " not a splendid shrine deserted by a great king, but a living body stirred by noble thoughts which cannot for ever be in vain."

This consciousness of the supreme greatness of humanity made him one of the prophets of his generation. In the Incarnation he found the key to all that social enthusiasm for which he is best remembered. " A critic asks me," he sadly complains at the end, " 'what has the Incarnation to do with war . . . with the organisation of industry, with buying and selling— with expenditure ? ' That such questions can be asked by a man of average intelligence is a terrible proof of our failure to make our message known." Religion must come from the twilight of the Churches, he was always insisting, and into the ways of men. So he preached Christian Socialism, and became founder and first President of the Christian Social Union, perplexing the orthodox and respectable with the sight of a bishop concerning himself with trade unions and an eight hours' day. He exhibited the rare combination, of the mystic with the practical man. The most spiritual of modern religious teachers descended most completely into concern with the petty questions of the day.

Some very pleasing pictures remain of scenes in Westcott's long and devoted life. There is the most touching combat in self-effacement between him and Lightfoot, each refusing to put himself as a candidate for the professorship before the other. There are the two sermons in Westminster Abbey preached by the solitary sorrower of the "triumvirate" over the grave of his lifelong friends. There is one aspect of the man in the somewhat eerie meditations in the great cathedral at midnight, spent in thought and prayer and communion with the dead; a silent figure in the moonlight, "when the vast building was haunted with strange lights and shadows, and the ticking of the great clock sounded like some giant's footsteps in the deep silence."

In sharp contrast, but all of a piece, is the dramatic scene at Auckland Castle, when the great coal strike, which had desolated a thousand homes, was settled by the personal pleading of the bishop. He invited the masters and men to the castle, presided at a joint conference, speaking earnestly for peace: then left them in separate rooms, himself acting as intermediary. The long hours passed, and no settlement arrived: the crowd which had gathered in the town pressed up to the palace, waiting with painful tension for any news. All the North was hanging on the result. He pleaded with the owners for concession, urging them to put aside all the aroused bitterness, to consider the question as it would be judged in the years to come. Finally, the force of sheer goodness prevailed: the owners consented to the compromise: the rest was a wild scene of rejoicing and gratitude in a thousand homes,

Effort, devotion, utter humility, shine through all. "If I had ever dared to form a wish," he writes concerning one offer. "Here I have learnt to feel my own deficiencies most keenly," he confesses to another, "and I have found, too, those who are willing and able to teach and to train me." With all this humility and kindness there is no essential weakness. He warned as well as encouraged. His occasional outbursts of wrath, as in the correspondence concerning the action of the bishops about the Revisers' Communion, are almost terrible in their intensity.

He saw and rebuked the vices of his age as well as its greatness. Many of his words were of doubt and warning. Here was no soft and easy gospel to be accepted by a nation living on the energies of the past and noisily proclaiming itself immortal. "Will the future say," he asked of this generation, "that crumbling heap, that desolate iron surface, tells of work performed only for the moment, which has cumbered the earth with ruins; those coarse and mean phrases which have corrupted our language, tell of men who had no reverence and no dignity; that class antagonism which torments us, tells of the selfishness of our fathers, who, when there was yet time, failed to bind men to men as fellow-labourers in the cause of God?"

Assuredly never was such warning more needed than in the time when the voice has become silent.

The keynote of this long life of single purpose is summed up in one of his great sentences, "To make of life one harmonious whole, to realise the invisible, to anticipate the transfiguring majesty of the Divine Presence, is all that is worth living for." To the end his unclouded optimism never failed him. He lived on the height. Something of the glory seemed to have

K

descended on him as, with rapt face and eyes which saw things hidden from the crowd around, he proclaimed the reality of an unseen world or the coming of the universal restoration. He lived in constant communion with spiritual powers. In the cathedral or his own chapel at night the dead seemed very near him. Those who have heard him proclaim his gospel will long remember how the little shrunken figure became transformed, and the almost painful humility vanished, and the voice took a sudden note of power, when, oblivious to the presence of the listening crowd, he proclaimed the spiritual message which he found almost too great for human utterance. Preceded by all his old comrades, leaving the memory of a great example, without fear, but with all his own humility and confession of sinfulness, he passed triumphant to his rest.

III

The life of Creighton presents a threefold interest. The first is the impression of the thought and change of a stirring time as reflected in the mind of a man of receptive and catholic sympathies. The second is the spectacle not only of history making, but of history being made, by one called to play a great part in the world's affairs. The third is the actual study of one of the most fascinating (in a sense one of the most baffling) of the great men of the later Victorian age, who would have been almost equally a subject of interest had he been Bishop of Mesopotamia or Valparaiso.

Mandell Creighton was the son of a joiner of Carlisle, who had made a runaway match at Gretna Green with a kind-hearted woman, "very quick with her tongue." Childhood "over the shop in Castle Street" was stern, hard, rather joyless. He passed to Durham, then to Oxford ; a brilliant career culminating in a Fellowship at Merton. The age was an age of wide disbelief, when all sane and clever men at Oxford were supposed to have abandoned Christianity. Creighton was chiefly renowned as a man who smoked multitudinous cigarettes and read multitudinous French novels, and in conversation held pre-eminent place for the audacity of his paradoxes. His ordination was "much commented on." He himself acknowledged "that it was the habit in Oxford to assume that a man who took orders must be either a fool or a knave, and that as people could not call him a fool they had concluded that he must be a knave." "He never wore his spiritual heart on his sleeve," is the judgment which would apply to all his life, " and for this reason many thought he had none to wear."

Then, too, as always, he never suffered fools gladly, and held a hearty contempt for the majority of his fellow-men. "We are told that all men are liars," remonstrates a friend, "we are nowhere told that all men are fools." "The strongest compound of grimness and tenderness that I ever saw or conceived," is a description.

"Dull and solemn people," writes a contemporary, "thought him flippant ; shallow people thought him insincere. No man of his time was so constantly, so freely, and so variously canvassed, not always favourably, but invariably as a rare and strange portent, not to be readily classified in any familiar category of human nature. I remember that once, on a tour in Holland with two friends, we talked of him daily and never exhausted the subject ; and years afterwards I was told that it had become so much the custom to discuss him at the shooting-lodge of one of his friends in Scotland, that some one proposed in fun to levy a fine on any one who mentioned his name."

From the early time he showed his entire concern in the practical life, in the historical method of approaching questions. Of Darwin's discovery, " the whole matter seems to me to be very ingenious and amusing," he writes airily ; " but I have not time for it, and would rather read some Italian history."

After his marriage he vanished from Oxford into a Northumbrian village, and was Vicar of Embleton for nine years—years of devoted work and incessant study of which the " History of the Papacy " was the main fruit. From thence he was called to the new Dixie Professorship at Cambridge, where he astonished the dull by his " frivolity." " Nowhere did he talk such nonsense as in our Combination Room on Sundays," was the admiring verdict of a friend.

After a canonry at Worcester, combined with his professorship, and a momentary exchange to Windsor, he was suddenly promoted to succeed Magee as Bishop of Peterborough. He had absolutely no wish for office. " My mind will go to seed," was his characteristic verdict. " I shall utter nothing but platitudes for the rest of my life, and everybody will write letters in the newspapers about my iniquities." The latter judgment was as completely fulfilled as the former falsified. His work at Peterborough first revealed to the general world same of his astonishing powers, and there was a universal approval when the call brought him to London.

His five years in London, in five of the most crowded and momentous years of the century, stamped themselves deep upon the history of the time. He always resented the time spent in curbing human folly. "Every ass in the diocese thinks that he has a right to come and bray in my study," was one characteristic complaint.

London he branded as "this inhuman spot." "The world which he defined as 'the activities of this life with God left out' seemed to him to invade everything in London." He found himself in the toils of interminable ritual disputes. He despised both parties—the one for their foolishness, the other for their bigotry and reliance on the secular arm; and scarcely took the trouble to conceal his contempt. His letters abound in firm common-sense which neither party found acceptable—which, indeed, he did not expect either party to find acceptable. "We are all agreed in regretting that there should be such a person as Mr. Kensit," he wrote to one party; "but the question how best to deal with him is a purely practical one." "There is no reason why your method should not be tried," he wrote to Sir William Harcourt on the other side, "except that no one wishes to try it, but only to abuse the bishops for not trying it."

His activity was astonishing. He went everywhere and did everything—generally two things at once. His sayings afforded unfailing copy for the journalists whom he so heartily despised. "I seem to be always talking," is his complaint. Men wondered when the Bishop of London found time to say his prayers.

It killed him in five years. At the end "he did not seem as if he wished to live." He passed away with "God" on his lips.

"For sheer cleverness Creighton beats any man I know" was Archbishop Temple's judgment. "The most alert and universal intelligence that existed in this island at the time of his death " was the verdict of Lord Rosebery.

All his life he remained aloof from contemporary politics, but his judgments are full of wisdom. In 1880 he definitely came out on the platform to support the Liberals against Disraeli's Imperialism, demanding that " we might go back from assertions of our ascendency to the duties which we met with at home." Later he is appalled at "the mess" the Liberals are making of it, and prophesies "a Conservative reaction that will last our lifetime." In 1881, with an almost uncanny foresight, he can foretell the future :—

"England is not healthy; she is going through a process of economical readjustment of which no one can see the end; it may result in the development of new forces, or it may be the beginning of a quiet decay—not decay exactly, but subsidence. All this sorely exercises the mind of the spectator and fills him with wonder. Trade and agriculture cannot any longer go on the old lines; will they find new lines or will they collapse? Already I see the doctrine of Protection taking a strong hold of the mind of separate classes. I believe that separate interests will coalesce against the public good and against the voice of wisdom. This, by bringing in a fallacious solution, will suspend the real settlement of the question and make a mess."

He distrusted Gladstone because of his enthusiasms and emotions. All his life he was an enemy of emotion and enthusiasm in public affairs. "Imperial policy will drive home affairs into a corner " was a verdict in 1885. He became a Unionist at the great disruption. In the Armenian agitation he branded the movement as " hopelessly Pecksniffian," because it refused the only practical step, " to hand the whole thing over to Russia." In the

South African trouble he condemned (as so many) the Chamberlain policy, but accepted the war when it broke out. "I don't like war with the Transvaal," he wrote just before the crisis. "It may be a short cut to great schemes, but we are great enough to wait." At the end he took a gloomy view of the future:—

"We are ignorant and refuse to learn. We are arrogant and refuse to sympathise. We believe in our general capacity: we rejoice in our national wealth. I think that in a few years our wealth will diminish in comparison with that of the United States: our commerce will be threatened by German competition, founded on better education and receptive intelligence. We must urge these considerations—and must not settle down, to live in a fool's paradise. I feel that the next ten years will be a very critical period for England."

He was the frankest and most natural person of the time. Whatever he thought he immediately spoke out or wrote down in his letters. The results were often disastrous. "If one stops to be judicious or wise or discreet," was his apology, "one simply becomes dull." He was undoubtedly "too clever": in many respects a kind of ecclesiastical Bernard Shaw; producing the same devastating effect on the plain man. He had no self-restraint, and to the end remained as one of those children whose company he most loved. He was inclined to treat all men, especially enthusiasts, as children; and the difficulties of the Ritual agitation were greatly increased by his inability to convince the violent partisans that he did not think them children quarrelling over toys and playthings. He hated all enthusiasm, all fanaticism. I remember hearing him preach a University sermon at Cambridge—a sermon on "Liberty," in many respects remarkable. He stalked into the pulpit, unrolled a conspicuous manuscript, read hurriedly in a passionless voice without ever lifting his eyes from the paper, and without a sign of emotion stalked out again at the end. It was impossible to imagine anything more chilling. Later, as chairman of the London Diocesan Conference, he sat at a table on the daïs writing interminable letters with an aspect of cold detachment, while rival factions howled at each other in the hall beneath. At the end he rose and dismissed the whole thing (so it seemed) with a few words of frigid contempt. He would go down to some suburb to bless the local hassock, and the Mayor and chief citizens and clergy would be gathered together, bursting with enthusiasm; and he would rap out some statement as that "this kind of thing bores me to death," or that "the horrible thought has just struck me that I shall be doing this sort of thing ten years hence"; and the fervour would somehow vanish from the ceremony.

"Bored" and "amused," as the greatest evil and the greatest good in life, run through his judgment. His view of his fellow-men, and especially of Englishmen, was of the lowest. "Sometimes it seems to me as if the world was made up of moral invalids and moral lunatics," was one verdict. The "heart of the English people" he described as "the very last place I should wish to be found in—a sloppy sort of place, I take it." Of history, "I know that we ought to believe," he wrote, "that mighty movements always swayed the hearts of men. So they have—when they made for their pecuniary interest. But I believe that ideas were always second thoughts in politics—they were the garb with which men covered the nudity of their practical desires. I mean that I can never ask myself first, 'What mighty ideas swelled in the hearts of men?' But, 'What made men see a chance of saving sixpence, of gaining sixpence, or escaping from being robbed of sixpence?' What man was clever enough to devise a formula round which men could rally for this purpose?" "The English mind has no grasp of ideas," he declared, "and no sense of proportion. Indeed, the Englishman has no mind at all; he only has an hereditary obstinacy."

He heartily despised our English education, from the elementary school upwards. He branded the nation as a whole as in that dangerous condition of "half-knowledge" which was more dangerous than ignorance. He exhibited no sympathy at all with the newer ideals of social reform, and seemed to care nothing for the problems of London's poverty. His real enthusiasms were reserved for knowledge, for liberty, and for that Church of England which he called "the nation looked at from the religious side," whose sober and unemotional piety seemed to him the type of all that is best amongst the religions of the world.

He was a wayward, always interesting, lovable character. He hated getting up in the morning. He hated the high mountains, "the rubbish heaps of Nature's workshops." He was passionately fond of children, who were entirely devoted to him. This love of children he never discovered till he was nearly thirty: more fortunate than Herbert Spencer, who pathetically realised the attraction of children's society only when an old man.

"Probably no one," writes Mrs. Creighton, "was ever a better hand at a romp than he was. He would toss the children about like balls, and allow them to ill-treat him in any way they liked. He was also an adept at telling nonsense stories ; sometimes on a walk with the children hanging round him, each struggling to get as close as possible, and their elders also trying to keep near enough to listen ; or lying full length on the hearthrug before the fire with all the children sitting upon him, making what he called a 'regular pie.' He seemed to enjoy his own inventions fully as much as his hearers, as he spun them out of his brain without a moment's pause."

At Sandringham, just after being appointed to the Bishopric of London, "yesterday afternoon," he wrote, " I was careering round the hall with the Duke of York's eldest son on my shoulder, and Lord Salisbury looking at my agility with amazement." A pretty story is told of an incident of Queen Victoria's last visit to London. Standing with his chaplain in the crowd, to see her pass, the Bishop noticed a child who was too small to be able to see ; so he gave his chaplain his hat to hold, and lifted the child to a safe seat on his shoulder whence it could see everything.

Beneath all the cleverness and scornful judgment of men—the brilliancy and glitter and capacity which astonished so many—was the inner life of affection and devotion. I remember being surprised by the sudden depth of feeling displayed in one of the last of his sermons—a Lent address to a small audience—upon the words "Incorruptible and undefiled and that fadeth not away." The purpose of life, his deliberate verdict, was "an opportunity for loving." "The longer I live," he wrote in those last years, "the more deeply I am convinced that the true and abiding qualities are not the intellectual qualities, but the qualities of absolute simplicity and straightforwardness, and the desire for the right."

138

"To me the one supreme object of human life," he confessed in a rare revelation of himself, "is, and always has been, to grow nearer to God; and I regard my own individual life as simply an opportunity of offering myself to Him."

IV

The main outline of Dolling's life is known to all. Here was a combination of diverse elements which caught the imaginations of men, and gave him a supreme interest amongst ministers of religion to the lay mind. Humanity in its larger aspects, naturalness, simplicity, a love of life and of all the varied men and women in the world, especially the sinners, the poor, and those outside the pale of the Church; these were some outstanding features of a life of single-hearted devotion to one high cause. He never felt at home until he escaped from the atmosphere of the theological college and the dull respectabilities of conventional society, and settled down in his Portsmouth slum, among the people whom he loved. There was always much wilfulness in him. The element of revolt was never far from the surface. The "dear street-corner out-of-work people," as he calls them, were always more congruous to him than the ordinary well-to-do ratepayer. Brought up in the old evangelical tradition, his was a mind naturally catholic, delighting in symbol and ceremonial expression and the light and colour of service and procession. He had little reverence for the past, and about minute points of ritual he cared not at all. But the possibility of the magnificence of church and ceremony in the midst of the huddled, squalid dwellings of the poor made to him an irresistible appeal. His artistic sense was limited. Elaborate music he always hated, and the æsthetic catholicism which combined contempt of the common people with the sensuous appeal of " Cathedral " service, he regarded as an enemy of mankind. But the Catholic discipline he frankly accepted. He held that irreparable wrong had been done to these common people by the practical neglect of the Sacraments for so many centuries. And he recognised that the dreary condition of minds vacant and dulled with an entirely material outlook and little power of resistance to the forces of evil—the condition in which he found great masses of the neglected poor— could only be broken up and restored to a living faith by the full inheritance of Sacramental worship.

The years at St. Agatha's were the great years of his life. The later period was more fruitful in lessons for the time. From the astonishing success of his Portsmouth parish, with the enthusiasm of all classes of the town for a vigorous social reformer, and the utter devotion of his own poor people, he passed, after a year of wandering, into the grey, dead atmosphere of East London. The earlier successes could not be repeated in such a dreary environment. " Religion has, so to speak," he confessed, " gone to pieces ; there is no opposition ; we do not care enough to oppose. God is not in any of our thoughts ; we do not even fear Him. We face death with perfect composure, for we have nothing to give up and nothing to look forward to. Heaven has no attraction, because we should be out of place there. And Hell has no terrors."

The conviction of the utter wrongness of such a condition of lassitude and of the disloyalty of a Church which allowed, without protest, the continuance and propagation of conditions creating this dreadful acquiescence, drove him in the last few years of his life to assume the function of a prophet. There is, perhaps, something a little incongruous in the idea of this exuberant, happy, rollicking Irishman, who retained through the whole of his life the heart of a child, thus warning grave and learned dignitaries of the menace of the time. But, indeed, it was just this childlike simplicity which gave force to his denunciation. He saw the wrong that was being done on the earth, not with the eyes of one who had grown up in its atmosphere and accepted its conditions as inevitable, but with the insight and clear power of judgment of a child suddenly confronting the things of the present with the laws of justice and truth.

Dolling was never a Church defender. He cared nothing at all for the Establishment and all the social influence which the Establishment represents. "If your heart is aflame," he said, "to defend the Church of England, first, at any rate, see that you cleanse her."

"As to the present so-called crisis," he declared, in the last time of upheaval, "the real crisis, the one that ought to make Churchmen, on their knees in penitence before God, confess their negligence, is that the vast majority of English people care nothing for the Church, many even nothing for God."

The smug respectability which Dolling's biographer brands as the evil genius of reformed Christendom, was his perpetual enemy. As the end approached and he felt the years passing without seeing any great change, as he measured the condition of such a parish as Poplar against the dull platitudes which he heard in high places, his denunciation took on a fiercer tone. The articles which he published in *The Pilot* just before his death are a scathing criticism of " the genius of the Church of England."

" She is tied to a perfectly unworkable system, with no power of adapting herself to modern needs. She has had now for many generations, and still has, a perfect genius for destroying all enthusiasm, a genius for getting rid of her best unless her best will become common-place. Is this too hard a description of the Church of England ? "

In the unhappy bishops he finds the centre and head of the offence. " They have but one opportunist canon of dogma : be commonplace, be respectable, after the sober-minded ritual of the Church of England." • "On no question of any importance, religious or social, have the bishops given any lead to their people unless they have been driven to it." We are left with " nothing but a complacent failure." Undoubtedly the strain of the work, the perpetual begging for the machinery of the parish, and the absence of colour and life, the intolerable weariness and content of his East London people, were here telling upon him. " We are as a whole bloodless and anæmic." " At Portsmouth our chief duty was to repress ; here it is to incite "—this is the burden of his cry. He saw wrongs unrighted all around him ; the poor perishing and no man laying it to heart. He found overcrowding, with the laws pro-tecting the poor always evaded. " My people," was his pathetic appeal, " have been dealt with unjustly." They have " never been given a chance. Think of the houses that they are born in, the overcrowding, the drains, the damp." " The law that safeguards the poor is always in the hands of those who do not put it into force." " Charity only makes people meaner and baser, and will never prove the solution of the problem."

He demanded in the names of these disinherited millions, not charity, but justice. The spirit of the child delighting in its life gave place to the spirit of the strong man having work laid upon him to do and straitened till it be accomplished. He went down to his death, appealing to the whole Church "for the righting of wrongs that cry continually into the ears of the Lord God of Sabaoth."

Dolling's radiant personality exercised a unique fascination upon all classes of men. The man was entirely sincere, filled with one persistent enthusiasm, the love of God and man. It is an Irishman with no respect for the sober conventions of English life. Sometimes he is singing comic songs with his boys in the smoke-filled atmosphere of cellar or attic. Again, he is leading an agitation against the liquor interest, or for some measure of social progress. Criminals are sent to him, and those who have failed, and all receive welcome. He kept the affection and confidence of Winchester through all struggles and for ten years. He encouraged dancing and healthy joy, and loved especially his riotous soldiers and sailors. His mothers' meeting—whom he addressed as " My Dears "—was one of the most unconventional of all his gatherings. In his church he varied simple extempore prayer with the elaborate procession and ritual in which his people delighted. He scandalised enormous numbers of respectable persons. "With your ultra-High Church proclivities on the one hand," wrote the Warden of Winchester, "and your Socialistic teaching on the other, no sober-minded and loyal citizen can be expected to support the mission." "Last came Father Dolling," wrote a Protestant paper, "a biretta perched on his most disloyal head." "He stirreth up the people," writes Father Tyrrell, "would,

I suspect, be the truest formulation of his ecclesiastical iniquities." And the opposition was not only stirred up among the Protestants. His social enthusiasms seriously offended numbers of those who supported his Catholic teaching. He threw open his church in Poplar for a meeting of protest against the East End Water Companies. " The withholding of rain from the district," wrote a scandalised shareholder, " is God's punishment, and to ninety-nine Catholics in a hundred, the present visitation upon the East End of London is consequent upon the appointment of Mr. Dolling to St. Saviour's." But at his death the opposition was drowned in the universal recognition that one had gone whose place could never be adequately filled. He has set a new standard in the possibilities of the Church of England and its relation to the life of the poor. He stands within this communion, a figure filled with passionate zeal for justice and love of those down-trodden by the world ; one of a class mainly, alas ! confined to other branches of the Catholic Church. " Many hard things are being said against us "—his farewell to St. Agatha's is a summary of his life—" many doubt our loyalty to the Church of England. But you will believe us, I am sure, when we say that we have had but one single aim, to bring some poor people in a slum in Landport to the knowledge of our Lord and Saviour Jesus Christ."

BEFORE THE DAWN

L

" They made me a keeper of the vineyards: but mine own vineyard have I not kept."

JUNE IN ENGLAND

I

THE station has been built where thin branches of railway shoot off on either side from the main stem. And hard by the station have gathered the habitations of men; so that the passing traveller sees a vision of little red houses nestling amid the cherry and apple orchards, with all round the long fields of hops and growing corn. Down these steel tracks, which stretch out straight over the level land till lost in the haze of the horizon, hurries all the traffic of Empire. As we wait, the drowsy afternoon is torn with a shriek and the earth shaken. In a whirlwind of smoke and fire the mail passes that is hurling through our quiet air passengers for Brindisi and Singapore. Then the train from which we have alighted gathers up its belongings and thoughtfully puffs its way after its violent comrade. Finally, in quite leisurely fashion, the quaint collection of carriages in the siding, with the antique locomotive at its head, makes up its mind to depart down one of the divergent branches. Drawing out from the little town sleeping so quietly in the June sunlight, it moves slowly upwards from the plain towards the villages which lie among the hollows of the hills.

147

BEFORE THE DAWN

The platform of each tiny toy station shows white in the sunshine, with green growing things and climbing roses pushing through the fences and over the white-washed palings. The town traveller, smeared with the hurry and dust of the cities, finds a sudden restfulness and serenity as he alights at one of these. When the train with its burden has passed onward, and the last echoes have died away, something of the great peace of the summer afternoon gathers round him, and envelopes him like a garment. In the little lane which leads from the station to the village the air is filled with the scent of grasses and the new-mown hay. On either side the full fields stretch upwards, with the clover and tall daisies making a tapestry of bright colours. There is no constant stillness. Now a light wind moves along the tree-tops. Insects with gauzy wings are dancing in the light. There is a rustling under the hedges and along the borders of the meadows. You can almost hear the music of the sap as it rises in its million tiny channels, pushing the growing life outwards into the buds and the petals of the expanding flowers. Life — life everywhere: the song of laughing, overflowing life is the melody sung in exultation and content by all the world in these shining summer days. It is heard proclaimed in the hedges crowded with honeysuckle and wild roses, and the climbing plants rushing upwards towards the sun. It speaks from the little gardens with their fragrant old-fashioned flowers— pinks and sweet-williams, and the glory of the tall white lilies. It riots triumphant in the weeds which have pitched their camps on the sides of all the country lanes, now waist-deep in tangled grasses : with shy blue flowers hiding in their depths, and above a blaze of yellow cups and white stars and crimson bells. A turn of the lane discloses suddenly the wide panorama of the plain from which we have climbed. Here is a good land and a large: a great green land with scattered red-roofed villages, and standing from their midst the white cones of the hop-kilns and the dark towers of village churches. In the boundaries of a remote distance brood the blue round-shouldered hills. Across the plain into some mysterious land beyond, run the straight white roads—the white roads which lead to the end of the world.

The land is fair always—in the later harvest, when the promise of the year is fulfilled, with the cornfields and their sheaves alternating with the hop-vines under the blue sky ; or in the autumn, when all the leaves are gold, and the distant church spires stand out from a background of fiery splendour ; but fairest in the month of expectancy, of preparation, when the year has first gathered together the pageant of the early summer. These are enchanted days, from the clear brightness of the dawn, through the splendid oppression of the mid-day heat, down the long afternoon, till the sun drops behind the pine-trees, and the light glances level along the world ; and in the gathering twilight a thousand fairy lights kindle over the great plain, and on a still evening you may hear the sound of many bells. "Then shall the earth bring forth her increase." Something of the exultation of the rich fulfilment of the promise has escaped in such seasons even into this island set in its grey northern seas. In the pollen-laden air, with all the scents and music of the world, the old apprehension of the miracle of the passing of dead matter into life, acquires a sudden vivid meaning. "He sendeth the springs into the valleys that run among the hills." "The valleys also shall be so thick with corn that they shall laugh and sing." "Before you the mountains and the hills shall break forth into singing, and all the trees of the field shall clap their hands."

II

In one of these broad fruitful valleys, facing the sun, and open to the delicate air of the south, stands the village which has held, since before the dawn of history, the homes of the passing generations of men. The houses gather round the green, and straggle in lessening avenues down the diverging roads. In the centre is the old inn, the focus of all social life, in the great parlour of which the ancients were wont to gather after the toil of day, smoking their long pipes in a soothing silence. Hard by is the blacksmith's forge; the pond, with the shadows of the tall trees over it; and the general shop; and the little primitive school, with roses trespassing on the palings and knocking at the windows. The little thatched cottages have their wooden gates and fences, and their red-tiled footpaths, and their gardens gay with flowers. On the hill-top is the home of a family with a high record of service in Church and State, a great white house with a little chapel by it, within all gold and jewelled with coloured glass; and the tombs of old knights in armour with crossed legs and folded hands; and the petition for the prayer of the passing stranger, that the place of those whose hearts once beat so high with passionate desire may at the last be found in peace. And up the road that winds through the woods and meadows is the little church, with its old Norman arch and square time-beaten tower, gathering round it the bodies of the humble, forgotten dead. Here was the centre of sorrow, exultation and pain: the home of mirth and weeping. The mysteries of Birth and of Death found here a meaning and significance. At length when the tale was told and the lights extinguished here were gathered enemy and friend, saint and sinner, in that sleep which henceforth nothing would disturb but the trump of the Archangel heralding the last judgment of God. Ever within the vision of each patient toiler were the graves of his fathers, the place where he also would one day be laid. The tombs and gravestones travelled backwards to a near past. Behind were the shadowy figures of the dead, resting through all the centuries, whose blood still beat in those now for a season enduring the sunlight and the winter rain. And with the old church itself, the ivy-covered windows and grey arches and tower, which had looked down on so many hurrying generations, thought is swept backward through the gulfs of time into a far-off England; which once hewed the white stone from the rock and raised these towers and high-roofed arches and swinging bells; that in all the long ages to come, through the great awakenings and voyagings which were to carry men into stranger and more hazardous regions than those first pioneers ever dreamt of or desired, this fair building should testify to the imperishable faith of those who thus could build.

III

It is all passing: crumbling visibly year by year, almost day by day: and the thought infects with a kind of austerity and sadness the glory of these rich June days. For into these remote valleys, long hidden unheeded amongst the hills, at length has entered Progress : and Progress with all the strange uncanny shapes which follow in her retinue. At first the rout came timidly, with hesitating footsteps : later with impetuousness and a certain arrogance as of those with an accepted supremacy and triumph. The old inn is going under, defeated in competition with the new house, glaring in the raw hideousness of red and white paint; the enterprise of a firm of neighbouring brewers, with the publican a hired servant ; and active catering for the stranger and the insatiable thirst of travel. The blacksmith is overshadowed by the corrugated edifice of the "Mid Kent Motor Company : Repairs executed at the shortest notice." The great house has been sold by the bankrupt heir of the old line to a family of German Jews. The chapel with its ancient tombs remains undisturbed : but the wealth of South Africa pours as through a funnel into the countryside, and converts the peasants who were sold with the estate into a race of parasites. Secure in comfort liberally dispensed, they are for the most part prepared to return deference and the aping of the old feudal life to masters of alien race and tradition. The little church is in the main deserted. Services are continued, but the bulk of the diminishing village population rarely attend. On Sundays they gather in aimless groups in service-time outside the new public-house or at the cross-roads to see the motors pass. The Motor is indeed the keynote of the newer changes. All these June Sundays a procession of wandering locomotives hustles along the roads and avenues. The air is vocal with their hooting and shrill cries, the ritual of the New Religion, as they clank and crash through the village, leaving behind the moment's impression of the be-goggled occupants, an evil smell, a cloud of grey dust.

JUNE IN ENGLAND

Despite this revival of the countryside, the newest industry and recreation which is finding a market for so many derelict estates and bringing a fevered energy along the old roads of England, the people are slowly vanishing from the village and the surrounding fields. No one notes their departure, nor greatly cares whether they go or stay. The new wealthy live in a life of their own, careless of any responsibility for the peasant peoples surrounding them. And the farmer, adjusting with astuteness his industry to the newer conditions, is basking in a brief spell of prosperity. The land is passing back into grass and pasture, cattle taking the place of men. In the new fruit farms and hop farms, during seed-time the work is huddled through by the old men and the children and the few who can be attracted to remain. And the harvest is reaped by nomadic hordes, lured out for a season from the slums of the cities, blinking in dull wonder at the strange world of sunshine and silences to which they have been conveyed. So first at fruit-picking and later at the hop harvest, the litter of their encampments is manifest in the day, and the lights of their revelry shine far into the night. The casual labourers of the lowest depths of the cities are spewed out over our green land riotous and rejoicing. The old inhabitants, secure in the pride of ancient heritage, gaze dismally at the pandemonium. With such double assistance from above and beneath—wealth which is the plaything of rich men above, poverty which is their scorn below— rural England confronts the exodus of its peoples with a stout heart and undismayed.

Only the magic of the evening becomes charged with a sadness in the memory of all the days that have gone and the homes henceforth for ever desolate. And in the stillness of the summer night, while the stars flash over the great plain and one by one the lights of the villages go out into darkness, the silence with its cool air and scent of flowers drives home to the heart something of the sorrow of other lights extinguished, as the children of England pass from their own land into the cities where June itself is but a memory.

IV

Far to the northward, as the shadow creeps over the valley, one can almost discern the great lights streaming up behind the hills. In a momentary picture appears the vision of the labyrinth of lamplit streets, the crowded thoroughfares, the crowded warrens and tenements, the restless life of those who have gone.

So in this June, with the magic of its passing hours, Time, which changes all good and evil things, fashions from the ruins of the old a newer England.

IN DEJECTION NEAR TOOTING

HOW to get there? That is not easy, because it is the place of all forgotten things. But across the river you may find municipal trams inscribed with its inspiriting title, and by elbowing out a few tired workgirls and edging away aged men of battered physique obtain the desired seat. You journey tardily for immense spaces of time past a moving show of shadow shapes of mean houses, in which airy nothing has taken a local habitation and a name. The texture changes from slum to suburb and from suburb back to slum. At length, amid an impression of rawness, public-house, and red brick, the final jarring outrage of the municipal brake announces your destination.

The cemetery made it first, established as far from human intercourse as was compatible with a reasonable fare for the conveyance of the remains of the departed. In the old English village the dead were buried in friendly fashion round the most frequented centre, the village church. In the old English town the houses gathered comfortably by the churchyard in a kind of sanitary reformer's nightmare. For in former days it was desired that the dead should be unforgotten, and death should be much in the minds of the living. But in the modern city, eager with its pursuit of material comfort, nothing is less desired than the evidence of the end of it all, the presence of those who before disquieted themselves in vain. The emblems of mortality are apt to weaken the zeal of the pursuit of a corner in pork or an accumulation of much goods in store. So it came to pass that the dead were hurriedly shovelled into the ground at Upper Tooting.

And as through the presence of the dead the place seemed secure, gradually there followed all other things that it is desirable should be hidden away. Wandering solitary in the Tooting uplands, amidst turnip fields and coarse yellow charlock, I lighted suddenly upon some of these. On every high hill towered a monstrous building of that particular blend of austerity and dignity dear to the municipal mind. Each was planned of vast spreading dimension, with innumerable blank windows, surrounded by high polished walls. Down below in the valley, conveniently adjacent to the cemetery, was the immense fever hospital, a huddle of buildings of corrugated iron. In front was a gigantic workhouse; behind, a gigantic lunatic asylum; to the right, a gigantic barrack school; to the left, a gigantic prison. Other shadowy and enormous buildings rose dimly in the background. Yet even the presence of these monuments of ruin could not arrest the eruption of mean streets, driven forward by the pressure behind them of unthinkable numbers. All round the fever hospital crept their red tentacles, the slums of the future—little red terraces leaning against each other as if reluctant to advance, yet pushed bodily forward, ending in builders' chaos and the indecent, naked skeletons of terraces yet to be.

The discovery of these fortress prisons threw sudden light upon a problem which had often proved difficult. In Italy and the South the English visitor is shocked and saddened by the spectacle of the old, incredibly withered and wrinkled, lying in the sunlight and begging of the passer-by. Where are the similar old of England? At last I had found them—behind high walls, at Upper Tooting. Here also are our brigands, enemies of society, where they can trouble society no more. In the South are the young also, begging, uncared for, unless subtly kidnapped by the Church. Our orphan young, safely guarded from that Church's activities, are secure at Upper Tooting. So by a smooth-working, efficient machinery all superfluous and unnecessary things are sorted out and ticketed and packed into the places prepared for them.

As I gazed at these large silent palaces on the cold winter afternoon I was able to frame some picture of this ordered and regular existence. All would be smooth, polished, spotlessly clean; warmed by hot water, and with a steam laundry. Particulars would be scheduled and classified; sanitation upon the latest methods; dietary calculated by a scientific scale, with bread weighed by the ounce and calculated to a crumb. Discipline would be perfect, and movements directed by the sound of a bell. Each institution had its chaplain. There was probably in each a library of edifying books. Hundreds of thousands of pounds had been expended upon every building, and the expense was borne universally, and, on the whole, contentedly, by the citizens who lived in the warmth far away. Gradually there rose before the inward eye some vision of the life within: and with that vision the apprehension of much before inexplicable. From the turnip fields of Tooting I apprehended the British Empire and something of its meaning; why we always conquered and never assimilated our conquests; why we were so just and so unloved. Amidst alien races we have brought rest and security, order out of chaos, equality of justice, a patient service of rectitude which is one of the wonders of the world. Yet there is not one amongst these alien peoples who would lift a finger to ensure the perpetuation of our rule, or shed a tear over its destruction. For the spirit of that Empire—clean, efficient, austere, intolerably just—is the spirit which has banished to these forgotten barrack-prisons and behind high walls the helpless young and the helpless old, the maimed, the restless, and the dead.

Night fell as thus dismally I mused amongst the vegetable gardens of Upper Tooting. The fortresses which marked the bulwarks of British civilisation loomed menacing in the twilight. A cold wind stirred the discoloured grasses. A bell clanged mournfully from the distant prison. I shivered and fled the scene : with a vague discomfort which did not disappear till I had again mingled with the procession of mean street and shabby edifice ; had recrossed the river and recognised again the kindly familiar buildings, the ample eating-houses, the crowds, if insurgent, unconfined. I shall never see Tooting again, but the memory of it will mingle with many a disordered dream. And when I hear, as hear I do daily for my sins, large men with chains and seals and rings discoursing upon modern Imperialism, the Empire, the decadence of Southern races, and the unparalleled results of modern progress ; I say nothing, for nothing could make them understand. But there rises the vision of the bleak hills and the fortress prisons crowning them, gaunt and silent in the dying day. And the eloquence becomes charged with an atmosphere of varying emotion : ironical ; a little fantastic ; not lacking in tears.

THE BURDEN OF LONDON

"DO not send a philosopher to London," wrote Heine, "and for heaven's sake do not send a poet. The grim seriousness of all things, the colossal monotony, the engine-like activity, the moroseness even of pleasure, and the whole of this exaggerated London will break his heart." The statement appears to the plain man but the sneer of the unpleasant foreigner, scarce concealing his eager envy. The stuccoed squares, the grave evidences of accumulation, the lines of terraces attesting a placid opulence—small wonder, thinks the plain man, that the unpleasant foreigner gnashes his teeth and rails in fury. And those to whom the plain man counts for nothing and the stuccoed terrace appears but vanity turn again, and yet again, to hymn the praise of "London." The city standing " at the entering of the sea," the picturesque centre of the commerce of the world ; the golden glory of Piccadilly in a summer sunset; the river with its dreams of a dead past that cannot die, immortalised in the " London Voluntaries " ; the mystery and magic of the November twilight in street and alley—who has not cut his tooth in salad days with the first proclamation of these discoveries?

Only with widened knowledge and the greyness which life brings does the aspirant learn that these are not London. He has fallen into the common error of mistaking "London" for London. London is not the City, spinning the financial web of the world. Nor is London the squares and parks and gardens westward, and the places of healthful or of desolate pleasure. These are but the accidents and chance development: alien to the essence, the soul of London. As a pleasure city "London" is surpassed by Vienna, as a centre of wealth by New York, as a home of art and literature by Paris or Pekin. But London is neither a pleasure city nor a centre of wealth nor a home of art and literature. London is an aggregation—amorphous and chaotic: six and a quarter millions of humanity. The aggregation is composed of a homogeneous substance: the City Dweller—a novelty in the world—gazing out upon the universe from a crowded street, in a swarming mob, from over the shoulders or beneath the legs of his fellows. He is coagulated into a broad smudgy ring round the city which lives and moves. He dwells apart from the city which desires and is satisfied. Realisation of his existence, in its aimlessness and acquiescence, chills as with a sudden bleakness the feverish enthusiasm of the minor poet for the glory and greatness of London.

Who will interpret the soul of this London—this condensation of the unimportant which for a century has sucked in the life of the country districts, and is now turning out a third or fourth generation crushed, distorted, battered into futility by perpetual struggle towards no rational end? Observers have attempted the task, and all acknowledged failure. G. W. Steevens, after sizing up America and India, is bidden to perform similar service for London. He walks through it from south to north, from east to west.

He notes its markets, its food consumption, its
drainage system; he finds himself bewildered, baffled.
He abandons the effort as beyond his powers. Charles
Booth assails the problem with a staff of helpers. He
issues seventeen stout volumes, life, labour, religion, or
the lack of it, of the people—Class A, Class B, maps of
blue, yellow, and red of brilliance and complexity. He
confesses he is no nearer estimation at the end of it all.
Figures by the hundred thousand, woven into curves, or
condensed into tables, statistics of overcrowding, of
drunkenness, of pauperism, of crime, all pass like a tale
of little meaning, though the words are strong. The
age still waits for the interpreter of this, the strangest
riddle of the modern world.

Yet this essential London should not be a complicated study. Knowing the life of one, you know the
life of all. Only no one has yet apprehended the life
of that one. The city is, for the most part, an endless series of replicas—similar streets, similar people,
similar occupations : crowded existence, drifting through
the choked and narrow ways. You journey on the
tardy tram by stages linking together conspicuous
gin-palaces, the only landmarks of successive regions :
now you are in "Walworth," now in "Peckham,"
again in "Deptford." The varying titles are useful but
deluding. The stuff is homogeneous, woven of drab
buildings and a life set in grey. Lay down an interminable labyrinth of mean two-storied cottages. Pepper
the concoction plentifully with churches, school-build-
ings, and block-dwellings of an assorted variety of
ugliness. Cram into this as much labouring humanity
as it will hold, and then cram in some more. Label
with any name, as Stepney or Kentish Town. You
have in essence the particular ghetto that you desire.

BEFORE THE DAWN

Beyond this ring the blotch we term London sprawls into still more unknown and desolate regions whose life is clogged and heavy owing to their distance from the central heart. On the one side, in a lopsided and monstrous outgrowth, the city spreads out into vast shallow suburbs of the labouring classes, stretched over the marsh land below the level of the sea. Here are districts so far removed from the place of work as to have become mere gigantic dormitories. Man rises up a great while before day to go forth to his work and to labour until the evening. The whole margin of life of the labourer disappears in the transit. The scuffle into the city, the prolonged and odorous journey, the scuffle out again, the hastily wolfed-up meal, curtailed sleep, represent the home life of the people. To these forgotten, nameless regions, apart from the inhabitants themselves and the occasional forlorn dust-collector, "no man comes, nor hath come, since the making of the world." On other margins of the city the texture insensibly is transformed into something quaint and strange. The lines of cottages protrude into bow windows. Children are scooped inside instead of discharged outside the houses. The population clothes itself in black coats, entertains yearnings after respectability, and attends on Sunday places of public worship. This is Clerkdom: Dulwich and Clapham and Harringay; where pale men protest Imperialism and women are driven by the tedium of nothingness into Extension Lectures or the Primrose League—an uncanny and humorous region, illuminated with perplexing ideals.

But these regions are also parasitic. London in its characteristic product is the city of the ghetto. Here gather the unparalleled masses of the obscure. They are members of no trades union. They are inspired by no faith in progress. They are forgotten, as it seems, alike of man and of God. Labouring populations, in which no one rises above the rank of the local publican, outnumber the inhabitants of many great kingdoms. The dreariness of their lives does not depend on their poverty. They are scourged with specific ills, of which no outsider knows or cares. But the tragedy resides in their acquiescence : the absence of eager revolt and protest : the listless toleration of intolerable things. They extend under sunshine and darkness, an interminable acreage, shabby, impotent, grotesquely negligible. They imbibe open-mouthed any specious illusion, cheering for blood when full of meat, when meatless clamorous for plunder. Few know of their existence : none realise its import. Populations of great colonies or European capitals could be torn from them without appreciable diminution. Who would even be conscious of change if, say, Wandsworth or Hoxton vanished with to-morrow's sunrise? A wave of human life has silently become pent up into a menacing congestion. There has been nothing like it before in the history of the world. Please God, after its destruction there shall be nothing like it again.

What of the race that is being reared in this stagnant marshland, lying aside from and unmoved by the stream of progress ? No one knows. It is a portentous vision of silence : a mob drifting from the cradle to the grave, without ever rising to articulate speech. No poet immortalises himself in " Ballads of Bermondsey," or " Lines written in dejection near Haggerston." No passionate protest from Pentonville rouses as with a trumpet-call. No Camberwell woman's love-letters disturb the serenity of the literary horizon. Visitors, indeed, from a different universe of being penetrate

163

these regions, attempt to crystallise into words the cloudy emotions of the ghetto. A Gissing will set himself to record the life of the decent and the ignobly decent. A daily newspaper will encourage the confession of their half-baked theologies and atheisms. A Davidson will proclaim, with a kind of scorching flame, the futility of life at thirty bob a week. But these interpretations remain, for the dissected subject, things distant and unknown. Noise, indeed, he makes in abundance in his brief passage between two Eternities. The play of children, the mirthless jest, the quavering militant melody, the sounds of contest and blasphemy, rises continually towards the quiet stars. He has been discerned emerging from beyond the river at daybreak, or trampling among his friends in a scuffle for the tram to convey him to his lair in the gathering twilight. But the mystery of the inner springs of his existence, the happiness, acquiescence, or discomfort of life as viewed from the sixth story of a block-dwelling or the half of a house in a mean street, are locked up beneath that harassed inscrutable face of his, a secret he will carry with him to the grave.

Such is the Burden of London: unfelt by the majority who pass by: weighing like a nightmare upon some of those who gaze forward towards the coming years. The vision is of London not, like the Holy City, at unity with itself: but a manifest object-lesson in a nation falling asunder, "being old." To-day we discern a race which is separating into communities profoundly ignorant of each others' existence : cities of artisans, cities of clerks, cities of labourers, cities of the wealthy. At bottom this is for the most part a parasitic population : from which the higher energies are not demanded, and by which in consequence these are not supplied : lacking the pushfulness of the artisan of the North as much as the obstinate endurance of the peasant of the fields. We apprehend hundreds of thousands engaged in the supply of artificial wants, in carrying people from here to there, in ministering to the changing fashion, or pandering to the unchanging appetites of men. And we recognise a population destined ever to extend. Greater London in less than thirty years is to amount to ten millions. The main part of the increase will be woven of this drab material. North, east, south, and west the aggregation is silently pushing outwards like some gigantic plasmodium : spreading slimy arms over the surrounding fields, heavily dragging after them the ruin of its desolation. And Tooting and East Ham, and Plumstead and Silvertown, are born into a world which shows no joy at their advent. Humanity staggers at the vision of the next generation : uninvigorated by the influx of the country life, ravaged by the diseases of overcrowding in dwelling and area, dulness, vacuity of labour, and lust for artificial excitement : dead to the faiths which once provided a tangible background to existence.

" Revolving this and many things," one can note the astonishing prescience of a poet of the far-back, long-despised, "early Victorian" era, who found in the blind Bull-god of the spoil of Assyria the image of the god of this people ; having wings but not to fly with : and eyes, but not to look up with : bearing a written image engraved of which he knows not, and cannot read it ; crowned, but not for honour :—

> " Those heavy wings spread high
> So sure of flight which do not fly,
> That set gaze never on the sky,
>   Those scriptured flanks it cannot see.

BEFORE THE DAWN

Its crown, a brow-contracting load,
Its planted feet which trusts the sod,

. . . . .

O Nineveh, was this thy god,
Thine also mighty Nineveh?"

But until the end is revealed no man can know whether
this or some other god be indeed the god of the city.

THE NEW REVOLUTION

"THE struggle between belief and unbelief," said Goethe, "is the only thing in the memoirs of humanity worth considering." And the problem of the religion and general outlook on the world which is likely to be evolved by an age of tranquillity and comfort is the problem which most immediately faces the civilisation of to-day and to-morrow. For the first time in many centuries, and especially in the Anglo-Saxon world, in England, in parts of America, and in the Colonies, we see a race developing who have experienced nothing but a serene and ordered existence. From the beginning they have been sheltered from the disturbing elements of life. They do not possess imagination necessary to realise that this is an abnormal and transitory phase of the world's development. All their accepted ideas in art, ethics, and religion, are inherited from times when this tranquillity was lacking. They are becoming vaguely conscious that for them the language is strained, extravagant, unreal. They have no conception of the meaning of such a cosmic upheaval, the disarrangement of a universe, as, for example, the great disturbance of '89 in France or the deliquescence of the whole social order before the invader in 1870. Even Nature's catastrophies have been sedulously removed. There is no fear of great epidemics, and only the occasional remote and unrealised echo of such an unexpected destruction as that of Martinique. Undoubtedly the contrast between such a life as that of Dulwich or Toronto or Dunedin and the life of all the past must implicate the coming of great changes in human life and its outlook upon the world.

Towards Nature, towards himself, and towards the apprehension of any spiritual principle outside and behind these, man's ideas are becoming profoundly modified. In Nature he has come to recognise the element of permanence. He is at home for the first time in an orderly world. The old fear—the panic fear—of some sudden menace no longer lurks in the shadows. The feelings of horror with regard to Nature and its operations and the feelings of insecurity are passing away from the minds of men. The general view of Nature which this new race is cultivating is that of the well-ordered watering-place which is the sole experience of most of them : a cleaned beach, breakwaters to temper the rough onslaught of the sea, with promenade and pier and safe playing-ground for the children, and the faint, emotional strains of the nigger minstrels in the evening.

And the progress of intelligence has drawn each man closer together to his neighbour. The world has become one. With an absence of any large and impelling impulse towards reform, men are vaguely desirous that all their neighbours should enjoy some sort of similar comfort to their own. Mr. Gilkes, in his little, most suggestive essay on the subject, has emphasised this restlessness in face of the evidence of pain. "They do not wish any longer," he says, "that regulations made by man should keep men from working and playing as they ought to work and play. A man can no longer eat his dinner comfortably when there are beneath him dungeons full of his fellow-creatures whom his own act has placed there, however strictly legal that act may be, and consequently there is a general impatience of all privilege, all excess of possession and of comfort."

With this altruism which finds its expression on the one hand in the largeness of so-called charity, and on the other hand in the general demand for the Churches to cease to strive towards impossible perfections and spiritual ardours, there has come a tendency to acquiesce in an average standard of attainment. In a recent controversy bearing the title " Do we Believe? " the populations of the suburbs poured out their hearts in the columns of a daily paper. It was instructive to note the general revolt from the violence and disturbance of religions which drove men and women out of their accustomed ways. The demand came more and more to concentrate upon a vague, amiable philanthropy. The less reputable sins were to be banished. The duty of man was to lead the life of the good citizen, voting in parliamentary if not in municipal elections, and at Christmas-time making liberal provision for the feeding and clothing of the poor.

The sense of sin and of a great humility and all the vast machinery of aspiration and penitence which have gathered around these, have become clouded in the minds of the dwellers in the modern cities.

But it is in the relation of man to God the greatest changes are evident. With the coming of this gospel of decency and good manners there has vanished those ardours and agonies of the soul whose interest now appears mainly pathological. No one can be blind to the process, accompanying this diffused ethic, of the weakening apprehension of spiritual things.

BEFORE THE DAWN

"If he received some sign," says Mr. Gilkes again, "to show him what he should do, some sign which showed him when he was in danger of doing wrong, which revealed to him his ideal, he might do right continually; but he receives no sign; perhaps once in a month or a year he sees his ideal plainly and God plainly, but often, even before he reaches the end of the road where he was when he saw it, the colour has faded from what he saw. He says the words which he said before, but they are dead words, and he would no longer go readily to death for the truth which they express."

When in time of order the new revolution is successfully accomplished, there are some who will look forward with longing to the change beyond the change. In the provision of elements of permanent value for the life of man periods of disturbance have always been more conspicuous than periods of certitude. The times of disorder and unsettlement when men suffered from oppression, trembled in terror before vague and inexplicable forces, were ravaged by great plagues and lived always in uncertainty, were the times which produced the highest developments of art and the finest flower of human character. When man was doubtful if he would see to-morrow's sunrise he built as if not dreaming of a perishable home. To-day when he cannot believe that death will touch him, and his orderly life stretches forward as an endless end of the world, he will leave for the amazement of future ages the Crystal Palace and the City Temple and the Peabody Building.

Dr. Arnold, in his "Survey of History," came to the conclusion that after all the changes of the past the world was now entering into a course of steady, orderly, and consistent development in a phase from which the unexpected would be abolished. Man would sit down

170

comfortably in a world whose forces at length he rightly estimated. It was a belief characteristic of an early Victorian Age unable to conceive of any more perfect life than that represented by its mahogany sideboards and its material opulence. It is a more hopeful view that we are on the edge of a process of profound change. Ruins if furnished with plush and alpaca and labelled Brixton and Holloway, will not provide a permanent habitation for the soul of man. Assuredly the condition of the ultimate flower of the process of evolution in the expanding middle class of England and America is not a condition of stable equilibrium. They cultivate habits of regularity. They weave themselves into other men's ideas. They are cut off from disturbing realities. They attend places of religious worship; but they hear language of ancient liturgies wrung out of passion and terror which seems to them archaic or meaningless. They are conscious of a vague, emotional satisfaction at an evening service or singing the hymns of childhood. Sometimes they feel a little queer at the death of a child or at the signs of the coming of old age. Occasionally, despite the avoidance of Nature and its mysteries, some old memories, the smell of Spring and Autumn, a wind blown into the city with the scent of flowers or up the river from the sea, stir into momentary disquietude emotions which have lain long buried under the weight of custom and routine. Love and Birth and Death, those divine Anarchists, are always disturbing, as Plato apprehended long ago, to any satisfied civilisation. These, with the exultations and agonies which form their " great allies," may be trusted to disintegrate any society which has banished mystery from its midst and turned its back on realities; and set itself down to use and wont, pitiful pleasures, and the obstinate fear of change ; and put aside the heavy and the weary weight of all this unintelligible world.

How the change will come it is impossible to foresee. Perhaps there may arise the sudden and unexpected outbreak of forces fermenting among the neglected populations, of whose existence and whose hunger for the material goods denied them this ordered state has but little apprehension. Perhaps, as in a former period of Imperial peace, a universally awakening consciousness may protest the futility and worthlessness of it all. Weariness will come of the "impracticable hours" of life divorced from passion and emptied of high, spiritual enterprise. However excited, those concerned with the soul's development rather than with the attainment of material comfort will be prepared to welcome the change. For such change will tear down the veil of comfortable things, velvet and cushions and fine clothes, which man will always raise if he can between himself and the unknown. Behind are the realities with whom he is never at ease, and whose acquaintance he is always anxious to elude ; himself : the world of real things ; God Who is the Beginning and the End of all.

THE BLASPHEMY OF OPTIMISM

TO assail one who has bewildered many decent people and added to life a new literary inspiration is a thankless and dismal task. To join issue with Mr. Chesterton, whose work is a perpetual stimulus to humility and astonishment, would appear but a mournful ingratitude. Nevertheless, it is time for some dull person to raise the banner of protest, however sober and grave, against the philosophy of life which Mr. Chesterton is steadily hammering into the brain of the English householder. The very brilliancy of his weapons, the paradox, the bold metaphor, the statement which leaves one doubled up and speechless, the divine lunacy of his intoxicated inspiration, foretells the success of his onslaught upon things customary, honoured, and secure. Avowedly in his criticism as in his poetry, as he acknowledges in his preface to his "Defendant," Mr. Chesterton is preaching a philosophy, maintaining an attitude, announcing a creed. We now possess in his collected works a consistent volume of doctrine which can be contemplated as a whole. Essays on "Chesterton as a religious teacher" will soon be utilised at the older universities to stimulate aspiring merit with mean monetary compensation. Before this consummation arrives it is well that the immorality of such a creed should be demonstrated.

173

BEFORE THE DAWN

With the side issues raised by Mr. Chesterton I am altogether in sympathy. It is but the main contention which is ultimately vicious. That Mr. Chesterton should seek to defend the obsolete and neglected virtue of Patriotism is a subject rather for praise than for blame. That he should endeavour to arouse Kensington to consciousness of its proximity to the Eternal fires should make for Kensington's righteousness if not for Kensington's equanimity. That he should attempt to interest the English people in the English Bible—a work much read by their forefathers—is a commendable if desperate enterprise. That he should hail himself as God is only to be deprecated by some rival claimant to the title. But that he should profess a blasphemous contentment, associate pessimism with minor poetry, and extol the average decent citizen for his average decency, partakes of the nature of that sin for which there is no place for repentance, though it be sought bitterly and with tears.

"I have investigated the dust-heaps of humanity," announces Mr. Chesterton, "and found a treasure in all of them." No one doubts the treasure in the dust-heap. The difficulty lies in the apprehension of the treasure in the drawing-room. The jewel is manifest in that which humanity discards. It is less discernible in that which humanity retains. Mr. Chesterton holds that all dross can be converted into gold by the believing mind. Nothing is either good or bad, he would say with the Danish optimist, but thinking makes it so. Assert in firm tones that all things are very good, and, lo! all things are very good. It is a simple creed, and yet pleasant when one considers it. In the spirit of his capering maniac Mr. Chesterton traverses the world charging himself everywhere with contentment and

174

triumph. A drunken man reels out of the beerhouse, zigzags heavily down the pavement, clutches wildly at vacuity, and flops into the garbage of the gutter. To himself he is a mass of internal discomfort, a dulled vacancy, and the earth an unkind stepmother springing up to knock him down. To Mr. Chesterton, observant, he is the living representative of the happy peasant, the modern pastoral idyll, and his soul is with the stars. The good citizen is journeying through the tube, portly, double-chinned, reading *Bright Bits* and breathing heavily. Should he but spring upwards, Mr. Chesterton holds, prance wildly down the carriage and spin round like a Dervish, he would inaugurate the golden age. Surbiton is a city of mystery and enchantment, Penge and Poplar suggest a restored fairyland, Wapping is the antechamber to the Kingdom of Heaven. All perspective is levelled in such a dreary morass of satisfaction. Mr. Chesterton is convinced that the Devil is dead. A children's epileptic hospital, a City dinner, a political "At Home," a South African charnel camp, or other similar examples of cosmic ruin fail to shake this blasphemous optimism. At the least he would design to make the Author of Evil die of chagrin at persistent neglect, or perish from the repletion of persistent flattery. The scheme is attractive but delusive. That ancient strategist has seen so many Chestertons flare and fade that he is unlikely to be entrapped by such naïve methods. Nor will the inclusion of good and evil in a higher synthesis, embracing both in a universal approbation, create any permanent or lasting peace in the war which is being everlastingly waged—on earth, as in heaven.

Progress has never been effected but by persistent toil and the emphatic demonstration of the wickedness and sorrow of the world. Mr. Chesterton's creed will act as a disintegrating force upon the never very secure foundations of this edifice. He will not, indeed, be able to convince a man that his own toothache is good ; but he may succeed with alacrity in assuring him of the sanctity and desirableness of the toothache of others. Here is a citizen who presents at times a singular combination of the hog and the hyena, with the seed of a god stifled beneath deep rolls of avidity and desire. All effort towards fructification of this seed is effected only by the sudden flashing into his face of some monstrous and unnegligible wrong. Show him a cab-horse about to trample on a child, and, at the cost of considerable bodily discomfort, he will effect a rescue. Raise a barrier of use and wont between him and the children which he dully knows are perishing and he will consume his dinner with withers unwrung. A holocaust of fourteen thousand children was demanded, with all the incredible accompaniments of bereavement, loss, and longing, before he realised in blear-eyed manner that away in South Africa his clumsy hoof was crushing something delicate and divine. Tell him that (say) Bermondsey is a blasphemy of stunted, distorted existence, outrage alike on God and man, and he may be startled into the effort towards reform. Tell him, as Mr. Chesterton tells him, that down in Bermondsey the gas lamps are fairy bubbles, the atmosphere is magical and charged with emotion, that each fuddled toper is in Paradise beneath the approval of the eternal stars ; with a deep content, thanking God that he is rid of a knave, he turns him again to slumber.

Mr. Chesterton holds that all things are very good.

He may assert that he has a certain reputable precedent for such a statement. The plea cannot be entertained. God found all things "very good." Such a discovery is a prerogative of divinity. No man can look on God and live; and no man can live who sees things as God sees them. Mr. Chesterton would urge us to believe that each man's life is illuminated by the same light which he himself discerns, though it were never on sea or land. It is the pathetic fallacy, eternally untrue. "The same sun shines on the windows of the almshouse as on the walls of the castle." Never was there a profounder delusion. The sun which shines on the castle is not the sun that shines on the almshouse. Contentment terminates in mortification. Complete satisfaction is indistinguishable from death.

Mr. Chesterton, alive himself, would fain persuade us that other men and women are alive. He assumes a point which he would find it impossible to prove. Men and women have been alive: there are intervals in the career of the most obscure when they should be alive. But the chief accusation against the modern city is that it has choked so many innumerable human lives: a mob moving who are dead. Compared with this outrage, the massacre of actual assassination fades into insignificance. At three periods, at least, humanity should rise above the line of life. For a moment they should live as children, in the world of fairyland peopled by a strange and kindly race who pursue generous action. For a moment they should live again when through sudden, passionate, inexplicable emotion men and women look into each other's eyes and realise their kinship with the stars. And for a moment they should live at death—though the experience, it has been noted, usually comes too late in life to be of much practical utility. But in the life of the modern crowd crushed into a mass of blurred humanity these avenues of the spirit are choked and blighted. Childhood is clumsily spoiled and broken by the misplaced ingenuity of the "Grown folk, mighty and cunning." Courtship is the panting pursuit of Phyllis by Strephon round the block-dwellings, or the sombre, nudging pilgrimage through a city of dreadful night. And most men die with a grunt or a bleat, lamenting the lack of gin, or protesting that they could drink pea soup. We have never seen a man die, was Thoreau's challenge; because we have never yet seen a man alive.

Once man apprehended that God walked with him in the garden in the cool of the day. Then he could lift his eyes to the magical world about him and Heaven's unchanging stars. Now the Archangel stands at the entrance with the flaming sword in His hand; attesting, on the one hand the effort needed for return, on the other the futility of acquiescence in any lesser aspiration. Mr. Chesterton would assuage the divine hunger by the pretence that outside the wilderness is fair. The man with the muck rake can obtain the golden crown, not by the painful effort to look upwards, but by weaving the sticks of the floor into a coronet and assuring himself that it is gold. Man has wandered into the wilderness and solitary places. It is well for him if here he finds no city to dwell in. Mr. Chesterton would urge him to build booths of boughs, assure him that Paradise is here or nowhere, expound to him the grandeur of the desert scrub, and the glory of the desert sand. Far on the horizon shines the Land of Promise, demanding first for its attainment a divine discontent and an eager pushing forward. Effort

178

unwearying, the sweat and blood of men, the wreck of a thousand lives, a world travail of pain, has been the price men have paid for permission sometimes to whisper to each other in the twilight that all things are very good. The ultimate tragedy of history, at which the sun veiled his face and the pillars of the earth were shaken, was necessary in order that humanity might be able to cherish for nineteen disordered centuries the desperate hope that God is Love.

CHICAGO AND FRANCIS

IN pursuit of my trade as a reviewer of books it befell
a while ago that I was reading two volumes dealing with subjects of especial interest. The one was a
description, compiled with enthusiasm and pride, of the
triumphs of the New America. The other was a record,
a little sentimental, but very pleasant and simple, of
the lives of the followers of Francis. And the chance
combination of two such subjects set one a-thinking.

The new America exhibits a nation definitely
organised for one purpose, straining every nerve and
sinew to attain that end. "Business" is the all-
absorbing interest; by the side of which nothing else
counts at all. The nation is joyously set on the commercial conquest of the world. As in former times the
people organised throughout as a military race was
enabled to trample down all rivals, so in a commercial
age the people which has with devotion moulded everything towards commercial energy is destined to crumple
up its less single-hearted competitors. The vision is
presented of a life where all other interests are ruthlessly planed away. In parallelogramed cities of
monotonous architecture, amid the shrieks of whistles
and the noise of telegraphs and monsterphones, a vague
impression appears of eager men in a crowd. They rise
hastily from sleep to rush from factory to counting-

house, consuming meals in their shirt-sleeves and toiling with a rude energy which is one of the wonders of the modern world. Leisure, solitude, art, literature, meditation, religion—all these are brushed aside as by-products, apart from the main business of life. Socialism has made less progress than in any other civilised country : with each man possessing the marshal's *baton* in his knapsack, why turn aside to raise all to the level of lance-corporal ! High above the throng tower the figures of those who have attained : a Jay Gould, a Vanderbilt, a Carnegie, who started with the proverbial penny. Such unified energy is producing its results. Already the old nations, with their militarism and their ideals, are feeling the commencement of the strain : the cry has gone forth for a Europe united against the common enemy—the new Barbarians knocking at its doors. But the flimsy barriers which such a Europe can erect are destined to be swept aside. The figures of commercial progress for even ten years in America are something stupendous ; in steel, in oil, in pig, in cotton, the output springs upward in a night. For the moment there is respite while the internal markets absorb the energies of the factories ; but in a few years' time America will once more leap forward to the commercial exploitation of the world. In the perfect adaptation of means to an end and the throwing over as lumber of all that does not subserve that end she stands unrivalled. We bow to our future conquerors.

America is changing beneath our very eyes. Yesterday's books concerning her are antiquated ; descriptions of ten years ago are hopelessly out of date ; between the writing of a book and its publication half its facts have changed. Yet the New America still awaits its interpreter. What exactly is the meaning of the events daily recorded ; not in terms of oil or pig, but in their inner and larger meaning ? What is the significance, *i.e.*, of the vast system of popular colleges in the cities of the Mississippi Valley ? What contribution to human welfare is provided by (say) Athens, Georgia ? What exact function in the spiritual progress of man- kind is performed by the Sixth Methodist Episcopal Church of Minneapolis ? These are the kind of problems upon which we seek light.

American civilisation has " come to centre about the conception of life as a matter of industrial energy." With rude strength, utter devotion, and boisterous energy, the American capitalist and worker have com- bined in alliance for the commercial exploitation of the world. Life itself vanishes in the terrific elaboration of the giant machine. In America there are "two kinds of slaves, the nigger and the white." Youth is everywhere evident. "Under the new strenuous *régime* there are no old men." Men as well as machines are thrown with reckless disregard to the scrap-heap. "America is paying more for her industrial success than we would care to pay; more, indeed, than humanity can afford." The women alone live. While these read books, discuss art, or pilgrimage through Europe, the men, in the midst of the shrieks of whistles and the clang of machinery, provide a panorama of a stampede from counting-house to factory, wolfing up meals of oyster-stew in an atmosphere of perpetual dyspepsia.

"Where are all your old men ? " asks the visitor as he gazes at young, tired faces everywhere. " Come up to the cemetery and I will show you," is the genial reply.

The Spanish war marked a deep-cut moment of change ; and the American nation is still intoxicated by the ease with which it crumpled up an historic military power. To the other nations of the world its entrance into *Welt-politik* has been like a descent of a brigade from the planet Mars, wielding a force singularly potent, absolutely new, and not quite accountable. The result has left the American people, on the one hand, with the legacy of great possessions : " an American Empire is arising." Forgetting their greatest President's dictum that "the Almighty never made a people good enough to rule over other people," stimulated by the alluring claptrap concerning the White Man's Burden and the Trustees of Progress, with the unlimited possibilities of trade exploitation that "expansion " always provides, they have set themselves to the task of elevating the Philippines and Cuba to the civilisation of Chicago. And on the other hand, with the taste for blood once whetted, their appetite for large interventions has been aroused. So they lecture Roumania on its treatment of the Jews, consider the possibility of intervention in Turkey, and elaborate a Navy for fresh conquests. In a few years the lectures are destined to find their fruit in action : and with that action the Coming Race enters into its heritage.

Turn from this vision of the complacent, shouting twentieth century to the pictures of the influence of an ideal in that strange Europe of seven centuries ago. Life is rude and troubled. Wars and brutalities abound, the Empire and the Church are fighting for a world mastery ; wolves, as in Salimbene's picture of the miseries of the time, howl under the walls of the little cities of Italy and at night enter the towns and devour men. There is little comfort and no content. Life has not yet come to revolve round an economic centre. But in all the chaos of a world but imperfectly comprehended, full of fear and strange adventure, there are interests leading to high spiritual endeavour and the triumph of the soul. The wonder is not in the unique and gracious figure of Francis. This, indeed, is a miracle. But similar if less complete miracles abound in the history of Christendom. But it lies in the spirit of the sons of Francis : in that madness from beyond the boundaries of the world, which fell upon so many quite ordinary men, merchants, soldiers, citizens, who in this century might have served a Beef Trust or engineered a corner in wheat. After twelve hundred years, attempts had again been made faithfully to follow the life of the Master. The living example of the Christian life had once more proved its appealing power. And the thirteenth century recognises for a moment at least the key to the secret of the transitory life of man. By the end the spiritual impulse is fading into the light of common day ; the followers of Holy Poverty are becoming less faithful in their allegiance. But even at the end, a hundred years after the Blessed Francis, the new Art is drawing all its inspiration from his life and teaching. Dante is proclaiming the greatness of the Franciscan ideal ; and such a miracle can happen as that strange pilgrimage of kings and cardinals to the mountains, to bring down from his refuge amongst the clouds a hermit who in a moment of madness or inspiration had been elected to the proudest position in the world, to inaugurate the golden age.

Haunting the whole of this tumultuous and fascinating time is the ideal of the Great Restoration : the sense of impending change in that visible revelation of the Kingdom of God to which the best minds turned with the eager longing of children. The third Kingdom, the Kingdom of the Holy Spirit, was about to dawn. To-day, or at furthest to-morrow, the Angel of the Everlasting Gospel would proclaim the entrance of the armies of God.

They are a fascinating company—these children of Francis, the members of the new order of spiritual chivalry enrolled in the service of their Lady Poverty. First are those who were with him, *Nos qui cum eo fuimus*, possessing some infection as it were of the altogether personal charm that surrounds the little poor man of Assisi. Bernard, who had loved him so, died protesting "I feel in my soul that for a thousand worlds I would not have been other than a servant of Christ. Hear my prayer, that ye love one another." Rufino nursed him at the end. Giles in his high perch at Perugia spoke his rough words of common sense and saw visions of eternal things. Masseo's life was broken by the death of his master. Leo, the *pecorello di Dio*, the little sheep of God, so humble and patient, could kindle into fierce anger at the violation of the rule in the building of the great Church of San Francesco, the wonder of the world. And after these came the long succession of those who gladly took up the torch from the first followers, rejoicing in the revelation of the secret. In front are a few selected figures : Salimbene, the kind-hearted gossip and traveller, in whose Chronicles lives all the life of the mediæval world; or John of Parma, the great General of the order, journeying on foot from house to house along the roads of Europe, taking the humblest place and the meanest duties at his visitations, as befits the greatest in this strong reversal of human standards : in the banqueting-hall of the king found amongst the tables of the poor. The strangest, most attractive figure is

BEFORE THE DAWN

Jacopone da Todi, with his austerities and his joyousness; his tender songs over the Christ Child and his poetry, through which breathes the open air and all the hot, coloured life of Southern Italy: " sun and sky and flowing water and flower-lined roads." Visions of unimaginable sweetness attend him in his prison; the End in Good unimagined and measureless Light is ever before him; he weeps " because love is not loved " and " would fain have suffered for the demons in hell and have seen them go before him into Paradise." At his death " it was believed," says the chronicler, " by those standing near that he died, not so much conquered by his malady, though that was grave, as from an extraordinary excess of love." And behind these greater figures is a multitude of forgotten common people who have caught fire at the message and whose life has become transformed; as those who set out to convert the Mohammedans, or the Friars that came joyfully singing into Stynkynge Alley in the city of London in England, or the obscure and shadowy figures who are discerned tending the lepers or following the track of the great armies to nurse the wounded and bury the dead.

Later there is conflict between the strict and the relaxed; the world rolls in again and stifles the ideal; and the faithful retire to the mountains with gloomy prophecies of ruin to become the soured and bitter Fraticelli of the fourteenth century. But in this early time the vision seemed not far away. There is a strange reason, a kind of disordered common sense, an unanswerable and rather distressing logic, subversive of the respectabilities and the gospel of success about these followers of Madonna Poverty. Here are none of the austerities and contempt of the world, the pitiless

186

laceration of the body of an earlier and gloomier time. Though pilgrims and strangers, seeking a country, they go singing through a land which for them is very fair. They love all natural things—the unclouded sky and the hot nights of Umbria. Lacking all possessions they are full of song in praise of God. They love all men and women, are passionately affectionate one to another. They are cheered by the abiding vision of the unseen world. Life when released from the intolerable burden of possessions they proclaim as very good. There is a blitheness here, somehow vanished from the modern manufacturing city ; an absurd satisfaction in the picture of the world as a cloister lacking in the more up-to-date picture of the world as a factory.

And despite the changes of the intervening years, how singularly contemporary is their appeal ! The *Sacrum Commercium Beati Francisci cum Domina Paupertate*, the prose version of Giotto's picture in the lower Church at Assisi—in its eloquence and shrewdness the summary of the whole spirit of the Franciscan revival—might have been written yesterday. St. Francis in his quest for Holy Poverty will go to the great ones and to the learned sages. This he did. But the great ones and the sages answered him hardly, saying, " What new doctrine is this thou bringest to our ears ? Let the Poverty thou seekest be thine and thy children's after thee. For us be the enjoyment of delight and the overflowing of riches. For brief and full of labour are the days of our life and in the end of man what refuge ? Nothing better have we found than to eat and drink and be merry while we live." And the temptation of Avarice, determining to take unto her the name Prudence and speaking humble wise, might have been delivered by any ecclesiastical dignity explaining the "twentieth century spirit of Francis" in Sabatier meetings.

"With all peace and quietness you can work your own salvation and others, if once your storehouse be full. . . . Will God not accept you if you have wherewith to give to the needy and. are mindful of the poor? . . . What fear for you in the contact of riches, since ye hold them as nothing? Evil is not in things but in the mind —for God saw everything that He had made and behold it was very good. So to the good all things are good. . . . O how many rich men spend foolishly, whereas, if you had wealth you would turn it to good use: for your purpose is holy and holy your desire."

An appealing vision was needed to combat a temptation so subtle and plausible. It was found in the vision of that Lady Poverty as Giotto painted her who "alone clave to the King of Glory when all His chosen and loved ones left Him in fear."

"I am not rude and unlearned, as many think; but ancient and full of days as I am, I know the nature of things, the variety of creatures, and the changes of the times. I have known the restlessness of the human heart, learning it now in my experience of the world, now by subtlety of nature and now by gift of grace. I was in the Paradise of God when man was naked, wandering through all that spacious realm fearing nothing. . . . There I thought to remain for ever. . . . Very joyful was I, sporting with him all the day, having nothing of my own, for all was God's."

Back one is driven to the old haunting question. Which of these have attained the real secret of success— these visionaries of Umbria long dead, or the solid live men who have made Chicago? those who get, or those who give? Truly if they were right then the modern world is altogether wrong. A modern novelist, M. de Coulevain, has attempted to represent the conflict of these ideals—the product of modern America in its most cultured and effective form with this dream world of the past. His heroine visiting Assisi only expresses regret that St. Francis and St. Claire never married. The language of the Saints towards the real things of the Eternal world is uncouth and alien to her. "There will never be any saints in America," she confidently asserts.

"No! No! I don't see an American divesting himself of his goods, preaching poverty and talking to doves. Instead of St. Francis we shall, may be, have men who will lessen ˙poverty and make the world a more comfortable place."

Wealth accumulated as a reality, wealth distributed as an ideal—here is the watchword of the spirit of the age. It may seem madness to cling to any divergent dream. Yet a certain suspicion still refuses to be stifled. "What shall it profit?" appears at times written large over all the monstrous buildings and shrieking factories. For long after Chicago and Birmingham and all the products of a complacent and mechanical age have become the habitation of bats and owls, men's hearts will still turn with longing towards the little brown cities of Italy, for love of those lives whose fragrance clings to their crumbling walls and appeals across the silence of so many dead centuries.

THE MAKING OF THE SUPERMAN

MR. WELLS and Mr. Bernard Shaw are our two living prophets. Both have entered the profession, like the shepherd of Tekoa, by unorthodox ways. Both interpret the function of prophecy as much in the diagnosis of the present as in the forecast of the changes of the future. Both follow the New Testament in preferring the wicked to the mean. Both have faith in nothing but youth. "Every man of forty is a scoundrel" is the cheerful aphorism of the one ; and the other appeals always to the young men to enrol in the crusade for the New Republic. They survey the squalid course of contemporary life in England, from the cottage to the castle, with a kind of disgusted pity. They find in the life of the average Briton, his complacency, his dull pretence of wisdom, his dull thirst for gain, the random routine of his unedifying day, something which cries to heaven as an offence. Both call for the Superman. But in the case of the one the call remains as a pious aspiration, a mere summary of revolt and weariness. In the other there is an attempt to ransack the springs of action, to drive down into fundamental things, to examine how, if at all, it is possible by breeding, by education, by social reconstruction to hasten the arrival of the Coming Race.

190

THE MAKING OF THE SUPERMAN

A figure famous in the literature of Europe has also in these later years joined the prophetic company. M. Maeterlinck has progressed steadily from the method and atmosphere of a dead past, through the wisdom and destiny of the present, to the proclamation of his faith in the future. Examination of three writers of such varied talent and temperament should throw some light upon the problem of the days to come.

I

Mr. Bernard Shaw, in his latest plays, reveals the attitude of revolt. He is tired of the tedious ineptitude, of the persistent muddle of life. It is the man of forty; disenchanted; the mocking spirit confronting existence with a grimace and a gibe. All the earlier illusions have vanished. The ideals of the time which he would term the " eighteen-eighties " have passed like a dream. He sees life in its grim and ugly nakedness, and he is filled with a hopeless disgust at the prospect. With one of his own characters he has " swallowed all the formulas, even that of Socialism," and found that he has eaten the east wind. The work of dramatic criticism commenced the process ; the completion was attained in experience as a Borough Councillor of St. Pancras. He heaps scorn upon progress, sentiment, all effort to regenerate the world. The foolishness and vapidness of the upper classes, the " cricketers to whom age brings golf instead of wisdom " ; the bourgeois with their respectability and their unclean reticence, the swinish multitude who are content to have it so—all are equally repulsive. The method of the Fabian Society and the method of the Barricade are both "fundamentally futile." " Enough," he cries, "of this goose cackle about Progress; man as he is never will nor can add a cubit to his stature by any of its quackeries, political, scientific, educational, religious, or artistic." There is merely an illusion of bustling activity; no real advance. "I do not know whether you have any illusions left," he writes to "My dear Walkley," "on the subject of education, progress, and so forth. I have none." The world to him, as, he gravely announces, it was to Shakespeare, is "a great stage of fools, on which he was utterly bewildered. He could see no sort of sense in living in it at all." *Vanitas vanitatum, omnia vanitas.* He turns round and roars with laughter at the absurdity of it all; the blindness of the little toiling race of men to the stupidity of its aspirations and the fatuity of its efforts. Like Gilbert's jester, when he has nothing else to laugh at, he laughs at himself till he aches for it. In the words of one of his characters in "John Bull's Other Island," he finds no jest so diverting as that of telling the truth. "The world will not bear thinking of to those who know what it is" is the burden of his cry. Huxley was prepared to hail a "kindly comet" which would sweep the whole affair away as a kindly consummation. But since, in Mr. Bernard Shaw's pleasant words, "the revival of tribal soothsaying and idolatrous rites, which Huxley called Science and mistook for an advance on the Pentateuch," Nietzsche, with the gospel of the Superman, has shown a more excellent way. Mr. Shaw calls for the elimination of the Yahoo and the breeding of the Superman.

In "Man and Superman," and "John Bull's Other Island," he has expressed in his own unequalled fashion this bedrock scorn of life. In "Man and Superman" the old illusions and the new fret and strut their hour upon the stage. Here are Roderick

Roebuck, of the eighteen-sixties, with his portraits of John Bright, Herbert Spencer, and Martineau, and his autotypes of allegories of Mr. G. F. Watts ; Mr. John Tanner, M.I.R.C. (Member of the Idle Rich Class), author of the Revolutionists' Handbook; Anne, a "Vital Genius," representing "the Life Force"; Hector Malone, an Eastern American, distinguished by "the engaging freshness of his personality and the dumfoundering staleness of his culture." The "new man" —the "man of the future"—is represented by one of Mr. Wells's engineers, Straker, the chauffeur, educated at a Board School and a Polytechnic, of a brilliant and engaging vulgarity. Behind this company is the machinery which pulls the strings and decides the issue. In a dialogue between the Devil, Mozart's original Don Juan, Anne, and the statue of her father, a temporary visitant from heaven, is revealed the gospel of Schopenhauer, and Nietzsche, and Shaw.

Briefly, this is the futility of all things except the blind but persistent purposes of Nature which subtly checkmate the plans of the individual for happiness or suicide, and direct all things towards the perpetuation of the race and the coming of the Superman. The Devil who had left heaven because he was bored represents the disillusioned spirit. "In the arts of life," he says, "man invents nothing ; but in the arts of death he outdoes Nature herself, and produces by chemistry and machinery all the slaughter of plague, pestilence, and famine." "The power that governs the earth is not the power of Life, but of Death." Each generation thinks the world is progressing because it is always moving. "Where you now see reform, progress, fulfilment of upward tendency, continual ascent by Man on the stepping-stones of his dead self to higher things, you will see nothing but an infinite comedy ot illusion."

To this Don Juan opposes his exaltation of Life, "the force that ever strives to attain greater power of contemplating itself." Against the citizen with his abject respectabilities and negations he uplifts the fanatic. He sings "Not arms and the hero, but the philosophic man." "Of all other sorts of men I declare myself tired. They are tedious failures." He sees modern pleasure-loving society dancing gaily to sterility. But he is confident in the victory of the Life Force, when "the plain-spoken marriage services of the Church will no longer be abbreviated, and half-suppressed as indelicate." With the expunging of the "unbearable frivolities" of the "romantic vowings and pledgings and until-death-do-us-partings," the real purpose of marriage will be honoured and accepted. The Devil gloomily promises a future of disillusionment and credulity. The Life Force will thrust mankind "into religion, where you will sprinkle water on babies to save their souls from me; then it will drive you from religion into science, where you will snatch the babies from the water sprinkling, and inoculate them with disease to save them from catching it accidentally"; then to politics, and other dusty and lamentable things. But Don Juan is persistent, and while the Devil deplores his failure with the Life worshippers, departs to heaven, of which a characteristic picture is given :—

" At every one of these concerts in England you will find rows of weary people who are there not because they really like classical music, but because they think they ought to like it. Well, there is the same thing in heaven. A number of people sit there in glory not because they are happy, but because they think they owe it to their position to be in [heaven. They are almost all English."

The scene ends upon the earthly stage. Anne, the Vital Genius, stalks and captures her prey. Tanner recognises that "the trap was laid from the beginning —by the Life Force," and yields while shouting his protests, and protesting that he would prefer to be hanged. He is gravely congratulated by the leader of the brigands. "Sir," says Madoza, "there are two tragedies in life. One is not to get your heart's desire. The other is to get it. Mine and yours, sir." And the curtain falls upon "universal laughter."

"Violet (with intense conviction) : You are a brute, Jack.

"Ann (looking at him with fond pride and caressing his arm) : Never mind her, dear. Go on talking.

"Tanner : Talking !

"Universal laughter."

"Universal laughter" is also the note of "John Bull's Other Island," and laughter that has no mirth in it, the only alternative to tears. The "anglicised Irishman" substitutes science for sentiment, and daily loathes himself more profoundly. The "Gladstonised Englishman" attains his heart's desire without ever apprehending the emptiness and foolishness of the figure he cuts in the sight of God. Heaven is once more pictured as a place of boredom and blue satin, mainly peopled by the English. Imagination curses one man, lack of it another. The peasant, freed, sets himself to squeeze the labourer. All are bought by flattery, which they know to be flattery, and yet accept joyfully. The dreamer who feels pity for all life is universally proclaimed as a madman. The world

worshipping efficiency is announced as creating effi-
ciently the machinery of labour and the machinery of
pleasure, all turning to dust. Hotels, golf-links, land-
purchase, membership of Parliament, ideals, desires,
dreams—this is the end of every man's desire. The
eye is not satisfied with seeing, nor the ear filled with
hearing. The thing that hath been, it is that which
shall be, and there is no new thing under the sun.
That which is crooked cannot be made straight, and
that which is wanting cannot be numbered. "I have
seen all the works that are done under the sun, and
behold all is vanity and vexation of spirit."

Mr. Bernard Shaw sees the world a den of dangerous
animals, amongst whom our few accidental supermen
must live as precariously as tamers do, "taking the
humour of their situation and the dignity of their
superiority as a set-off to the horror of the one and the
loneliness of the other." His cry for the Superman is
little more than the cutting of a stick with which to
emphasise the ultimate impossibility of the finite life of
man. Amidst his world of supermen, undoubtedly one
rebel against the common superiority would be Mr.
Bernard Shaw, convicted of a horror and loneliness all
the more real because there would be less obvious
material for his pleasant and bitter discontents.

II

The stories of Mr. Wells have thinly veiled, under
the guise of scientific romance, an impeachment of present things. In the history of the " Sleeper " he shows
in the future all the forces of the present ten times
multiplied—more noise, more confusion, more wealth,
more poverty, more separation from nature, more blind-

ness to aught but material things. Society has again passed into the condition of the later days of Rome, when, having attained an end and with nothing to anticipate, the springs of action have been choked with a world weariness. Later, however, in "Anticipations," and "Mankind in the Making," and a "New Utopia," he has attempted a saner estimate of actual possibilities. The forces of life are estimated, as well as the forces of death : the revolt from the present and its unclean poverty and routine, the mess that man is making of life, becomes itself a guarantee that effort will be directed towards a better existence for our children's children.

Mr. Wells is a master of the suggestive phrase which suddenly opens great issues. He pictures the student of divinity to-day coming "into a world *full of the ironical silences that follow great controversies.*" There is a whole universe in that single phrase. " To state these questions," he says of the Republican ideal, "is like opening the door of a room that has long been locked and deserted. One has a lonely feeling." Many a man with a youthful dream of noble things " peers to-day from between preposterous lawn sleeves or under a tilted coronet, sucked as dry of his essential honour as a spider sucks a fly." In his discussion of the sex question—a sane and clean discussion of one of the most baffling of human problems—he sees common human nature with a really dreadful insight. "I had purported to call this paper 'Sex and the Imagination,'" he says, "and then I had a sudden vision of the thing that happens. The vision presented a casual reader seated in a library turning over books and magazines, and casting much excellent wisdom aside, and then suddenly, as it were, waking up at that title, arrested, displaying a furtive alertness, reading, flushed and eager, nosing through the article."

By such unflinching observation of the facts of the world around him does Mr. Wells justify his claim to preach the gospel of the New Republic—of the Superman.

" Call ye that a Society," cried Carlyle seventy years ago, " where there is no longer any Social Idea extant ? " " One writes ' our present civilisation,' " re-echoes Mr. Wells to-day, " and of previous civilisations, but, indeed, no civilisations have yet really come into existence." With a kind of smooth and polished bitterness, Mr. Wells heaps up his indictment of the men of his time. It is all a little cruel ; too detached to be entirely pleasant : the author surveys the scrambling horde as the observer surveys the ant-heap or the locust crowd with a cold resentment and contempt. He has known something of the foulness of the struggle. He has been near to be himself suffocated in the swarm. He has escaped with no illusions concerning the heroism and loveliness of the average citizen of the Imperial race. All his onslaught could be summed up in a single challenge. Stand in the street of any modern English city and watch the stream drift by of shuffling, shabby bodies, of dissatisfied or vacuous minds. Or contrast in thought the ox-like seriousness over trivial things, the compromise and gross living of the prosperous middle-class citizen and his wife, with the vision of their radiant childhood. Mr. Lowes Dickinson has summed up his fundamental dissatisfaction with life in a picture of the active and graceful lambs transmuted by time into the stolid and silly sheep. It is to-day's progress of mankind. And the play of malign forces upon these beautiful children, with their possibilities of rational and refined existence, points all the sombre warnings of the message of this modern prophet.

His purpose is to seek for remedy. He has been compelled to rule out, though with reluctance, a method that would appear easy and pleasant. Why cannot we artificially " breed " the Superman as we breed strong horses or fat cattle ? Because, in part, of our ignorance of the subtle laws of inheritance and the strange sports and variations it produces. Because, again, our Supermen will be different the one from the other, will embrace a combination of qualities, so that even in the case of mere superficial physical beauty it is quite impossible to choose a particular pair to produce a particular type in the second generation. And, above all, because it is the abnormal and the variation which are most useful to mankind : the genius trembling on the border of insanity, often flowering on a tainted stock ; the fiery mind of a Stevenson or a Henley pent up in a diseased or battered body ; the eccentric distortion of the saint or the hero. You can breed out, but you cannot breed in. You could conceivably eliminate all lopsided personality and produce a gross acreage of decent citizen. But the result would be a kind of a nightmare of the mediocre, a universal Brixton.

At the conclusion of the record of Mr. Lewisham's somewhat squalid life history, his creator discloses a sudden illumination almost in the form of a revelation. The coming of the Child, with all its possibilities, reaching down to endless generations, takes this shabby little clerk from the cramped surroundings of his personal life, and gives him somehow a pathetic but real dignity as the steward of the heritage of all the future. In his later social appeals Mr. Wells attempts to awaken in his readers some thrill of the same emotion. In a whimsical picture he presents " all our statesmen, our philanthropists, our public men, gathered into one great hall," and regarding perplexedly "a huge spout that no man can stop," discharging " a baby every eight seconds." " Our success or failure with that unending stream of babies is the measure of our civilisation." As in the dream of a great novelist, he sees the might have been, the fair vision of an ideal of individual life which will never be realised, contrasted with the mean and pitiful reality ; and with something of the fervour of a Hebrew prophet, he confronts the men of his time with the inquiry, Why these things should be ?

" With a weak and wailing outcry, that stirs the heart, the creature comes protesting into the world." Already it is handicapped by ancestral sins and scars of body and mind. But from the first we increase that handicap, according to Mr. Wells, with our selfishness, our clumsiness, and our ignorance. First we slay an enormous proportion by preventable squalor and disease. The statistics of infant mortality reveal a holocaust of children, a " perennial massacre of the innocents "— 161 children out of 1,000 in Lancashire—which is alone evidence of the survival of barbaric conditions. In one of the few passages in which the author has allowed his feeling to emerge from beneath the polished and scornful invective of his denunciation, Mr. Wells arraigns society in the name of these murdered children : " stiff little life-soiled sacrifices to the spirit of disorder against which it is man's pre-eminent duty to battle." Our civilisation has neither the courage to kill them outright, painlessly, nor the heart to give them what they need.

THE MAKING OF THE SUPERMAN

" There has been all the pain in their lives, there has been the radiated pain of their misery, there has been the waste of their grudged and insufficient food, and all the pain and labour of their mothers, and all the world is sadder for them because they have lived in vain."

But those who have run the gauntlet of this hazardous infancy are in hardly a better plight. Mr. Wells shows by tables and statistics the far falling away, which is the destiny of the children of the poor, from any reasonable standard of physical development. The consequences endure—the fruit of bad feeding, mothers "battered and exhausted with child-bearing; insanitary, ugly, inconvenient homes; absence of fresh air and sunlight." These figures "serve to suggest, but they do not serve to gauge, the far graver and sadder loss, the invisible and immeasurable loss through mental and moral qualities undeveloped, through activities warped and crippled and vitality and courage lowered."

But the child grows; reason awakens the imitative faculties, the beginnings of will. In Mr. Wells's indictment of the cunning grown folk everywhere these are waiting for him: with bludgeons and clubs, with pitfalls dug for his unwary feet, with the grosser cruelty of their kindness. We begin by using the child as a plaything for ourselves: giving him foolish toys that he may be amused, talking " baby language " to him because' it causes us vague satisfaction. As he grows older, we infect him with our mean compromises and shabby virtues. We rear him in the terrible sham genteel homes of the middle classes, which the author describes with a kind of cold fury. " A raging father, a scared, deceitful mother, vulgarly acting, vulgarly thinking friends, all leave an almost indelible impress."

Then comes education. Of all Mr. Wells's hatreds the dreary farce we term middle-class education perhaps occupies the supreme position. With no thought-out plan, with a thousand inherited shams and inconsistencies, with an unctuous boast of moral influence and the teaching of a religion which we do not ourselves believe, we thrust the developing soul through the period of awakening passion. Some collapse and go under. Some hold on and develop into the kind of creatures of compromise which make up the horde of average men and women. It is all wrong—all fundamentally wrong. The child, with all its infinite possibilities, has become even as one of us: a "suburban white nigger," with a thousand a year and the "conceit of Imperial destinies"; or full of "the haughty incapacity, the mean pride, the parasitic lordliness of the just-independent, well-connected English."

It is a sombre picture of the raw disorder and meanness of average English life. The kind of picture when painted half a century ago by John Ruskin or Matthew Arnold, left English readers speechless with furious amazement. The men of to-day, with a less good conceit of themselves, will possibly receive it with a gloomy acquiescence. By the side of the "clean and beautiful child" Mr. Wells places in cruel contrast "the mean and graceless creature of our modern life, his ill-made clothes; his clumsy, half-fearful, half-brutal bearing; his coarse, defective speech; his dreary, unintelligent work; his shabby, impossible, bathless, artless home." The author lifts the curtain for a moment on some phase of this creature's typical activity, "enjoying himself" on a Bank Holiday, or "rejoicing, peacock feather in hand, hat askew," on "the defeat of a numerically inferior enemy." The conversion of the one into the other he upholds as the persistent tragedy of modern life.

No discriminating observer can contemplate the particular type of civilisation, or the lack of it, which is developing in Anglo-Saxon communities without profound disquietude. "He gave them their heart's desire, and sent leanness withal into their souls," might be written over all the vast material success and the fundamental spiritual poverty of the dominant race. Mr. Wells, passing to his remedy for these discontents, has found a less eager following. The astonishment and rather poor humour which have been evoked by the sweeping nature of his suggestions may indeed be put aside. Such criticism is merely the result of a lack of imaginative foresight. No social system could ever be more entirely incredible than the social system of the present day, if explained on paper to the denizens of another world. No possible changes in the immediate future could ever be more revolutionary and profound than have been the changes of the immediate past. A Government, by an adapted jury system, replacing the universal democracy; the State subsidy to selected authors and critics; the development of the "New Republic"; the deliberate attack on the problem of poverty and low-grade life; the large reorganisations of education—all these which, to the dull mind, appear but fantastic dreams, will certainly be paralleled by equally disturbing changes before the century has closed.

It is rather in his fundamental theory of life and of human well-being that one would join issue with this acute critic. He believes, as ardently as the newer Fabians, in efficiency, that latest of the cries which Mr. Shaw covers with the violence of his scorn. He has a really remarkable faith in the power of revised organisation and government to modify the life of man. Strangely enough for such a shrewd observer of the tragic comedy of human affairs, he appears still to believe that the intellect, the human reason, counts for much in human progress ; that men may be reasoned into sanity, cleanliness, order, and an ardour for all excellent things. Whole pages of his books burn with the same generous fire as that possessed by the eighteenth-century French writers, or the English reformers of the early Victorian school. The vast catastrophe of the revolution in the one case, the prolonged sunset of hope deferred in the other, emphasised a lesson which humanity is always being compelled to re-learn : that as the razor to the granite rocks or the mooring thread of silk to the vessel, so is human intellect and reason confronting "those two giants, the passion and the pride of man."

This pleasant intellectual enthusiasm extends even to free libraries, towards which Mr. Wells exhibits a devotion shared, one would think, by no one but the admirable Mr. Carnegie. "Give books," he cries with fervour ; diffuse useful knowledge ; increase "the amount of intellectual activity in the State." "Thought is the life of a community." "For three thousand years and more the book has become more and more the evident salvation of man."

He has failed to realise the practical difficulties of amelioration and reform when the people, as a whole, are content to have things otherwise. He demands, for example, a "minimum standard of soundness and sanitation " for houses and "legislation against overcrowding." We have such minimum standard at present, and such legislation ; but the law is a dead letter. It is no one's interest to put it into force : it lies undisturbed on dusty shelves. He assails again our present system of treating the children of vicious and drunken parents : using "the quivering, damaged victim" as our instrument for punishment of the parent. He would take the child away to an institution (though, as he wisely recognises in another place, those "institutions" are but "aspects of failure"), and debit the cost on the parent. The system is at present at work in the industrial schools. There is a continuous pressure on the part of undesirable parents to get rid of their children. But, as every poor-law guardian knows, the parent very shortly skips off and is lost in the crowd of the city, leaving the State to rear its ill-fated offspring. Nothing but a German system of classification and registration could overcome this difficulty. But, in fact, as Mr. Wells recognises in his revised scheme of Government by Juries, we are faced, not as the prejudiced assert, with a breakdown in Democratic Government, but with a breakdown in all Government. You call for a Dictator, you organise a central Executive, and you get—the English War Office. You delegate authority and create local interest, and the result is—the London Borough Council. It is a kind of deliquescence of character and responsibility. "The National energy is falling away." "Our workmen take no pride in their work any longer ; they shirk toil and gamble. And, what is worse, the master takes no pride in his work ; he, too, shirks toil and gambles." In his onslaught upon philanthropic institutions Mr. Wells indicates the truth. "They do not work" is his severe but just summary. "In cold fact it is impossible to get enough capable and devoted people to do the work." "Able, courageous, vigorous people are rare, and the

world urges a thousand better employments upon them."
It is the creation of "able, courageous, vigorous people"
which is the crying need of the modern world; with simplicity, tenacity, clean minds, and, above all, a personal
responsibility and devotion for the gifts of body and
soul.

There is no indication of the method by which such
character can be obtained, only a message of desolation
at its loss.

To all the modern claim for character building and a
moral training, Mr. Wells is frankly scornful. Religion
is kept out of his survey, but there are enough occasional
asides to show the direction of his thought and his contempt for the claims of "religious" instruction. "In
spite of a ceremonial adhesion to the religion of his
fathers," the author says of the modern man, "you will
find nothing but a profound agnosticism. He has not
even the faith to disbelieve." Till some such internal
change or faith has come to him, and the society in
which he moves, it is difficult to see how he can be
saved. All manipulations of machinery will leave the
heart cheerless and cold.

Mr. Wells's books are crowded with excellent suggestions of social reorganisation, the clearing away of
lumber and refuse, the oiling and cleaning and polishing
of crank and wheel. But at bottom Mr. Wells is
appealing to a spirit behind the material change.
With the great eighteenth-century dreamers, he desires
a fresh start. With Carlyle and all the school of the
prophets, he demands a new heart; in the old theological
language, a mind set on righteousness, a will directed
toward harmony with the will of God. He appeals
to the young men. "After thirty there are few
conversions and fewer fine beginnings; men and women

go on in the path they have marked out for themselves." What man over thirty—so rings his challenge—dares hope for the Republic before he die? or for an infantile death-rate under ninety in the thousand, with all the conquered desolation that such a change would mean? or "for the deliverance of all of our blood and speech from those fouler things than chattel slavery, child and adolescent labour"? With the young men and women lies all the hope of the future. A refusal to acquiesce may be in them a generous ardour for reform. Clean thought and a vision of better things may lead forward to a newer day. With this new spirit, which feels something of the sorrows of the world and its confusion alike as a reproach and a call to action, the fulfilment of the coming years may be "better than all our dreams."

III

In sharp contrast to the bitter humours of the one and the energy of the other comes the serene outlook of the third of the prophets. M. Maeterlinck also is watching the night for the signs of the dawn. His attitude also is one of acceptance of modern progress, and its transfiguration. He finds good in the world of the present. He will have nothing to say to the cry of disenchantment. He believes this present itself may be charged with significance and high ardour, adequate to all the demands of the human soul. With a note of triumph he turns from the long courses of human history, already hurried into a vanished past, to confront with eagerness and longing the flower and consummation of man's effort in a life more desirable than man has ever known.

Much of his writing upon modern things is the work

of fancy—fancy not simple, but carefully elaborated—rather than of imagination. Efforts to personify the motor-car, the "wonderful beast," "the dreadful hippogriff," with description of its soul, its "terrible complex heart," "the mighty viscera," appear artificial and overstrained. His summaries of the flowers, the begonia, "pretty but insolent, and a little artificial"; the double geranium, "indefatigable and extraordinarily courageous"; the nasturtium which "screams like a parrakeet climbing up the bars of its cage" are more quaint than illuminating. The reader recognises that the author feels compelled to make a certain effect, and the results attained are forced rather than spontaneous.

But behind it all is that philosophy of practical life and outlook upon human affairs which bring M. Maeterlinck's writings as a real inspiration to many perplexed minds. He sees a universe from which the old lights have fallen. The schemes of salvation, the control of benignant spirits, the manifest presence of a Deity concerned with human welfare, having suddenly vanished from man's outward survey. He sweeps the heavens with his telescopes, and finds no God. He is driven to take up the business of life with no pillar of cloud by day or pillar of fire by night to guide him on his journey. "We are emerging (to speak only of the last three or four centuries of our present civilisation)," he says—"we are emerging from the great religious period." The background, the "somewhat gloomy and threatening background," which "gave a uniform colour to the atmosphere and the landscape," is to-day "disappearing in tatters." And the space—the abode of our ignorance, "which after the disappearance of the religious ideas, had appeared frightfully empty, is gradually becoming peopled with vague but enormous figures."

THE MAKING OF THE SUPERMAN

The "Void," the "Infinite," the blind and meaningless schemata of the sciences which have assumed the thrones of the elder gods, continue to put unanswerable questions to the bewildered minds of men. They put questions to us "and we stammer as best we may." But the "active idea which we conceive of the riddle in the midst of which we have our being" is opening gradually a "luminous and boundless perspective" which is destined to transfigure all man's activities and dreams.

"We were, it might be said, like blind men who should imagine the outer world from inside a shut room. Now, we are those same blind men whom an ever-silent guide leads by turns into the forest, across the plain, on the mountain, and beside the sea. Their eyes have not yet opened ; but their shaking and eager hands are able to feel the trees, to rumple the spikes of corn, to gather a flower or a fruit, to marvel at the ridge of a rock, or to mingle with the cool waves, while their ears learn to distinguish, without needing to understand, the thousand real songs of the sun and the shade, the wind and the rain, the leaves and the waters."

On the one hand there is this vision of hope and the enlargement of the human mind which comes from the apprehension of infinite horizons. "Though we no longer count, the humanity of which we form a part is acquiring the importance of which we are being stripped." The greatest dangers that awaited this humanity at its hazardous infancy have now been over-passed. "The instability of the seas and the uprising of the central fire" are to-day infinitely less to be feared. We may be permitted to believe that the peril of "collision with a stray star" may be averted for "the few centuries of respite necessary for us to learn how to

ward it off" : till we have learnt to "lay hold of that
essential secret of the worlds which for the time being
and to soothe our ignorance (even as we soothe a child
and lull it to sleep by repeating meaningless and
monotonous words) we have called the law of gravitation." We feel, therefore, in this age the greatness of
expectation—looking towards a revealing glory. "We
are in the magnificent state in which Michaelangelo
painted the prophets and the just men of the Old
Testament on that prodigious ceiling of the Sistine
Chapel : we are living in expectation, and perhaps in
the last moment of expectation."

"Expectation, in fact, has degrees which begin with
a sort of vague resignation, and which do not yet hope
for the thrill aroused by the nearest movements of the
expected object. It seems as though we heard those
movements ; the sound of superhuman footsteps, an
enormous door opening, a breath caressing us, or light
coming ; we do not know ; but expectation at this pitch
is an ardent and marvellous state of life, the fairest
period of happiness, its youth, its childhood. . . ."

The one attitude is this of expectation, of inquiry, the
sense of vast powers and purposes almost revealed. M.
Maeterlinck's essays have the best quality of reverie.
There is much directly reminiscent of Sir Thomas
Browne ; reveries of life and death, of the mystery of
things, of symbols and colours, and the secret meanings
of signs and numbers. A fascination for the occult distinguishes his latest work, for the spells and enchantments
of the modern spiritualisms and thought-reading, and
oracles and teachings which blossom now, as in former
times, on the ruins of the great systems of religion. He
will inquire concerning the mysteries of chance as seen in
the dancing of the tiny ball on the roulette table at

Monte Carlo. He will inquire again how it is, if the future, arising naturally from the changes of the present, is as real as the past, that the veil is never withdrawn which hides this real world from us.

The other attitude is the attitude of contentment with the common things of life; the conclusion of the philosophy of the eighteenth century that "it is necessary to cultivate our garden." Under the mysteries already unfolded, amid the conflagrations of worlds and systems, undeterred by the vast solitudes of space and their enormous cold, M. Maeterlinck will cultivate his garden. Lightness and brightness are added to the vision of natural beauty. On the "motionless road where none passes save the eternal forces of life" spring comes and autumn, the rain and the sun, the silence and "the night followed by the light of the moon." It is no small thing that the world should grow fairer year by year, and men's hearts and the weather more gentle. "We live in a world in which flowers are more beautiful and more numerous than formerly; and perhaps we have the right to add that the thoughts of men are more just and greedier of truth." "We are mastering the nameless powers." We are making our planet all our own. We are "adorning our stay"—we should rejoice at it—"and gradually broadening the acreage of happiness and of beautiful life."

The curtain rises upon the violent revolt against the things of the present which Mr. Shaw voices—the voice of a generation's disgust and weariness. The action of the play is along the lines of deliberate improvement outlined by Mr. Wells with such energy and appeal.

BEFORE THE DAWN

And the curtain falls upon a vision of gentleness and tranquillity in the garden of flowers.

Is this a forecast—or but a challenge—of the courses of human life in the civilisation of the West during the century which has opened with such uncertain dawn?

THE CHALLENGE OF TIME

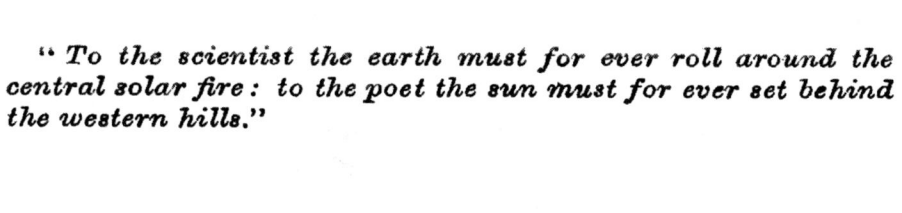

" To the scientist the earth must for ever roll around the central solar fire: to the poet the sun must for ever set behind the western hills."

THE CHALLENGE OF TIME

TIME corrodes all weakness and stamps strength with the guarantee of its approval. Examination of its fretting upon the work of earlier enthusiasms is a task always fruitful, always mournful. Science, Literature, Religion alike are compelled to encounter its salt winds and subtle forces of decay. Science rests, it would appear, upon knowledge secure when attained, and henceforth indifferent to its ravages. Literature is the expression of man's soul in which Time can effect no change. Religion and its experience belongs to a timeless universe. Yet the man who, with candour, will examine the work of the years immediately past will find in none of these regions of human action that serene security. I can think of three authors which each at one time burst upon the mind with an overmastering domination. Huxley had said the final word of the sciences. Mr. Swinburne represented the supreme expression of all that passionate youth desires of literature. Newman had penetrated to the ultimate recesses of the human soul within, and the revelation without of a hidden God. It is no unprofitable task to review after a decade what of these ardours still endures.

I

How is time treating the man of science, whose name sounds through all the great intellectual conflicts of the past half-century? Huxley was indeed more than a scientific investigator. Writing a pure and nervous English, he plunged into varied fields—philosophy, theology, sociology, the struggle for intellectual freedom. In all these many hailed him as leader. Here time has already commenced the work of destruction. The enthusiasm stimulated by the vision of successive scientific advances has become less strident. The "fairy godmother" whom he praised has proved powerless to abolish the evils of life. Pain and poverty still remain to trouble the little life of man. The Golden Age has been relegated to a remoter future. In face of a seven-million peopled Abyss of lives austere with want and crime, the famous alternative which Huxley himself suggested, the "kindly comet" whose advent he would hail as a "desirable consummation," might seem a not unwelcome alternative. In this and in other matters the spirit of men has undergone a profound change. His was an age of faith without belief; ours, of belief without faith. He fought for a dismal nescience with the fervour and devotion of a Puritan. We have witnessed a spiritual revival, a reaction towards constructive belief and a faith in the unseen. But this faith is languid and spiritless. Men for the most part hold these things only tedious, and marvel at the excitement manifested by their fathers.

Beyond the changes of the age, the work of Huxley can be seen in a clearer perspective. His vigorous certainty, the power of popular controversy which he possessed, the transparent honesty and truthfulness of the man, exercised a dominant influence upon his contemporaries. It seemed impossible to conceive that he could be in the wrong. To-day certain limitations appear. He was never a Liberal, either in politics or in the world of thought. He held in a real abhorrence everything represented by the name of Gladstone. To the most heroic and sincere of all English statesmen he found it difficult to award even the common virtue of honesty. Huxley joined issue along the whole line from Home Rule to the Gadarene pigs. He read into the political action some of the rather complicated and tortuous methods of the theological controversies. He became convinced that he was dealing with a mind evasive and rhetorical, overrated, leading England down slippery paths. Towards the end of his life he recognised that a kind of sacred duty was laid upon him to assail the Liberal leader at every vulnerable point. Nor was he a Liberal in thought. He fought, indeed, for tolerance. But he desired the toleration, not of opinion, but of his own opinions. His attitude, as Herbert Spencer told him unkindly and in a famous controversy, was that of a theologian rather than a philosopher. He refused resolutely to defend the baser and more popular atheisms. His treatment of the newer sciences of mental disturbance and obscure aberration was essentially similar to the treatment against which his own sciences had slowly struggled to recognition. His attitude to the Psychical Research Society to the last was one of contempt. One can imagine the disgust with which he would contemplate the respect and welcome which have been given in later years to the work of this body of explorers.

Sure of himself and with a power of relentless analysis possessed by but a few, he became the terror of all weak adherents of traditional creeds. Certainly he cleared the ground of much encumbering rubbish. Yet his philosophy, when viewed as a whole, shows strange inconsistencies, and his theological knowledge presents startling gaps. In philosophy he knew the English thinkers well, Hume and Berkeley; he could estimate upon the traditional English lines the problems presented by the newer knowledge. But he never understood Kant. All German metaphysics he dismissed as moonshine. He spoke for the moment, upon set occasion, and it is impossible to unify his often sensational, always noteworthy, lectures and essays into one consistent body of doctrine. In one place he pictured human beings as "conscious automata" with all future changes exactly determined by the past, and consciousness but as the shadow of the locomotive, accompanying but uninfluencing the progress of change. At another he breaks into a passionate assertion that human will "counts for something as a condition of the course of events," and urges each of his hearers deliberately to set himself to lighten the world's load of suffering. On the broad question of ultimate reality he fluctuated in quite an extraordinary fashion between an idealism and a materialism. At one time he compared the advance of law in the spiritual world to the advance of an eclipse upon a terrified sun-worshipper seeing the extinction of his god. At another he is roundly dismissing all these "laws" and compulsions as gratuitously invested bugbears. On the moral question he definitely changed. At first he was laboriously pleading for a purely natural system of ethics, and the handy and serviceable garments which science would provide. Later, in his Romanes lecture, the most brilliant in style of all his work, he is tearing to tatters a "cosmic process" consummating only in the instincts of the ape and the tiger. In his theological excursions, acute and suggestive as they remain, his limitations are no less manifest.

He knew the work of Baur and one or two other German scholars. The opponents he fought unfortunately knew less. But he was convinced that the whole fabric of the accepted religion stood as one piece. He had been brought up to hold verbal inspiration as the only legitimate theory. The rejection of a Garden of Eden or a Noachian deluge seemed to him the rejection of the whole of Christianity. Those who treated these stories in any but literal form he branded as disingenuous and " wrigglers." He appeared never to have heard of Clement or Origen, or a time when while Christianity was making its greatest advances, these early legends were frankly accepted as allegorical.

Such are the losses. What remains? The man still stands as a great figure and character, for which the world is richer. He was strong, hewn from rock, trenchant of all shams and sophistries, honest as the day, stern often, but with a fund of passionate tenderness only revealed to the outside world after his death. Ever a fighter, he delighted in battle with his peers. He loved the combat for the combat's sake. Yet he was ever courteous, generous, scrupulously fair, determined never needlessly to offend. The honesty and utter devotion to truth is perhaps the outstanding feature. His letter to Charles Kingsley, in which, under the sudden agony of a strong man's suffering, he poured out to his friend the secrets of his heart, stands as one of the great utterances in the history of the life of the spirit. From the grave of his dead child he refused to delude himself with a hope which, could he only accept it, would have changed the face of the world. Like George Eliot, he resolved to do without opium. It was this resolute truthfulness which gave him the power to destroy with such sudden and overwhelming destruction such as Samuel Wilberforce. The scene at the British Association meeting at Oxford has become historic as one of the great episodes in the conflict between authority and progress.

The record of friendships which kept such a body as the X Society dining together for so many decades; the touches of home affection, the very human outbursts of impatience at stupidity and ignorance in high places; the tenderness of the strong man towards children and the weak; the occasional passages of almost startling self-revelation, of half-wistful hope moderating the truculent agnosticism as he confronts the mysteries of Life and Death—these are the elements which reveal a character of an unchanging attraction.

It is the strenuous life devoted to high ends. There is a very pleasant picture in his life of the Sunday evenings in St. John's Wood in the latter years. In summer the family are gathered in the garden. Friends drop in, there is talk of the latest scientific results, of progress, and the smiting of the enemy. It is the afternoon of the successful man, golden, but with a touch of evening and the approaching night. There is that in plenty which should accompany old age: honour, love, obedience, troops of friends. Only in the end something appears lacking. Perhaps the outlook entirely narrowed to a fragment of time and the success of a lifetime stands judged by a sense of larger issues beyond. It is Sunday evening. Outside the walled garden is a chaos of confusion and pain. And as the twilight falls there comes the sound of a world-old appeal renewed ever in humility and patience: "Pitifully behold the sorrows of our hearts. Mercifully forgive the sins of Thy people."

THE CHALLENGE OF TIME

II

Mr. Swinburne in the preface to the collected edition of his work, has surveyed the long progress from the day when "Atalanta" revealed a new and magnificent force in literature, and later the first poems and ballads astonished and scandalised the world. He found nothing of which to repent, nothing to withdraw. He described the whole succession of changing subjects : the early poetry of passion, the songs of sunrise, the national faith and its heroes, the dramas, the poems of spiritual revolt, and the celebration of the coming dawn ; and after these the poetry of natural things and of childhood ; and, above all, the voice of triumph and longing which runs through the whole series, the "light and sound and darkness of the sea." Of the first, "there are photographs from life in the book," he asserted, "and there are sketches from imagination. Some which keen-sighted criticism has dismissed with a smile as ideal or imaginary were as real and actual as they well could be ; others which have been taken for obvious transcripts from memory were utterly fantastic or dramatic." To all that hubbub of anger of "the spiritually still-born children of dirt and dullness," the author was as indifferent then as he is to-day.

But in the poems of freedom "there is no touch of dramatic impersonation or imaginary emotion." They were inspired by "such faith as is born of devotion and reverence" ; reverence to a cause and to its leaders ; especially to "the three living gods, I do not say of my idolatry, for idolatry is a term inapplicable where the gods are real and true, but of my whole-souled and

221

single-hearted worship "—Landor, Hugo, Mazzini—the last "the man whom I had always revered above the other men on earth."

The appeal of the new spiritual sunrise, with the signs of the passing of the night of the older religions Mr. Swinburne gathered up especially in "twin poems of antiphonal correspondence in subject and sound," "the 'Hymn to Proserpine' and the 'Hymn of Man'—the death song of spiritual decadence, and the birth song of spiritual renascence."

Such a defiant re-assertion of the faith of a lifetime is a challenge to all the memories of the past. I commenced, a boy at school, with the earlier selections, reading in mingled perplexity and tedium. The long sea poems of the second series of the "Poems and Ballads," with their difficult metres, their rhetoric, and their frequent obscurity, serve as about the worst possible form of introduction to Mr. Swinburne's poetry. And a volume which contained scarcely anything from the first "Poems and Ballads," and none of the greatest of the Atalanta choruses—a volume omitting "The Garden of Proserpine" and the "Triumph of Time" and "Hesperia," with the "Songs before Sunrise" very inadequately represented, failed altogether to reveal the magic of the master.

My conversion was effected later, at Cambridge, and at a lecture upon Swinburne by Mr. Frederic Myers. The instrument of the sudden change was the end of "Tristram" recited in the deep, impassioned chant which I suppose Myers had learnt from Tennyson. I can still hear the throb of the music as the emotion deepened to the splendour of that imperishable close:—

222

THE CHALLENGE OF TIME

" Nor where they sleep shall moon or sunlight shine,
Nor man look down for ever ; none shall say
Here once, or here, Tristram and Iseult lay ;
But peace they have that none may gain who live,
And rest about them that no love can give,
And over them, while death and life shall be,
The light and sound and darkness of the sea."

From that moment commenced an allegiance which speedily passed into an unfaltering worship.

Then came the period, which most young men have passed through, of intoxication, when we would hurl Swinburnian imprecations upon "whatever gods may be," or in the interval between a football match and a hearty meal proclaim our thirst for annihilation to the unconscious stars. Time and the experience of sorrow wore down these earlier ardours ; much of the swinging stanzas began to appear as rhetoric, or at best eloquence, rather than poetry. Much also was revealed as so detached, cold, and separate from " the labouring world " as to give the impression of a hard, inhuman glitter and brilliance ; the brilliance of the Arabian Nights, the hardness and cruelty of the stories of fairyland.

But still the old spell in part remains. To-day one can again recall the fascination of the buoyancy and ardour, the waves of passionate eloquence, that violence of triumph and weariness which will make Swinburne always the singer of the springtime, and only pass when youth has vanished from the world.

No poet has attained such general recognition of supremacy with less general acceptance of his ideals in life and literature. In a secure vitality, and with Death a thing incredible, we were all intoxicated with the poems of its praise. Later, with life passing, and the shadow lengthening on the hills, " the end of every man's desire " seemed something less desirable. It says much for the spells and sorcery of the enchanter, the magic of an outburst of music, alike mournful and triumphant, that the accepted verdict could even for a moment be denied, and men at the last gather to enlist under the defiant banner of defeat.

For it is not death alone which is here commemorated in song. Not only the fascination of sleep and silence are celebrated in the hymn to Proserpine, and revealed in the unforgettable vision of her garden, with its bloomless poppies and dreams of forsaken days. Here is also the elevation of Destruction as against Creation, the denial of the desirability of life itself, the deliberate rejection of that exultation of Being for which the morning stars sang together, and all the sons of God shouted for joy. Mr. Swinburne took the work of the Revolution and pushed it home, without that faith in a universal restitution which broke the seals and poured out the vials and loosened " the thunder of the trumpets of the night." He tears down King and Priest. He rages against all the ancient oppressive laws. He demands the clearance of the accumulated refuse of the dead. But this alone will not content him. Destruction, renunciation, annihilation must be elevated in the place of the gods dethroned. And in the end he passes to a world vision of the work of dissolution accomplishing itself to its far conclusion: the earth and all its peoples passing, its hopes and hates, its homes and fanes, the bones of the grave and the grave in which they have been laid ; sun, moon, and stars crashing into the abyss : hell and the palaces of heaven and the older and the newer gods, and everything that is and has been and is to come crumbling into darkness and silence, with all that remains an enormous nothingness, an enormous cold. Others have gazed upon this picture with shuddering, while deeming it but a dream and a vision. Modern theories of Evolution have suddenly endowed it with fierce and insistent life. It was left for the century which felt the thing gripping at its heart to produce a poet who would confront it not with horror, but with exultation, proclaiming with a passionate violence the ending of all violence and passion.

This is new in literature, and this must endure, for the vision is not yet destined to vanish. A civilisation becoming more and more divided from sane and rational things is destined more and more eagerly to welcome a *Götterdämmerung* which will involve not only itself, but all existence in a cosmic desolation. Two great and emotional appeals against this assertion of an elemental despair lie in the early work of Mr. Swinburne. In the choruses of the " Atalanta " is the revolt rather than the acquiescence of man in such an ending. " Because thy name is life and our name death "; because " thou hast fed one rose with dust of many men " ; therefore " all we are against thee, against thee, O God most high." And in the " Songs before Sunrise," with their celebration of national resistance to Imperial supremacy, a resistance congruous with " the actual earth's equalities, air, light, and night, hills, winds, and trees," manifested in the European struggle for the liberation of the smaller peoples, the worship of Proserpine vanished before the vision of a splendid dawn.

Later Mr. Swinburne turned back upon the national cause : and with that desertion his inspiration fell from him like a garment ; so that with each successive volume of fluent verse men said sadly to one another : " There was a Swinburne." These later productions form a study of profound sadness. With the poems arranged in order of writing, and surveyed as a whole, the volumes might not untruthfully be labelled " the dying of Genius." To turn from the opening of the " Poems and Ballads " to the close of the " Channel Passage " is to turn from life to death. Youth has gone, and with youth the passionate faith in high, disinterested causes. The poems leave a nasty taste in the mouth ; the taste of a snarl and a sneer. Much might appear as a parody of Swinburne written by a reporter of the journalism of the day. The injunction to the Russian revolutionists upon the accession of the present Czar—to " smite and send him howling down his father's way "— may perhaps be passed as, at least, in the tradition of the terrible sonnets of 1870 upon " Napoleon III." But what is to be said of the jeerings at the Irish Nationalists, the clamorous invective dashed against Gladstone ? Or those deplorable sonnets in which the poet acclaims the sailing of the soldiers against the Boer Republics ? The foes of England are chivalrously described as " like wolves," " dogs agape with jaws afoam," with " foul tongues that blacken God's dishonoured name." The poet cries for vengeance and destruction and screeches shrilly for blood.

The emotion aroused in the reader is that of Japhet towards the drunken Noah. These poems are already dead. In the future they will be mercifully forgotten. To escape from this fog and foulness to a cleaner air and the sight again of sunlight and the stars you have only to turn back to the former things :—

" Content thee, howsoe'er, whose days are done ;
There lies not any troublous thing before,

THE CHALLENGE OF TIME

Nor sight nor sound to war against thee more ;
For whom all winds are quiet as the sun,
All waters as the shore."

It is welcome to turn from so indecent a spectacle to the memories of the earlier time. For here is the outburst of an inspiration's dawn ; before a too passionate spring tide and time which changes all good things had left nothing but scentless autumn flowers, and of all the year's earlier promise " only dead yew leaves and a little dust."

III

Newman, of all the pilgrims of Eternity, absorbed in a world alien to the common interests of man, stands alone in the fascination of his influence upon those of entirely incongruous ideals. Amongst all the strange problems of his personality, none are more perplexing than that of the origins. That " typical Englishmen " should have inherited traditions long imbedded in the past. The writer of the most perfect and simple English prose since Bunyan, the child of the English Church, with enthusiasm for her ancient ways, the voice through which the very spirit of Oxford and the old University ideal became articulate, should have originated, one would think, in some secluded line of ancestry, an historical family of the landed classes, or with memories of ancestral services to learning and religion. The facts were entirely otherwise. Newman was a stranger, an alien, with scarcely a drop of English blood in his veins. On his father's side he was descended from a line of Dutch Jews ; on his mother's, from a family of French Huguenots. He appears as the son of a clerk in a banking firm, in straitened circumstances. His childhood was passed near Richmond. He attended a middle-class school at Ealing. His sister's name was Jemima. He was reared in the typical evangelical piety of the middle classes, which, turned stagnant, gave cause later for such merciless satire in "Loss and Gain." Two rough deductions from history to which Newman seemed an exception, are indeed confirmed by the discovery of this ancestry. The one is that genius is the child of the mixture of races. The other is that the great religious leaders and saints of England, from the days of Anselm or Hugh of Lincoln, the "humble and heavenly stranger," have been for the most part of alien stock. The pure Saxon blood does not easily turn to the high endeavours of the soul.

Those who would fully estimate the life of this extraordinary man, are confronted with a difficulty at the present insuperable. In the first half of the story, the material is superabundant ; in the second, almost entirely lacking. "The going out of '45" cut through the life history, severing all the strings of friendship and tradition. From existence passed in a glare of sunshine almost pitiless, revealing every spot and wrinkle, Newman suddenly passed into silence and grey shadow. For over forty years there remain but a few scattered letters : the Manning correspondence, occasional notes to Lord Acton and others, and such chance reminiscences as have appeared in the biography of others. The published books alone for the majority revealed that Newman still lived on. These years were of tranquillity indeed, and confidence in the haven attained after rough voyaging. But there were schemes of service always checked and baffled, and the failure of many designs whose influences might have been incalculable. The plan for his retranslation of the Catholic Bible was sanctioned by Wiseman, then withdrawn in obedience to the protest of the booksellers. The daring project of a return to Oxford, which might have changed the history of the future, was checked and finally destroyed by Manning in a piece of ecclesiastical intrigue which the friends of Catholicism would fain forget. "A painful correspondence" ended in "a lifelong estrangement." Seven years were spent in a kind of nightmare struggle in Ireland, endeavouring to create a Catholic University, amid a chaos of political intrigue and religious bigotry. The history of this he has left in a volume privately printed. The true history of that troublous experiment would make a record at once entertaining and piteous. He was torn between two parties, each demanding the support of his great name, each indignant when he refused to throw in his lot with them. The Liberals, under Lord Acton, held that he had deceived and betrayed them. To the last, Lord Acton could never afterwards speak of Newman without reproach and bitterness. The opponents of Liberalism on the other hand, were never likely to forgive the spirit which found expression in the denunciation of their methods in the letter on the Vatican decree. A criticism, says his latest biographer, "which includes all his opponents," is "that they failed to comprehend an intellect greater than their own, busy with problems to the vast horizons of which their view could not extend."

The great works which remain to-day for our estimate and judgment are in fact but polemical pamphlets called forth by the controversy of a day. But for the madness of the Catholic aggression, we would never have had the "Present Position of Catholics," one of the great books of the nineteenth century : a plea against mob-rule un-equalled in its mingling of pathos, irony, and restraint. But for the call to impossible work in Ireland, the lectures on the " Ideal of a University " would never have been given ; and the world would have been poorer by the most magnificent of appeals for knowledge as in itself an end, for theology as an essential of true learning, for education in its true and not its accepted meaning. And but for Kingsley's random and reckless onslaught the " Apologia " would never have been written, and Newman would have gone to his grave unvindicated ; the product of six weeks' white-heat emotion having produced, as by a kind of miracle, one of the most convincing of all records of the pilgrimage of the soul.

Still to-day, however, abides unchallenged the supremacy of Newman's English prose. For mingled refinement, simplicity, gentleness, this stands unrivalled in his time. Specially concerned and entirely congruous with the deeper things of existence—sin and its consequences, the mysteries encompassing human life, its uncertainty and future, the longing of the soul for God —it possesses qualities which would have made Newman triumphant upon the plane of the controversies of the world. His power of irony, indeed, is unsurpassed ; triumphant in all its expressions : from the more delicate irony of the description of the English gentleman, through the broader satire upon the English view of " Don Felix Melatesta de Guadaloupe," to the savage and awful irony of the lost soul's awakening in the " Sermons to Mixed Congregations," at which the reader is moved against his will to a kind of metallic laughter.

It is as a mysterious, majestic figure that Newman

appears in the history of his age : at heart solitary. Life for him was "a dialogue not a drama." Turn where you will in his writing, you find the same spirit : an inner life of absorbing interest, a grave wonder at the ends and ideals of man, his folly, his aspirations, the confusion he has made of his world. The music of that voice holds the listener enchanted, as it appeals from all transitory things to those which alone are secure and abiding ;—

"The world goes on from age to age, but the Holy Angels and blessed Saints are always crying alas, alas! and woe, woe! over the loss of vocations and the disappointment of hopes, and the scorn of God's love and the ruin of souls. . . . Times come and go, and men will not believe that that is to be which is not yet, or that what now is only continues for a season, and is not eternity. The end is the trial : the world passes : it is but a pageant and a scene : the lofty palace crumbles, the busy city is mute, the ships of Tarshish have sped away. On heart and flesh death is coming ; the veil is breaking. . . . O, my Lord and Saviour, let me die as I desire to live, in Thy faith, in Thy Church, in Thy Service, and in Thy love."

The curtain of that quiet life is torn aside for a moment at intervals as the years go by. At each revelation Newman appears, still expecting, looking outwards at the tremendous turmoil of the world with pity, sadness, surprise. In his own chosen epitaph, he turned " *Ex umbris et imaginibus in veritatem.*" That world then and afterwards has been at once attracted and baffled : as the world is ever attracted and baffled by one who possesses both a secret which it cannot penetrate, and an indifference to all it holds dear.

OF DEATH AND PITY

" Nil nisi Divinum stabile est, cætera fumus."
—MANTEGNA.

OF DEATH AND PITY

THERE are books and writers which command a universal attention. The critic immediately can assert a supremacy. Here is literature, unchallenged, secure. The world may be indifferent, the comment of the crowd perplexed or doubtful. But the decision is confident and final. There are others, for which no similar high claim can be advanced, which yet may appeal to the individual with a particular entreaty. There are weaknesses obvious, flaws, limitations. The legitimacy of another's criticism must be recognised, as the claim is dismissed with scorn or aberration, and direct interest is suggested as the cause of the extravagant praise. Nevertheless every writer who is compelled to pass under review any large quantities of prose and poetry must of necessity find some which, through temperament or common interest, comes with a special appeal. Henceforth this work is placed upon a particular shelf of the memory. He can listen unmoved to all analysis and depreciation. To you these are nothing, or but ruins of great effort: to me they have come with something of the force of an inspiration.

I can think of certain tiny volumes—in all a few hundred pages—which in the past few years, amongst literature still unrecognised, have given me this special delight. Here I can describe some of them : a volume of gloomy, almost morbid, self-analysis by an author terming himself "Mark Rutherford" : a series of little impressionist sketches by Mr. Lewis Hind : the "Sonnets of the Wingless Hours" : the poems of Mrs. Marriott Watson.

All of these penetrate beneath the outward show of things. All present a picture of a world of tragic import unheeded in the traffic of men. There is the soul's hunger behind the visible pages, a vision of longing and baffled purposes. The spirit which unites them all is the sense of the greatness and the sadness of the life of man, pent up in the kingdoms of Pity and of Death.

I

My first reading of the "Autobiography" was at Cambridge, and my marked copy is the fifth edition, dated 1892. I took the book home from the booksellers and read it through at a sitting, and immediately hurried out and ordered the "Deliverance," which, when it came, received the same treatment. I thought then that the two books represented in their intimacy and sincerity and simple, refined style something unique in modern English literature. For perhaps the seventh time I have read this life story again. And I would entirely endorse the earlier verdict. If this be not literature "of the centre," then all our accepted standards of taste must be abandoned, and the test of greatness sought in the popular rhetoric and the largest circulation in the world.

OF DEATH AND PITY

Yet "Mark Rutherford" has never entirely come into his own. Many who are familiar with that thin stream of literature which still trickles through the parched and blackened land of present printed matter, have failed to recognise the greatness of this life history of one of the unimportant. I remember once discussing with Professor Henry Sidgwick these and other works. He told me that as he was getting older he came more and more to limit his novel reading to those books which gave him pleasure, and that he could not find pleasure in such works as the "Autobiography of Mark Rutherford." And indeed the standpoint has to be somewhat detached—an appreciation of artistic excellence, of one thing set to do, and supremely well done— if pleasure is to be obtained from this haunting picture of man's futility and his failure. "Mark Rutherford," as Bagehot's old lady said of Thackeray, is "an uncomfortable writer." The passionless detachment of the narrative makes the resultant impression all the more challenging and sorrowful. The reader finds himself suddenly confronted with pictures which he would fain forget, with questionings which he has generally managed to put by in the bustle of business or pleasure. A modern scientific writer has announced a transformation, through the growth of a newer knowledge, of the last words of the ancient wisdom. "Man, know thyself," has been changed into the counsel, "Man, may thou never know what thou art." If this verdict is to be accepted as final, the work of "Mark Rutherford" may well be placed on some future index of proscription of a race determined to life always in the summer days.

This dreary outlook, in his case as in the case of another painter of modern life and its failures,

George Gissing, may be the chief cause of the lack of recognition. In the city civilisation of the present there is an element of boisterous and lively fancy, noisy and cheerful and untroubled by the pale cast of thought. Hampstead Heath and Margate Sands, the popular election scrimmage, the *Daily Telegraph*, give together that note of exuberance which Mr. Boutmy has found most characteristic of the English middle class. This note is altogether absent from Mark Rutherford's pages. In one of the late chapters of the " Deliverance " the author describes how one Sunday, on " a lovely summer's morning in mid July," he and Ellen and the child Marie took an excursion to Hastings. " Our pleasure was exquisite, we had a wonderful time." " To be free of the litter and filth of a London suburb, of its broken hedges, its brickbats, its torn advertisements, its worn and trampled grass in fields, half given over to the speculative builder, in place of this to tread the immaculate sea-shore, over which breathed a wind not charged with soot, to replace the dull, shrouding obscurity of the smoke by a distance so distinct that the masts of the ships whose hulls were buried below the horizon were visible—all this was perfect bliss."

" We wanted nothing, we had nothing to achieve." Later, on the return home, " all the glory of the morning " was forgotten in a huddled, overcrowded carriage, with drinking women roaring obscene songs. The incident is symbolic of a life history, or, rather, of a temperament. His companions on the excursion were probably profoundly bored by the sun and the sea, and only happy in the intervals of eating, rollicking merriment, and the joys of the return journey. Lacking this rollicking joy through all discomfort, the single isolated toiler, trampled under in the modern struggle for existence, may be forgiven if he thinks that he has anticipated the tortures of the Inferno. And the type of all civilised existence is gathered up in one pitiful figure here exhibited for a moment in the waste of London. A clerk in a gallery, four foot from the ceiling in a gas-lighted office, his life consists in addressing envelopes ten hours a day. He is bewildered by the perpetual foul grossness of his fellow-slaves : and only able to endure the awful monotony of his existence by changes from steel pens to quills, or variations in the walk to the house of his servitude.

Modern England appears in these pages, modern England, indeed, under grey skies, and interpreted by one to whom the passing of the dreams of childhood and its high hopes for the future has brought none of the customary apathy and numbness. In the " Autobiography " the scene is mainly in the provinces. The interest is in spiritual combats amongst the ultimate questions of existence. Here is an unforgettable gallery of portraits of the types of the lower middle class in provincial cities. These, it must be confessed, are in the main unpleasant with narrowness and hypocrisy. Sordid love of gain is dominant, with an incredibly low standard of culture and of honour. They include the students of the theological college, the worshippers of Water Lane, Mr. Snale, the " Christian tradesman " and bully, and Mrs. Snale, " cruel, not with the ferocity of the tiger, but with the dull insensibility of a cart-wheel," and Mr. Hexton, with " not a single chink, however narrow, through which his soul looked out of itself upon the great world around." They come, they go. Of few are more than a few words said. The narrator passes from the college through the Baptist chapel at the little provincial town to the Unitarian chapel in the country, and so to the private school and the Atheistic publishing office. But in each chapter appear these clear-cut characters, drawn with a confident, firm hand. So that the reader is convinced that all these societies still live on. Beyond his interests is enduring that strange world of obscure and complacent human lives, carried through an existence to whose meaning and possibilities of kindliness and high endeavour, in its brief passage between two ʳeternities, they seem destined to be for ever blind.

In the "Deliverance" the scene has passed to London. The spiritual struggle has become replaced by revolt against the meanness and monotony and squalor, the material ills of ugliness and poverty. The problems here presented of degenerating life appear "round and hard like a ball of adamant," and men and women move through time, helpless, disconsolate, " with great gaping needs which they longed to satisfy." In two or three chapters a gaunt and desolate picture is drawn of the modern city, the isolation of its inhabitants each from the other, its confusion, its carelessness of pain. London on Sunday afternoon in autumn fog, or the cold winds of spring; London in shadow; the actual slums with their outrage on the senses, and the gaudy sign of the undertaker as the sole evidence of the survival of human aspiration ; the solitary sufferers who have been trampled under and flung aside, John, the waiter, Cardinal, burdened with his jealous wife, Taylor, the coal porter, working always in the dark—all these in a few pages call up a pageant of maimed and broken lives which remain long after the book has closed as a troublous vision.

240

OF DEATH AND PITY

The picture, indeed, is not entirely grey. The world of which "no theory is possible" is seen to contain besides "children sickening in cellars" and "the rain slowly rotting the harvest," no less obvious "an evening in June, the delight of men and women in one another," love and human kindness. Something like tranquillity is attained before death enters as with a bludgeon, and suddenly and clumsily makes an end of all. There is acceptance of life's simple pleasures, gratitude for any kind of response and affection, a wearing down of the harsh fretting of the enigmas into a patience which can even cherish a kind of hope. Human life, here and now, with the age of belief in a future restitution dead, and the age of a satisfying present not yet born, appears in the life history of Mark Rutherford not unlike his own picture of the Essex marshes. The land stretches low and level into the far horizon ; with thick yellow clay clinging round the bitter weeds and discoloured yellow grasses ; and stagnant, scum-covered pools mingling with the smell of the earth the rank odour of decay. But there is a crimson light in the west at evening : the wind that blows at sunset is laden with the breath and salt scents of the sea ; and all the long night in the high heavens wheel and flash the unchanging stars—the stars that shone in Eden, and will shine again in Paradise.

II

The language of the famous "Conclusion" rises naturally to the mind as the reader turns over the pages of "Life's Lesser Moods." Here, indeed, "not

the fruit of experience, but experience itself, is the end."
" With this sense of the splendour of our experience
and of its awful brevity, gathering all we are into one
desperate effort to see and touch, we shall hardly have
time to make theories about the things we see and
touch." Walter Pater, afterwards in " Marius,"
showed the practical workings of a life thus startled
by magnificence and the apprehension of death into a
" constant and eager observation." Moving detached
through field and forest, or along the city ways, the
observer drew from the things seen—autumn leaves,
the sun behind the pine-trees, the face of a child—the
apprehension of " some passionate attitude of those
about us," and the " tragic dividing of forces on their
ways." The experience is won from common things,
in the appeal which the labouring world passes by : a
sudden revelation of hidden emotion ; a colour that
flares, and in a moment fades ; " a breath, a flame in
the doorway, a feather in the wind."

The attitude of Marius eighteen hundred years ago
is the attitude of Mr. Hind to-day. He, too, is to be
reckoned among those who looked on, a little perplexed,
a little diverted, sometimes sorrowful, as they confront
the noise of passing things. Men are planting and
building, busy about material things, eager for wealth,
and crying for fame, for the heaping up of wealth
which another shall inherit, for a fame which is but
the ripple of a moment in the midst of an Eternal
Silence. Conscious even in the grey city of the
splendour of our experience, with the sense also of
its awful brevity ever before him, he sees the thing
pass like a panorama in which the shouting becomes
shrill and presently dies away, and all the gold and
glory crumbles to a little dust. Immediately, however,

is the present experience, directly apprehended. There resides an appeal as insistent and compelling in the labyrinth of London as in the autumn of dying Rome ; the setting sun reflected in the roadside puddle ; a night of rain, a night of stars ; high emotion in meeting and parting, ten minutes in a railway carriage, the sights of a street on a winter morning. The flame of outward life, of the unchanging beauty : the flame of inner passion : the inscrutable mysteries of each individual separate soul, knowing its own bitterness, knowing its heart's particular joy ; these make up the world of the wanderer, as he roams with hungry heart through England and Spain and Italy, and records impressions of life's lesser moods—" a breath, a flame in the doorway, a feather in the wind."

The attitude of detachment, a refusal to judge, is written on every page. An impression is given, here and now, recounted as truthfully as may be. And there each is left ; standing isolated in the past, a picture ; without any attempt to co-ordinate it to the entire scheme of things, glad or sorry ; to estimate, to approve, or to condemn. The method is so un-English that it is difficult to prophesy its development or popularity. We write for edification. We never rest on the experience without demanding its fruit or teaching. Each particular incident must carry thought from itself to the boundaries of things. The record of a child shivering in the rain would appear to us intolerably cold without an appeal at the end for free breakfasts, or an impeachment of a society which can allow such things to be. The gleam of a golden sunshine must attest the goodness of God. Thunder and the bitter frost must certify the presence of evil in the world. To stand aside is to acknowledge indifference. To accept all is to enlist amongst those who neither for God nor for His enemies, are " scorned alike of heaven and hell."

An actual example will best illustrate this un-English attitude. In one of Mr. Hind's sketches he pictures the " Unemployed " marching through the West End streets. The dingy red banner, the meagre figures, escorted by the stalwart, indifferent policeman, the rattle of the collecting-boxes, the clang of many foot-steps along the frozen roads, the scornful comment of the bystanders are woven into an impression of con-tempt and pity with an undernote of fear.

"Later in the day I met them again. It was twilight time ; but the fog had made an end of the day early in the afternoon. Over everything hung that murky gloom, over the procession of the unemployed, over the faces of the employed who left their work to watch. The day's tramp was ending ; they were going east-wards—home—but the fog was so dense that I could see only those who slouched close by. Somewhere far in front the head of the procession felt its way through the dim streets ; somewhere far behind the tail followed obediently ; and out of the thick night came the rattle of the coins in the collecting-boxes. A woman near me pushed the box contemptuously away. ' Want work, do they ? ' she cried. ' I've been a week trying to get a man to mend a window-sash.' "

" The barrow with the naphtha lamp passed on. I watched the last straggler of the London unemployed disappear into the fog." There is no approval. There is no condemnation. There is no denunciation of society or appeal to Charity Organisation. There is no effort to weigh merits or pardon offences. There is merely an extraordinarily vivid picture of an actual experience, for a moment present, in a moment gone.

OF DEATH AND PITY

The author, like the ancient magicians, can reveal the vision. No more than they can he reveal the interpretation thereof.

The danger of the method is sufficiently obvious. Life has a tendency to become a mere variegated pattern, pleasing or discordant; a Persian carpet; or a succession of sense impressions, in which the picture, or any meaning which the picture can convey, is lost in the search for agreeable combinations of curves and colours. Against this danger is here set the sensitiveness to the emotional background, the conviction that even if the impression be but for a moment, that moment must represent the illumination of forces of eternal significance. Love and Death, the passing of Change and of Time, the high ardours of the spirit, the questioning ironies of man's existence and helplessness and unknown destiny, are written over all these experiences of life's lesser moods.

So that the experience itself is found to unfold large issues. A vision is given, if for the moment only and without judgment or approval, down the long vistas of human life towards far horizons. A " Citizen " presents the type of a life vanishing from England. The life of effort, unwearying, narrow toil, acceptance of responsibilities, is set over against " the zest for pleasure that marks these days, the refusal to accept responsibilities, the petulant protest against irksome tasks." A companion picture is that of a woman pursuing always " The Way," with " the glow of spiritual awakening and expansion that came when the particular duties of her life were fulfilled, and she could invite the whisper of the mysteries." There are visions of the " Time of Buttercups," with children dancing in the sunshine; of the death of a child of genius, a cripple, born in a humble peasant home; of the fires of an unforgettable sorrow luminous after nineteen years. There is much of London, its vastness, its desolation; of its sombre magnificence; of its callousness and its charity, the emanations of its million lives, the problem of its present and its incalculable future; of "her loneliness," "her littleness," "her magic," "her terror," "her silence." And at the end the scene shifts into the South, Spain and Italy, the little queer incidents of travel, the conflict of diverse civilisations; and the living, blinking, blear-eyed, or with thoughts of memory and of pity, around the memorials of the dead.

Everywhere Mr. Hind shows himself particularly attracted to the revelation of some inner springs of serenity, the secret of a life hidden from the modern world. This he apprehends in the Salvation Army lasses collecting alms in the Strand, in the old priest upon the mountains, the monks as he sees them in his garden, the poor who acquiesce and are content. The apprehension of the permanent in the transitory, the Divine unclouded by the "little smoke" of men's mad wants and mean endeavours is the end of the story.

"I had entered Italy through Genoa," he concludes, "her stainless marble palaces soaring proudly into the sky. I left her by Venice, her stained marble palaces shimmering sadly down into the water. I had seen the fireflies all along the Umbrian valley, that candle flickering in the dark church of the Frari, and Mantegna's last picture, on which he had inscribed, 'Nothing but the Divine endures; the rest is smoke.'" The vision was complete.

OF DEATH AND PITY

III

"The Sonnets of the Wingless Hours," that tragic sequence of bewilderment and pain, have now been revealed as born of the intimate experience of life's sorrows. The protest and perplexity everywhere present in them drives home under the force of this knowledge, with a renewed appeal. Mr. William Sharp, in his preface to the Canterbury edition of Mr. Lee Hamilton's poems, has taken the world into the secret of the laboratory in which were fused these shining jewels. The author—half-brother to "Vernon Lee"—at the beginning seemed to have all life before him in most favoured circumstance. In the midst of his work as diplomatist he was suddenly seized with that dreadful disease from which Heine suffered years of martyrdom. "From the first definite collapse in 1874 all hope was practically abandoned." He lay in a semi-paralysed condition through the months and years of agony. "For a long period suffering was too acute to enable him to be read to; conversations, messages, letters, had to be condensed into a few essential words." So passed twenty of the best years of manhood "in the posture of the grave," years he compares to the old torture of prisons whose walls steadily closed in upon their victims, a little nearer every day. Pity itself can only stand silent before such a tragedy.

And from this tragedy were born the "Sonnets of the Wingless Hours." Nowhere is there weak complaint; nor any hope for a future which will vindicate the purpose of the punishment, and provide adequate compensation for the ruin of a lifetime. Charon now sleeps, asserts the author, in the rushes by the deserted

247

shore, and no souls demand the services of the ferry of the underworld. Heine, from his mattress-prison, like some old heathen defying his tormenters, went down into his grave hurling mockery and imprecation at the God whose irony had overwhelmed him. But here even the consolation of defiance is denied. For the gods themselves have vanished into vapour, and the walls of Heaven crumbled into dust. Henley deepened the poignancy of his hospital rhymes by deliberate roughness and jagged edges, telling of sudden agonies; and by the attitude, as of a startled child, towards all the apparatus of pain. But in the sonnet which demands more than any other medium perfection of form, this method is impossible. The very smoothness and simplicity of the language of this sequence of suffering deepens the sense of sorrow and tears. His muse has brought him

> " A branch of dead sea fruit, not bay,
> Plucked by the bitter waters of the soul."

Sometimes " bitterer is the cup than can be told," and the only hope is for the quick coming of " death's unstarred and hospitable night." Sometimes a sudden passion of regret for a life thus wasted catches him by the throat:

> "And now my manhood goes where goes the song
> Of captive birds, the cry of crippled things;
> It goes where goes the day that unused dies."

But for the most part there is patience and endurance, gratitude for the little golden cup of " Poesy's wine of gold," as the sufferer watches the years go one by one in

> " A garden where I lie beyond the flowers,
> And where the snails outrace the creeping sun."

248

OF DEATH AND PITY

These fruits of the wingless hours, the children of endurance and pain, have the intimacy and distinction which should give them permanence in literature. There are, indeed, flaws; hardly a sonnet is quite perfect; and flaws so obvious that one could mark, as it were, with a pencil, the weak line or, in most cases, the single word which mars the perfection of the whole. But there is a splendour of style and thought charged with an emotion sometimes passionate, always sincere, which lift these sonnets from the ranks of the ephemeral, and justify comparison even with the greatest.

Two qualities in particular they possess. The first is the very sharp-cut impression of beauty of form and colour. As all things stand clear in a storm-swept atmosphere, so in the heightened sensitiveness of this life of suffering Nature has become charged with a shining brightness unheeded in the common ways of men. The verse throbs with the colour contrasts of Italy, Siena with its dizzy belfry stabbing the fiery air; evening in Tuscany; the rich, hot scent of " old fir forests heated by the sun "; and all the magic of an enchanted land.

Such a sonnet as " Twilight "—containing, indeed, two obvious weak lines—abides in the memory for a particular luminous atmosphere, for a moment harmonious with a mood in which sorrow itself has become serene.

> " A sudden pang contracts the heart of Day,
>   As fades the glory of the sunken sun.
>   The bats replace the swallows one by one;
> The cries of playing children die away.
>
> Like one in pain, a bell begins to sway;
>   A few white oxen, from their labour done,
>   Pass ghostly through the dusk; the crone that spun
> Beside her door, turns in, and all grows grey.

OF DEATH AND PITY

And still I lie, as I all day have lain,
  Here in this garden, thinking of the time
Before the years of helplessness and pain ;

Or playing with the fringes of a rhyme,
  Until the yellow moon, amid her train
Of throbbing stars, appears o'er yonder lime."

The greater poems are those in which these outward
visions are used to create an imagery conveying thought
charged with human emotion. The appeal of a personal
suffering passes into a universal cry. The sadness is
in the April air when a "breeze from Death's great
wings Shakes down the blossoms that the fruit trees
bear." The note of sorrow is heard, which runs through
all the music of the world. There are poems of most
delightful, child-like fancy, and a whole series of
imaginary experience of historical incident. But the
sonnets which stand out with a strength of emotional
power are those translating the individual experience
into the human cry. The eternal subjects of loveliness
and longing, time hurrying into nothingness the transitory generations, the sadness of the memory of all
vanished joy, the great dreams and desires of a race
which passes from essaying the walls of Heaven to the
silence of a little grave—these are interpreted each in
terms of some visual picture. Such are the sonnets
that already have become famous. In " Sunken Gold "
long lost hopes are seen lying as on some reefy shelf,
" the gleam of irrecoverable gold " in the twilight of the
dim sea forests. All Souls' Day in the wintry evening
mingles the memory of the multitudes of the forgotten
dead with the figure of the sower, " grey and lone " in
the autumn fields. And the sonnets entitled " The
Wreck of Heaven " unfold a majestic vision of the ruin

of Paradise and its battlements and towers, with an echo of the closing music of the *Götterdämmerung* in its mingled exultation and despair.

> "Ay, ay, the gates of pearl are crumbling fast;
>   The walls of beryl topple stone by stone;
>   The throngs of souls in white and gold are gone;
> The jasper pillars lie where they were cast.
>
> The roofless halls of gold are dumb and vast;
>   The courts of jacinth are for ever lone;
>   Through shattered chrysolite the blind winds moan,
> And topaz moulders to the earth at last."

Behind this vision of the destruction of the most wonderful dream which has ever comforted the hearts of men, there stands the earth and its realities; and man, uncheered by hope of a future glory, but enduring with the old brave patience all the accidents of time, flinging the grain into the furrow in hope of another harvest.

All admirers of the "Wingless Hours" must rejoice at the wonderful thing which came at last to their creator. "After twenty-one years of this prolonged half-life, the miraculous happened. The disease commenced to wane. The invalid arose from a bed to a new life; thereafter, recovery to health became complete." He travelled; love came to him; the note of sadness and patience in his verse gave place to joy and a renewed sense of the beauty of the world. In a little volume called "Forest Notes," in which he has collaborated with his wife, also a distinguished writer, he has given the first taste of the product of this new life. These little poems lack the sombre magnificence of the sonnets, but they possess a delicacy and a charm which will be welcome to all oppressed with the unanswerable questions which the sonnets inevitably raise. That happiness and a great contentment may be given to the author of this little book for many years must be the hope of all who can appreciate an indomitable courage and suffering heroically borne. That this contentment may be as fruitful in song as the bitter past must be the desire of all lovers of poetry.

IV

Modern poetry is feeling after the expression, in varied form, of one of two emotions. The first is the ultimate exultation and triumph of being, "the glory of the sum of things." The second is the ultimate sadness and regret of all that changes, the "idle tears" of "the days that are no more." It is to the latter class that Mrs. Marriott Watson belongs. Her work demands recognition for its simplicity, pathos, and a rare gift of sincerity. The influence of Henley is strong. The inevitable word is not indeed so successfully attained. Many of these little detached lyrics leave the reader with a sense of imperfection owing to some weakness often in the last line or stanza. But in many there is a haunting melody and beauty. "I am weary of all that passes" is the cry of a great modern writer; and something of the pathos of that passing—regret over the coming of age and the death of the flowers—at times poignant, more often quiet as the sadness of a summer evening, illuminates these little songs of loss and longing.

"After Sunset," the title of her latest volume, would serve as a title to the whole. The light has fallen, and there is silence; only the shadows are creeping over the hills and the signs are manifest of the coming night. The song of the blackbird again and again recurs: "in

the dusk of the cold spring dawn," " Singing the Song
of Songs by the Gates of Dream," or telling the oft-told
story of " dreams and the dying spring." The verse is
woven of the material of sorrow :—" the poor dead whom
none remembereth " : Death's black pavilion in the
Unshapen Lands, and all the grey flowers in Death's
garden : the old wind which

> " Goes murmuring still of unremembered seas,
> And cities of the dead that men forget."

But more than the tragedy of death it is the tragedy
of change which has here found expression. There
will be many fairer days, but never again yesterday.
Flowers will again blossom, but not those flowers
which have faded. Other generations will rise into
exultant life, with perhaps the days of summer unending
and the roses blowing earlier in those after, happier
years. But the generations of the present are going into
silence and the generations of the past have gone.
That time itself should triumph over love and hope and
endless desire : that childhood should vanish and all its
absorbing interests ; that youth should be hurried forward
into age, and no effort stay the march of the intolerable
hours ; this is the irony of life which makes all human
experience a thing so helpless and piteous and transitory.
" Alas, that Spring should vanish with the rose " might
have been written on the title-page of all her poems.

> " They are mowing the meadows now, and the whispering,
>   sighing
> Song of the scythe breathes sweet on my idle ear,—
> Songs of old Summers dead, and of this one dying,
>   Roses on roses fallen, and year on year."

With this also comes the almost blinding contrast

between the renovating powers of Nature and the little life of man. "You are not here, and yet it is the Spring." No temporal consolation can satisfy the hunger aroused by the mute mocking of such a contrast.

> " Youth comes no more for ever—even although
> The fields take flower again, and lilacs blow,
> And pointed leaf-buds gather on the vine;
> Even although the sun should sail and shine
> Bright as of old."

Here, indeed, is the protest which has rung down all the centuries since that distant dawn when Moschus, crying for his dead friend, found himself but mocked by the mallow and the parsley and the renewal of all the splendour of field and flower.

To the vigorous citizen desirous above all of banishing uncomfortable thoughts, this emphasis of the tragedies of change will appear morbid and futile. Outside the garden life goes roaring by. In the dust and bustle there is little time for the hauntings of memory or the cultivation of the sorrow of passing things. With this world Mrs. Marriott Watson has little concern. There is a strange sense of incongruity in the intrusion of such a masterful figure as Lord Kitchener into her poems. In her enchanted land the vision is of the ruined altar, the deserted home, the white way that winds down the hill, the cry of children that are gone out into the night.

Above all here is the cry of the children. The songs of childhood have an especial grace and charm. Some have the tenderness of mingled smiles and tears, as in the sight of the discarded toys and all the child's forgotten world. Some have the deeper note of longing for the childhood vanished in the natural growth to maturity:

the disappearance of the "small, down-vestured head":
"the innocent eyes": "the sweet, impetuous little
feet." And some have the note of anguish which wails
round the most unendurable of all the outrages of death,
in the calling through the night of the ruined heart for
a little child struck down by those merciless hands—

> "Leave the door upon the latch—she could never reach it,
> You would hear her crying, crying there till break of day,
> Out on the cold moor 'mid the snows that bleach it,
> Weeping as once in the long years past away."

Such is the garden "after sunset." The night and its
shadows have not yet come. The sadness is tempered by
the charm of the dying day. Tenderness and compassion
walk more blithely than in the glare of the afternoon.
And all the magic of the evening gathers round that
land of longing and tears, which stretches its horizon
into far distances when once the sun has dropped behind
the hills.

THE RELIGION OF THE CITY

" *For the world is not to be won by anything except on those conditions with which the Kingdom of Heaven first came. What conquers must have those who devote themselves to it: who prefer it to all other things: who are proud to suffer for it: who can bear anything so that it goes forward.*"

—R. W. CHURCH.

THE RELIGION OF THE CITY

A T the beginning of the twentieth century two attempts on a large scale have been made to estimate the religion of London. The results have in the main confirmed the statements of those who assert that the condition of these familiar, crowded populations is in reality as obscure as that of China or Mexico. The one was statistical, the other impressionist. Facts limited to bare numbers were given by the *Daily News* census. A vast complexity of conversations, testimonies, experiences was provided by Mr. Booth's seven volumes.

It is to the student of opinion and social change that the first of these—the numbering of the religions of London—will prove of lasting value. Only advertisement, cynicism, or vulgar curiosity benefits from the announcement that Mr. A's church (heralding itself as exercising enormous spiritual influence) gathers four hundred worshippers every Sunday, or that Mr. B's church (proclaiming a similar success) gathers forty. The tabulated results of the Census have been used as the basis for crude and ill-informed deductions. They will form the material in the future for the demonstration of all manner of preconceived ideas. But this is the common fate of statistic. Let the figures be taken for what they profess to be—the record of the numbers of attendance, men, women, and children, at morning and evening service on certain Sundays in the years 1902–3 in every public religious edifice in London. No claim is made that these figures give adequate basis for comparison of the spiritual influence of different individual churches or of the aggregate of organised religions. One church, in a poor district, attracts a congregation by a distribution of cocoa and slabs of bread at the commencement or the conclusion of the service. Another, in a comfortable suburb, fills its pews with an audience to whom church-going is the custom and the fashion, a display of smart clothing, the occupation of a seat hired by the year, or a method of killing the boredom of an idle Sunday. A third, hidden in a back street, gathers together thirty or forty poor men and women who support the expenses with their scanty earnings, and meet for edification or for worship outside the sphere of both fashion and material benefit. There is no common denominator of religious aspiration which will measure three such congregations as these; but in dispassionate estimate of figures they are of necessity weighed together as if each individual attendance were of similar account.

Yet the figures themselves are of quite extraordinary interest and value—an interest and value which will increase as the memories of London in 1903 fade into an almost fabulous past. They have stamped in permanent form certain facts of the spiritual energies of this strange and perplexing city in this particular period of change. Corrected by personal knowledge, and retranslated from their bloodless skeleton of information into terms of human effort, tenacity, and aspiration, they become charged with a romance and significance paralleled by few other such tables of numbers and names.

Mr. Charles Booth's investigation has not been received with so universal an acceptance. Comments, often angry, have been evoked by the somewhat sweeping strictures of his investigators. The personal impression of curate or minister seems often to have formed the main basis of judgment. Pretentiousness, noisiness, vulgarity, produce emphatic condemnation ; the critics would have done well to remember that pretentiousness, noisiness and vulgarity have often been associated with a real and vigorous religion. Mr. Booth deliberately (I am inclined to think, rightly) rejected the statistical method as misleading in the estimation of something so elusive and intangible as spiritual influence. But as a corrective to many of his statements the Census figures are quite invaluable. No serious student can neglect either the one or the other. Read first the seven volumes of Mr. Booth ; examine and analyse the figures of this Census; make yourself personally familiar with at least a few selected districts of different types—the wealthy, the suburban, the artisan, the poor : you will then be in a position to offer at least some tentative suggestions towards an estimate of the religious condition of this great congeries of cities which we term London.

I

In the commencement of examination it is desirable to attempt an estimate of the characteristic classes of the people of the city. We may omit the specialised class of the West End : that particular " golden " area in which is condensed the product of all the spoil of Empire. Religion has never been the serious concern of the wealthy. They play with it as they play with life. They contribute the funds of impersonal charities, they discuss the sufferings of the poor, they patronise all creeds offering a new sensation—Christian Science, Æsthetic Catholicism, Spiritualism, Revivalism. It is sincere in so far as any sincerity in such a life is possible. But it in no way essentially differs from the homage which this class is always prepared to pay to the accepted gods of a nation. The real problem of the future of religion in the city is being fought out amongst those classes which make up the grey matrix of labour of which that city is composed.

For purposes of investigation this solid background of the city's energies can be split into four main divisions. First we may note the " poor " in the proper sense of the term ; those, in Sir Henry Campbell-Bannerman's now famous phrase, living "on the verge of hunger " if not "on the verge of starvation." These are. the subjects of Messrs. Booth and Rowntree's dismal statistics. They are a class which only emerges above the political horizon when some energetic statesman is composing a moving peroration or essaying a new policy. They are the forlorn multitude of those who have failed. They are most numerous in South and East London, forming great wedges and masses along the riverside, and collecting in scattered pools or isolated streets in all the other boroughs. They form the ready prey of church and mission. Each particular district in which they herd is swarming with rival agencies essaying their bodily sustenance and the salvation of their souls. A continuous vast river of charitable help pours through the channels of these missions into every corner and crevice of their homes. Bread, clothing, boots, vegetable soup, grocery tickets, monetary assistance, fall sometimes, like the rain of heaven, upon the just and unjust, sometimes only upon those who are willing to make a decent return in attendance at public worship or mothers' meetings. This source of supply is eked out in most cases with casual labour or the more desolating forms of unskilled employment, with outdoor relief, with the products of home industries, the earnings of school children, and the munificent wage earned by the free unorganised labour of women. The children are innumerable. The death rate of infants is high, but a sufficient number survive to ensure the transmission of the rickety type, stunted physique and fragile or diseased constitution, to the generations of the future. The individuals rise or fall. The class remains, a stagnant pool of low-grade life which is slowly extending its borders, and swelling its multitudes to a bulk which finally will compel attention to the menace of its futility.

The second class makes up the matrix of which the great mass of working London is composed. It is the class of decent working men, from the highly paid artisan to the better paid labourer. Here is the "poor" as it appears to the rich, lumping into one common category all below the status of retail tradesmen. It more than fills the block dwellings and cottages in which it is housed, and it is continually flowing over through leaks and gaps into the suburbs which surround it on all sides, to the infinite disgust of the original inhabitants of these desirable regions. It works for the most part away from its residence, and spends much of its leisure in journeys to and fro. It is on the whole contented with its life. But its intel igence and vitality seem partially sapped by its crowded city existence, and it manifests none of the somewhat aggressive social and political vigour which is characteristic of a similar class in other cities of England. At present it is largely country bred. It still shows traces of the open air and the life of the fields. But each year the rural elements diminish, the urban increase. It is a race passing in bulk through the greatest change in the life of humanity, the change in which nature vanishes from the horizon and is replaced by the perpetual presence of man.   It represents at the present a stage in this transition, with stability, acquiescence, and the peculiar city characteristics not yet fully attained.

The third class is one often overlooked, whose neglect has originated some of the more absurd generalisations upon the life of the poor.   In all the boroughs, poor as well as rich, lining all the main roads and many of the side streets is the class of tradesmen who minister to the needs of the vast populations which are hidden behind. These form a prosperous bourgeois class, possessing considerable vigour and enterprise, and very sharply divided in interest and outlook from the poor and the artisan who do business with them.   In the poorest boroughs they form an aristocracy of wealth.   In the wealthier boroughs they are less conspicuous, and there are social grades from which they are excluded.   But they are numerous in all, and in all offer a very marked contribution to the religious life of London.

Lastly, in the outlying districts we find the suburban dweller, forming, on the hills principally of the South and the North, a class of quite peculiar and specialised life and characteristics.   He is a product of those economic conditions which have made London the banking centre and clearing-house of the world.   He is a dependant of the City, to which he journeys every morning.   He leads an entirely sedentary existence, writing other men's letters, adding other men's accounts, each a cog or link in the machinery of other men's ideas· The energy pent up in this remarkable toil is reserved for the hours of freedom.   There is active home life, strong family affection, little gardens and ornamented villas, ambition for the children.   A certain artificiality distinguishes such an existence, a divorce from reality which only intrudes at intervals of love or suffering or death. Vigour may be more conspicuous than breadth of outlook or intellectual agility, and there are often set up quite astonishing standards of "respectability" in politics and religion. But there are compensating elements in a widespread material comfort, enjoyment of simple pleasures, and a very real and active religious life, probably stronger here than in any other class of the community. It is here that the churches and chapels are crowded, that their activities blossom out on weekdays into mutual improvement associations, debating clubs, and innocuous amusement. The orthodox religions receive a willing adherence which has resisted successfully all the disintegrating forces of changes in thought and environment. This is the class beyond all others where the particular characteristics find expression in the edifices it has reared for its worship and the nature of the services it generously maintains within them.

Let us see what light the Religious Census will throw upon the spiritual condition of this world of working humanity. Although it would be quite inaccurate to judge the influences exercised from particular churches by the simple comparison of the numbers of worshippers; and although, undoubtedly, a religious enthusiasm focussed in the Sunday gatherings diffuses through great numbers who never or rarely are actually present; yet on the whole we may say that the organised religious and ethical bodies stand practically for the active spiritual enterprise of London. Once I had expected it otherwise—thinking that the widespread break-up of faith and the influence of destructive criticism would have created a large class of persons unable conscientiously to attach themselves to church or chapel, but eager for ethical progress and the assertion of the supremacy of the things of the spirit. But experience has failed to discover any number of such individuals. Many, indeed, pass through a stage in which all definite religions are judged and condemned as insincere or untrue. But either interest in all ultimate questions vanishes, or the inquirer in time finds himself drawn to some church or congregation. Even those who are unable to make any positive spiritual affirmation may unite in some positivist society or ethical fellowship. The influence of such bodies, indeed, containing some of the most sincere and devoted of men and women, is altogether underestimated by the meagre numbers of attendance. Outside there is much vague social discontent, and often a feeling of bitterness against all organised religions. But such feelings, however praiseworthy, are not in themselves guarantees of spiritual or moral energy. The man who will abstain from church-going, and informs you with complacency that his religion is that of the Sermon on the Mount, is usually distinguished by little but an amiable unwillingness to do conscious injury to those who have not injured him, and by a determination at least not to love himself less than his neighbour. As symbols and representatives of whatever spiritual life still remains in London, we may quite confidently limit our outlook to the religious bodies who are dealt with in the Census return.

To come then to the facts. Let us first consider the bare aggregate of numbers.

In the County area of London one man out of every twelve, and one woman out of every ten, attends some form of Divine worship each Sunday morning ; and one man in every ten, and one woman in every seven, attends each Sunday evening.

THE RELIGION OF THE CITY

And if we may accept the figures given by the superintendent of the Census of 38 per cent. making a double attendance, we can lead on to the further statement :

In London one man out of every six, and one woman out of every five, attends some place of worship at least once every Sunday.

I must confess that this is a far larger proportion than I should have anticipated. Living amongst a population which has practically abandoned churchgoing, I had mechanically interpreted my own experience into the larger whole. The twelfth man who goes off to church at eleven o'clock on Sunday morning had escaped my vision. As a rough estimate I should have given anything from 1 to 4 per cent. as the total actively Christian population of labouring London. One is grateful to the Census if for this alone—the revelation of larger numbers of attendance than one had dared to hope—however much later examination may show such attendance to be meaningless and conventional.

Let us pass from these massed aggregates which mean little to the more interesting and difficult analysis of classes—to the attempt to estimate how these worshippers are divided amongst the main grades of society. Here is the ready field of wild deduction. Many critics knowing dimly that Southwark (say) is poor and Chelsea wealthy, have concluded that the statistics of the borough of Southwark show the statistics of church attendance of the poor, and those of the borough of Chelsea that of the rich. Some have thus discovered a fixed proportion of church-goers in all classes. Others will tell you confidently of the demonstration by such numbers of the strength of some particular denomination amongst the poor or the rich. Such

267

crude deductions are entirely erroneous. On the one hand, a poor borough may contain places of worship which attract well-to-do worshippers from a wide area. Southwark, for example, contains an Anglican and a Roman Catholic cathedral, as well as the great chapel made famous through the English-speaking world by the pastorate of Charles Spurgeon, whose enormous audience of 3,625 represents a similar cathedral gathering. In the poorest district of Lambeth, again, is the great church presided over by Mr. F. B. Meyer, which draws a well-to-do and intelligent audience from all the southern suburbs. And on the other hand, such a statement altogether neglects the comfortable class of tradesmen and the middle class who live in all the poorer boroughs, and provide perhaps the most ardent adherents of many flourishing religions. Any one intimate with such a district will know that it is this class in the main which contributes such worshippers as the churches and chapels are able to gather together in working-class districts. The places of worship line the main thoroughfares. Their frequenters are respectable, well-dressed men and women, the dwellers in those main thoroughfares and the better-class squares and streets that remain undestroyed. Investigate every place of worship down (say) Walworth Road from the " Elephant " to Camberwell Green—the heart of a poor district. In all the varied centres of religion, whose buildings are thickly studded at close intervals, you will find no signs of obvious poverty. In the districts behind, in some obscure gathering of Primitive Methodists or Bible Christians, you may discover the class you are seeking. But in all central South London, the district with which I am most intimate, I have only seen the poor in bulk collected at two places of religious worship—Mr. Meakin's great hall in Bermondsey, and St. George's Roman Catholic Cathedral at Southwark—an object-lesson in (amongst other things) the wisdom of the permission of the late Archbishop of Canterbury for the use of incense "for fumigatory purposes." In London as a whole—apart from certain isolated and exceptional instances—I have no hesitation in asserting that it is the middle classes which attend church and chapel, the working-classes and the poor who stay away.

This can be illustrated by comparison, not of the large areas of the boroughs, but of some definite working-class area with some suburban district. I have been at some pains to make such a comparison, whose figures are appended. The working-class area I have chosen is a triangular patch in the centre of South London, bounded by three great thoroughfares. It is a normal crowded district with which I am personally familiar, varying from the lowest poverty to the comparative comfort of skilled industry, and bounded by the middle-class shopkeepers in the main roads. If anything, it should be unusually favoured in its religious effort, for it is the scene of some very interesting experiments. Several of the public-school and Cambridge College missions are here, and the well-known Browning Hall settlement. The churches are high, low, and broad. The clergy are Tory, Radical, and Socialist; they include amongst them borough councillors, guardians, and two of the best known Radical parsons of London. All types of Nonconformity are represented, including a flourishing Baptist and a flourishing Wesleyan Chapel.

To compare with this I selected a suburban district in South Dulwich and Forest Hill, which is as yet

comparatively free from the inroad of the working
man.

The figures for the two districts compare as follows :—

ADULT ATTENDANCE.

	Pop.	Church.	Noncon-formist.	Total.	Percent-age of Pop.
Working-class District .	99,261	2,289	4,255	6,644	6·5
Suburban District. .	32,096	6,686	3,147	9,833	30·6

The figures become more striking, perhaps, if areas
of equal population are compared. The single parish
of St. Mary Magdalene, Old Kent Road, contains almost
as large a population as five of the suburban parishes.
But the church attendances are different.

ADULT ATTENDANCE.

	Pop.	Church.	Noncon-formist.	Total.	Percent-age of Pop.
St. Mary's, Walworth .	20,142	189	1,089	1,278	6
Five Dulwich and Sydenham Parishes	21,373	3,320	2,858	6,178	29

When it is further remembered that the suburban
district undoubtedly also supplies worshippers to a
number of churches and chapels outside its borders,
and that by scraping off a layer of middle-class houses
from the main streets of Walworth you would probably
diminish your church attendance by at least two-thirds,
I think the illustration is striking of the difference in

270

habits of church attendance between the prosperous and the poor.

An isolated example such as this is indeed not conclusive. But I would ask any critic still doubtful to work out similar calculations from the Census returns. Let him compare Bermondsey with Lewisham, inner with outer Lambeth, Deptford with Blackheath—he will find similar results. The results were, indeed, well known to those familiar with the life of the poor, and are continually asserted in Mr. Booth's investigation. The new city race of workers is developing apart from the influences of religion. The spiritual world has vanished from their vision. The curtain of their horizon has descended round the life of toil which constitutes their immediate universe. Here and there, widely scattered, you may find a successful religious community of the poor; but these are mere isolated instances in an area of grey indifference. The energy, determination, and devotion put forth by adherents of all the religious bodies to convert some portion of this vast multitude, is one of the most noticeable displays of self-sacrificing effort to be found in modern England. Every expedient is essayed, from the guilds and fraternities, processions and banners of "advanced" churches to the antics of "Jumping Jack" or "Salvation Joe" of a different school of Christianity. The wealthier members of the varied religions generously pour subscriptions and material gifts for the same arduous task. The best of the younger members of the Church of England undertake work amongst the poor, and certainly the standard of the clergy in the central districts where the churches are empty need not fear comparison with the standard in the outlying suburbs where the churches are crammed. If the works done in London to-day, one is inclined to assert, had been done in Sodom and Gomorrah, they would have repented in sackcloth and ashes. To all this the great unknown multitude remains unresponsive. So far as a conscious spiritual life is concerned the results seem almost negligible. The key to the heart of the City has not yet been found. Its interminable streets and desert of crowded dwellings wait for some outpouring of the spirit as yet withholden. Against its amiable acquiescence and passive resistance to the exhortations, threatenings, and promises of the churches all these energies beat themselves in vain. The indifference to religion is, indeed, accompanied by indifference to all intellectual effort, to political and social action, to the advancement of any ideal cause. " It was supposed," is one verdict, " that as men would not come to church they would go to the hall of science. Not a bit of it. Of the two they would prefer the church, but what they really want is to be left alone." " The fact is," said a lady to a friend of mine who was canvassing for a vote, " me and my 'usben' don't take no interest in anythink."

Amongst the third class of residents—the middle classes, stretching in a kind of skeleton framework through the cities of labour, so strangely members of this unique community, yet alien from all its hopes and desires—we can recognise a strong and vigorous religious life. It develops mainly an individualistic gospel ; stern ; a doctrine that every man should help himself, and that if he fails it is his own fault. It recognises an "old-fashioned" teaching—heaven and hell as realities, unaffected by the destructive influences of modern ideas. Here, if anywhere, is the survival in London of the Puritan element, the distrust of worldly pleasures, the looking forward to the salvation of the elect, escaping, though hardly, from a world destined for everlasting fire. This population fills the great Nonconformist tabernacles which occupy so conspicuous a position in the religious life of London. It is interesting to see how its existence causes a reversal of the standards recognised elsewhere—clergymen, for example, repeatedly explaining to Mr. Booth that their wealthy people were "too well off" for the Church of England, or that the edifice is "placed in a wealthier part among people who are Dissenters or nothing." "These churches," is the verdict on one district and one religious body—it may be extended to all—"are mainly supported by the lower middle class; with the working class their difficulties begin, and in the streets that show a really poor element all religious efforts fail, here as elsewhere." The summary of a particularly successful Baptist tabernacle in Camberwell is written large over the whole of London. "Few are rich, for the rich have left the neighbourhood; none are poor, for the poor do not come, and a mission started for their sake has not been a success. But as a middle-class organisation the church is the centre of a vigorous congregational life." In these districts at least, Nonconformists form the aristocracy, and the Church and the Roman Catholics work with a lower social stratum.

In our fourth class—the residents of the suburbs—we have perhaps the largest proportion of church attendance in any district in London. Practically the whole population attends religious service on Sunday. Places of all religions are crowded with overflowing congregations. The disintegrating influences which have swept over Society and the West have here as yet scarcely penetrated. Sunday amusement is still sternly discouraged. Sunday is made as unpleasant a day as is possible for the ungodly who refuse to recognise the obligations of worship. The record everywhere is of activity and enterprise. Munificent sums have been spent on new buildings and endowments. Church attendance is the fashion, pews are rented for families ; the chief difficulty is to provide accommodation for the increasing demands. Adjacent to each other, indeed, we have here two populations, each inhabiting an entirely separate universe. In the centre the minister may talk with the tongue of man and angel, and the church remains deserted. In the suburbs he may roll out commonplace platitudes, and the church is crammed. "A certain class will come to church," is the summary of one minister, "provided you do not positively repel them ; while another class cannot be induced to come at all." In the suburbs we hear of districts in which "almost every one in this neighbourhood goes to some place of worship"; others where "you have only to build a church and it will be filled, unless you drive the people away."

The conclusions of Mr. Booth and the statistical Census now further sift themselves under classes.

In London the poor (except the Roman Catholic poor) do not attend service on Sunday, though there are a few churches and missions which gather some, and forlorn groups can be collected by a liberal granting of relief.

The working man does not come to church. A few small communities of Primitive Methodists, Baptists, Salvationists, and similar bodies, as a general rule represent his contribution to the religious life of the nation.

The tradesmen and middle class of the poorer boroughs exhibit an active religious life, mainly gathered

274

in the larger Nonconformist bodies, especially the Baptists.

The residents in the suburbs crowd their churches and chapels, and support with impartiality and liberality all forms of organised religion.

Before passing to conclusions, there are some further points of interest to be noted concerning the region of religious effort and failure.

First, I think the statistics conclusively demonstrate the failure of what I may call the "mission" system. The original conception was an idea of a very attractive simplicity. The parish church or the mother chapel was to be the place of meeting of a cultured and comfortable audience. These paid for the seats, and were edified by the ministrations of a cultured and comfortable pastor. "The poor will not come to church." The presence of their squalor, if they found their way in, would, indeed, be a little embarrassing. So in the poor part of the parish a "mission-hall" is built, where the curate or the faithful laymen of the church may extemporise popular and breezy addresses, and conduct with the aid of an harmonium popular and breezy hymns. The mother congregation will contribute generously to this necessary supplement to their efforts, the lady members will assist in the singing or become district visitors, and the hall will be a centre for the liberal distribution of meat, clothing, and coals. One may perhaps rejoice at the failure of this vicious system, as revealed by these investigations. Mr. Booth brings a sweeping indictment against the whole collection of shabby, dilapidated mission-halls of tin or drab brick, which he found offered as homes for the spiritual nourishment of the poor. And in practically every borough the attendance of adults at these lamentable erections is found to be approaching the vanishing point. Rarely does it reach a hundred. 43, 34, 16 in the Anglican, 8 in the Baptist, 41, 41 in the Congregational, I find the mission-hall attendance in one district. In another are ten Baptist missions with an average morning adult attendance of 7, and evening of 33 ; in another five Anglican with a morning average of 13, and evening of 50. Not on such lines, it may safely be asserted, will the news of the kingdom of God come to the working populations of London.

A second noteworthy feature is the power seemingly possessed by the old parish churches to gather congregations within their walls. They stand, for the most part, of a Georgian or early Victorian architecture, like great ships washed by the flood of humanity which has swept around them ; built for a time when Walworth was a fashionable suburb, or Stepney surrounded by gardens, or Woolwich a flourishing, self-centred country town. They awaken memories of a vanished past, before the torrent of poverty swept down on the fields and marshes and destroyed, like the lava stream, all green trees and every living thing. Something, however, of their quaintness and old-world atmosphere seems to have clung around them. The services themselves are nearly all of a "moderate" type, most characteristic of an Established Church and early Victorian religion. Most of these parish churches, with their type of worship now almost superseded by modern, energetic innovations, exhibit a noteworthy number of Sunday attendances.

A third item is the manifest tendency of the Nonconformist worshippers to collect together into strong centres—that centralising system which is inevitable where preaching is so emphasised and the stimulus and guidance of the pulpit so much desired. I have no doubt the tendency implies loss as well as gain—that the smaller chapels round, which are emptied to swell the great congregations, must inevitably suffer from depression and a sense of failure. In Woolwich, for example, we may note Mr. Wilson's great tabernacle, with an adult attendance of 1,669; and ten other Baptist chapels dividing 1,520 between them, or an average at each service of 76 persons. In Southwark Mr. Spurgeon attracts a magnificent congregation of 1,054 adults in the morning and 1,954 in the evening; the seven adjacent Baptist chapels obtain between them 873 in the morning and 1,769 in the evening, an average of 188 per service; while the adjacent four Congregational churches are occupied by but 628, or an average of 78. Mr. Meakin's hall in Bermondsey, again, with its 1,217 evening attendance, presents a sharp contrast to adjacent Wesleyan churches with congregations of 12, 130, and 19, and to the desolate condition of churches and chapels of other bodies in the same desolate region. Undoubtedly there are high compensating advantages. The power of the great preacher is multiplied. The stimulus of these vast multitudes is invaluable to the bodies of Christians scattered and small in the surrounding indifference. The sight of the congregation of the Newington Tabernacle singing hymns on Sunday evening on the steps of the great edifice is a guarantee to the heedless stream which passes by that there are some who still believe in their religion. But work under the shadow of these cathedral gatherings in the humbler chapels is a depressing experience. The congregation slowly melts away, as the old faithful depart and the younger members are drawn to more obvious attractions. I know of few more depressing sights than the gathering of the few score dejected faithful scattered through buildings of size and pretension from which all the life has departed.

The parochial system of the Established Church, with its strong emphasis on local ties, is a resistent against this tendency in the Anglican community; the comparatively unimportant place occupied by the preacher is another. Undoubtedly, however, the Anglican attendances suffer as well as the Nonconformist from the attractive influences of these gigantic tabernacles and mission-halls. One is driven more and more to the conclusion that under present conditions the percentage of attendance at church to population in London is about a fixed number. You may, by special effort of preaching, music, or excitement, draw a large and active congregation. But you have done so by emptying the churches of your neighbours. The water is not increased in quantity, but merely decanted from bottle to bottle. In the cases mentioned above, the great chapels with their allied branches and their immense activity, I can very gladly testify from personal knowledge to the real spiritual enthusiasm and benefit which they diffuse. There are, however, other popular attractive services which must be received with less unqualified praise. Efforts are made, wholesale, reckless, sensational, to excite an emotional vigour. The influence in any case appears transitory. The adherents of the churches are lured from their less exciting services, dosed with a kind of spiritual intoxication, and left to recover from the debauch as best they can. Energetic, well-meaning persons, seeing London as a heathen city, hire large halls, flash lantern slides before the eyes of the crowd, advertise "Salvation Jack" to preach on the subject "Catch 'em alive." The success is phenomenal, and they go to sleep at nights convinced that they have advanced by their efforts the conversion of England. People who had attended humble churches and chapels, often miles away, are drawn to this new spiritual excitement. In many cases they never return to their old membership, finding the old methods humdrum and unstimulating. I am sure I am in agreement with the majority of the ministers in London when I say that experience has created a distrust of the large "undenominational" mission, with its lavish charities and sensational appeals, the special advertisement and religious excitement, and all efforts to reach "the outcast who has never heard of the Gospel" (who scarcely exists in London) by the satisfaction of his stomach or the adaptation of the methods of the circus and the music-hall.

Another feature of interest is the evidence of the progress of Ritualism and "advanced" doctrine amongst the suburbs of London. This was a surprise to me. I had thought these energies mainly exhibited amongst the rich who were attracted by its ceremonial and the poor who welcomed its gospel of Socialism and fellowship. But here are strong churches among the middle classes —churches mostly built in recent years, and by the worshippers themselves without external assistance— evidently providing something which their congregations desire. Here, if anywhere, is to be found the Ritualistic grocer whom Sir William Harcourt once challenged his ecclesiastical opponents to produce. The suburbs, I should have thought, would have remained the last home of Protestantism, and around the northern boundaries of London they remain entirely faithful to the evangelical tradition. But all through the south and the west we find largely attended " Catholic " churches. All new districts of mixed population seem to be efficient fields for these newer energies. It is a noteworthy factor in the estimation of the changing aspects of London's religious life, a movement still progressing towards an end no one can clearly foresee.

Many other striking features are revealed as by a sudden light thrown into a universe of cloud and darkness. There is the smallness of number and magnitude of congregation of the Roman Catholic churches, revealing both the poverty of this body and the readiness of its members to travel considerable distances to fulfil their obligations of attendance at Mass. There is the astonishing blossoming out of offshoots and branches of the main stream of Christian life into all kinds of quaint minor sects, each with its own specific doctrine and place of meeting. These become most pronounced in the suburbs, as in Camberwell, where we find the New Jerusalem Church with 45 morning worshippers, the Calvinistic Independents with 153, the Christadelphians with 49, besides such less conspicuous bodies as the Holiness Gospel Mission with 15, the Christian Band Hall with 70, and two branches of Spiritualists with 13 and 89 adherents. Again, there is evidence of the comparative failure of " undenominational " services, with a series of minute attendances ; the inability of the Salvation Army to attract inside audiences ; and the great contrast, in the case of the Wesleyan Methodists, between attendances at the new centres of the forward movement and the old circuit chapels.

Finally, it may be asked, What is the relation between the figures of attendance and actual religious influence ? How far can the activity of a Church in districts be measured by or limited to the number of adherents here given ? This is a question largely a matter of personal impression for which there are no exact data. My own opinion is that, in translation into the world of real values, the numbers for the central districts are considerably too small, those for the suburban considerably too large. This is due, on the one hand, to the far wider diffusive influence of the Church in the poorer districts than that which is represented by the handful of worshippers ; on the other, to what I might call the greater religious *intensity* of the worshippers who do attend where church-going is out of fashion than of those who attend where it is the recognised custom. The Church in the vast city is a great engine of civilisation. There is a network and machinery of social organisation—clubs, guilds, boys' brigades, mothers' meetings, improvement societies. It may indeed be questioned how far a Church is justified in turning its energies from its definite spiritual mission to the more practical work of the provision of pleasure and the amelioration of the hard life of the poor. But certainly it is undoubted that civilisation would be considerably delayed were this apparatus removed. This activity has earned for the Church the friendliness and toleration of vast populations still impervious to its spiritual message, and a few years ago in an attitude of open hostility. An overwhelming proportion of the children attend catechism and Sunday School and are launched into life with such cloudy religious conceptions as these institutes are able to provide. The clergy are frequent and often welcome visitors. Each individual is present at service at least at his baptism, his marriage, and his funeral ; and occasionally on other special occasions—harvest festivals, confirmations, and the last night of the year. The services of the minister of religion are requisitioned in times of trouble or illness, and few would willingly die without at least one visit from the clergyman. All this means a real if diffusive influence. Religious ideas are still " in the air " ; and the message of the Church, the consciousness of sin, the need for repentance, and the expectation of future judgment, have not yet entirely vanished from the horizon of London.

I should be inclined to assert again that, in quality, our attendance within the congested area more than compensates for the quantity of the region beyond. We come, if at all, because our religion is real, and amid the manifested contempt of our neighbours. In the smaller churches and chapels at least there are no meretricious attractions to lead us thus to defy public opinion. Suburban religion is largely of a different character. Much of it is the mere conventional homage to the accepted gods of the community. And even the section that is honest and deliberate is often partly lacking in certain essentials of an active and aggressive Christian endeavour. It upholds a decent life and a clean moral standard, with much individual personal piety. But it is far too content to limit its outlook to its own family or church, heedless of the chaos of confusion and failure which lies at its very doors. It regards with disapproval and often with contempt this world of poverty with its dumb demand for aid. It is generous in charity, but no appeal for justice in the name of the forgotten poor goes forth with united voice from the churches of London. It is content to cultivate its own garden, to save its own soul. It is loth to identify its interests with those of its less successful neighbours. The challenge, " Which think ye was neighbour to him that fell amongst thieves ? " remains unaccepted. For this neglect of obvious Christian duty its loss is at least as great as the loss of those it declines to aid. It becomes more and more cut off from the realities to which a living religion has always appealed. It draws the line tight round its own border, and endeavours to satisfy with missions and gifts of money the obligation of personal service and of a campaign for justice to all the desolate and oppressed. It has remained up till now unaffected by destructive criticism and the changes of thought and outlook which have so ravaged the orthodox religions in other regions. But there are not wanting signs of the approach of the disturbance. It has still to pass through a time of trial in which it will be tested to its foundations. Materialism, the lust for pleasure, the modern impatience with a definite creed, are slowly creeping into this vigorous suburban area ; and the negative assertions of science and biblical criticism are creating centres of local disquietude. If the prevailing type of religion largely withers before such forces as these, it will be because it has set itself apart in comfort, content with a personal creed of salvation ; because it has felt no passionate impulse to assert a common fellowship with the less fortunate who are lying at its doors—no call to right the wrongs which, in the words of a modern reformer, " cry continually into the ears of the Lord God of Sabaoth."

We have enough facts, I think, to justify us in the statement that the religious life of England at the dawn of the century occupies a quite unparalleled position amid that of the nations of Western Europe. In the case of all other countries, religion has been practically abandoned by the rich and successful, and is still grasped with tenacity and devotion by the masses of the poor. In the cities, indeed, amongst the male populations of the working classes, the historical faiths of Christianity have been replaced to a large extent by the newer creed of Socialism. But Socialism, with its sense of fellowship, its demand for the merging of the individual life in the success of the cause, its uplifting of an ideal condition of justice, and its effort towards a day of better things, in many ways provides a background to life and the vision of a larger horizon. But in England exactly the reverse conditions prevail. The claims of religion are still acknowledged by the rich and governing classes. They are inoperative amongst the lives of the poor. No dreams of a renovated society have entered the chambers left empty by their absence. Few can doubt that in this contrast ours is the greater loss. Religion to the rich is a by-product—a luxury or a plaything. Religion to the poor is an essential ingredient of lives at the best stunted and confined, oppressed by the perplexities of existence and limited by the day's toil or the evening's pleasure.

It is not an encouraging picture which is finally stamped upon the mind in the investigation of human life in London. It is a vision of vast and shadowy multitudes of human beings driven by some blind impulse to the struggle for material comfort and the needs of a day. Happiness is there, family affection, the play of children, even ambition and a high moral standard. But it is the life of a day with a narrowed outlook. There is light to work by, but no clear radiance of dawn or sunset. At the end comes nightfall, with no vision beyond. Vague hope of a better time for the children seems rarely to develop into a conscious effort after the attainment of a new social order. Vague acknowledgment of a phantom and tenuous life beyond the grave is the sole representative of that hunger for immortality which in every age has refused to acquiesce in the visible ruin of death. Those who have lived with and learnt to love its labouring peoples, with their indomitable cheerfulness, pluck, and endurance, will be the first to affirm that their predominant need is the sense of a larger life, without which human existence is as that of the gnat or the midge; an uplifting of the material surroundings to show, if but for a moment, an encompassing spiritual horizon; and an ideal cause able to illuminate even the scene of contemporary failure with a kind of glory

II

It is interesting to note how, in the discussion of remedies for the ineffectiveness of religion in modern England, almost all critics plunge straightway into the question of machinery. The worship of machinery, as Matthew Arnold continually asserted, is a national characteristic of Englishmen. And each observer appears to hold that if that particular section of the machine in which he can detect a flaw could be repaired, or if a particularly up-to-date invention replaced some antiquated adjustment, the machinery of the Churches would once again grind out religious enthusiasm. With one it is the edifice. He deplores the cold, Gothic building, repellent to the poor. He would substitute large lighted halls of the remarkable and dignified style characteristic of the later nineteenth century, with plenty of carpets, paint, and colour. With another it is the edifices themselves. Let the leaders of religion come out into the street, he holds, and the problem is solved.

THE RELIGION OF THE CITY

With one again it is the service, antiquated, unintelligible to the vulgar. Collect a band, he urges, sing the " Holy City " and other moving modern melodies, weave into your prayers allusions to politics and incidents of the day. With another it is the sermon ; the minister is too cold, or speaks with stammering tongue. Let us place a great preacher in every pulpit, and the masses will vehemently fight for entrance to our churches. Some advocate, some deprecate, the methods of the theatre. Some would abolish pews altogether, and let the men stand. Some see the inevitable advance of religion if pews are made more comfortable. Each one has convinced opinions as to what " the poor " will come to—the large hall, the small mission, the street corner. Few seem to care to face the question what " the poor " are to be offered when they come.

All this would be very relevant if we could recognise large populations with real desire after religious devotion on the one hand, and a Church with a living message which can satisfy this desire on the other. The whole problem would then exhibit itself as a consideration of the method by which the one can be most effectively brought in contact with the other. But the conditions are quite otherwise. On the one hand are masses of people to whom the spiritual world has no meaning, and from whose lives the fundamental bedrock appeal of religion seems to have vanished. On the other are Churches whose faith has grown cold, and whose good news sounds far removed from anything approaching the passionate enthusiasm of earlier Christian centuries. Were this enthusiasm present, the problem of machinery would soon be solved. Preachers would be speaking with a conviction itself eloquent. The services would take upon themselves a character of infectious courage.

THE RELIGION OF THE CITY

The people would themselves build, as always in the past, edifices reflecting in the very stones the characteristics of their faith. Religion would impetuously flow forth from their limited spaces into the open ways. Until such a wind of the spirit can animate the dry bones of religious organisation with some such violent life, all conscious modifications of machinery become but attempts at creating a soul through the body, the artificial galvanising from without of an organism from which the inner life has fled.

Yet, even with such imperfect message as we have, it is well to criticise the vessels in which it is conveyed; more especially if these be but survivals of antique furniture, or symbols of class distinction and a dead faith. How far and in what particulars, we may profitably inquire, is the message of the Churches hampered by its methods of deliverance?

First in regard to the services. Undoubtedly we are here suffering from the dead hand of the past. The morning and evening services of the Church of England, as normally performed, with their complicated and mysterious variations of canticles, prayers, and irrelevant readings of Scripture, are altogether bewildering to those not intimately familiar with the books from which they are compiled. The reformers of the sixteenth century endeavoured to restore worship to the people in the vulgar tongue. Unfortunately the Reformation was in essence aristocratic, never, as the Reformation abroad, awakening response from the masses of the population. The churches passed from the hands of the people, who ceased to take a pride in them. The Church services became more and more an inheritance of a limited aristocracy. The longing for something warm, human, inspiring, contributed largely to create the independent bodies which in all the subsequent centuries have formed minor centres of worship. I have no hesitation in saying that, for the majority of the poor, to-day's services are as incomprehensible as if still performed in the Latin tongue. The central service of the Roman Catholic Church, indeed, with its dramatic and appealing character, is far more intelligible even to the humblest worshipper. The Reformation changes provided the essentials of the Mass in the English Communion service, a service for dignity and beauty quite unparalleled. The monkish matins were never intended for formal parade one day in the week, swollen by elaborate music into intolerable dimension. Any one concerned with the religious life of the poor will welcome most heartily the increased honour paid to the feast of the Lord's Supper in recent years, and the progress towards its restoration to the central position of the Sunday worship. Such a change alone would, I believe, remove one of the chief obstacles to Church attendance.

We may welcome also the renewed efforts after light, colour, and beauty ; the introduction of symbolic action, procession, and some elements of movement and drama into the drabness of our churches. Religion is independent of such adventitious aids, and the essentials must never be lost in the attractions of sensuous imagery. But I am sure that, in the acres of desolate hideousness of the streets of our working populations, all the appeals of sense and sound and colour should be associated with a worship which is to lift the minds of tired men and women to some other vision than that of their material meanness. I should like to see the churches of the wealthy studiously plain ; not vulgar, indeed, like the " up-to-date " religious edifice, a building which will serve as a record and a warning to future ages of the condition of religion in twentieth-century England; but with whitewashed walls and scant decoration, that the worshippers may contrast this simplicity with the splendour of their own homes, and acknowledge one standard of reality in man's judgments, another in those of God. And I would see the churches of the poor rich with colour and light—with great paintings on all the walls and the freest use of every artistic appeal —that these also might learn from day to day that the monotony and meanness of the grey streets in which they are confined, and the grey lives to which they are destined, is not a destiny which was designed for them, nor a bondage from which they will never be freed.

In passing from the ceremonial to the character of the service, we are confronted with a manifest difficulty. Living in a transitory time or order, and with a vision limited to our own settled and decent lives, much of the language used by men who dwelt amongst the enduring facts of human existence appears to us archaic and meaningless. "Agony and bloody sweat"; "widows and orphans and all that are desolate and oppressed"; "battle, murder, and sudden death"; "the hour of death and the day of judgment"—how faint and far away all this seems to the rational and settled life of suburban London! The difficulty, indeed, will endure but for a time. The persistence of comfort in a world of illusion has never existed but for a few generations. Here, if anywhere, the absence of sympathetic imagination, and the faithlessness of the Churches to the larger vision, has produced an aspect of make-believe. If these congregations could be roused to apprehension of something of the real world outside—of Ireland or South Africa in the immediate past, of Macedonia in the immediate present, of the life of the poorest always—these exclamations and cries of appeal would become charged with an awful significance, a demand urged with violence in the name of fear and pity for the vindication of the government of a righteous God.

And as with the service, so with the sermon. I would not reiterate the demand for "good preaching," which seems to me utterly to confuse the purposes of the services of the Church. We meet, not for edification, but for worship—to confess our sins, to obtain spiritual succour, to renew the visible guarantee of fellowship. Eloquence will attract everywhere, in the pulpit as in the market-place. But the crowds which run after a popular preacher, which purchase his portraits and finger his clothes and pry into his family life and the contents of his larder, seem to me somehow alien from the sincerest forms of religion. Yet there is no doubt that the patient layman has a right to appeal for better preaching. The pulpit in many cases is not only not an attractive, but is actually a repellent, force. We have no privilege to insist upon eloquence. But we can demand sincerity, the frank facing of difficulty, freedom from the conventional machinery of the popular exposition of doctrine. The prevailing theology, even more perhaps than the prevailing liturgy, is wrapped up in an ancient language. The very terms are technical— grace, justification, conversion, perseverance. They flow out glibly from the student who has soaked himself in their historical meanings; they are Greek to the general. They were once living realities for which men fought gladly and died. They still symbolise realities, the permanent elements of the life-history of the soul. But they are wrapped around in cobwebs and the complications of a technical system, frozen into sterility.

They have no more meaning and no more appeal to the audience at whom they are thrown in such profusion than the details of the performance of the Mosaio ritual, or the genealogies of the legendary heroes of the Hebrew Bible. We want neither edifying lessons drawn from the wanderings of Israel or the Book of Joshua; nor brilliant "word-painting" of some of the scenes of the Bible with a more up-to-date eloquence; nor the exposition of the machinery of schemes of salvation once real from which the life has departed; but some message concerning the things of the spirit, delivered in simplicity and humility and sincerity to men who would fain be simple and humble and sincere.

A special question has been aroused by the impeachment, with significant emphasis, of the methods of modern charity and its alliance with religion. Mr. Booth discovers over the whole town a persistent and undignified struggle between competing religious bodies; and in any particular choice slum area a competition, rising into an almost open warfare, for possession of the field. One half of London seems engaged in entertaining the other half with soup and bread with a view to its subsequent spiritual edification. Round the city he finds the whole population visibly tainted by the corrupt influence of competitive charity: "'Irreligion,' said one incumbent, 'is the result of all this bribery; we are all in it, church and chapel are equally bad. It begins with the children; buns to come to Sunday School, and so on, so that they grow up with the idea that the Church is simply a milch cow for tracts and charity.'"

The typical East End, the happy hunting-ground of the slummer, is "overdone with religion and relief." In St. Luke's on Sunday afternoon "visitors from five different agencies in the buildings are found bribing the people to come to their meetings." In Soho, "nowhere is the clash of rival doctors so great as here." But even the far-off regions at the limits of the city tell a similar tale. In Deptford "the poor parts are indeed a regular Tom Tiddler's ground for missions, and we hear of one woman, busy at the wash-tub, calling out, ' You are the fifth this morning.' " In Greenwich there is "too much competition for the moral health of the people." In Woolwich the inhabitants are "fought over by the various religious bodies with more than common vivacity." Even in the new districts, whose development almost immediately into slum areas is one of the most appalling revelations of Mr. Booth's book, the same astonishing competition is shown. Down in Wandsworth "religious activity takes the shape very largely of missionary efforts, competing with each other, not without mutual recrimination." In Kilburn "there are four churches after every poor family," and the observer wonders at the strange struggle "fought over men's bodies for their souls."

These competitive charities become most pernicious when they are definitely used to wean adherents from a rival faith. It is a somewhat dismal commentary on the nature of the forces behind the distribution of modern charities to find that while a particular mission in a neglected district fails to evoke support, a mission planted down to combat the influence of some rival Christian body never seems to lack money or adherents. This is especially true of the opposition to the new Ritualistic energies which in the past twenty years have swept into all the poorer quarters of London. "The record of the Evangelical mission," says Mr. Booth of one district, and a similar commentary is repeated all through the volumes, "is simply that of a struggle with the High Church for the souls and bodies of the children. It is dole *versus* dole and treat *versus* treat, and the contest openly admitted on both sides, while people taking the gifts with either hand explain how careful they must be when attending service that the other side knows nothing about it." "This atrocious system," as Mr. Booth rightly calls it, is a very distressing revelation of the superior power of religious rivalry to religious charity.

This enormous stream of charity flows down through the various religious agencies from the rich to the poor. We hear of mission funds with incomes of ten or twenty thousand a year; some business-like, some not audited at all, or "audited in heaven." Twenty-five thousand children are fed in one winter by one mission; over a million men receive shelter, cocoa, and bread from another; in a third to all comers is a free night-refuge. Yet the problem of poverty is no nearer solution. Nor do the attempts to bring men within the reach of the Gospel by means of the offer of food and gifts appear to create permanent results. That the whole system does more harm than good is the verdict of those familiar with its results. One would think it was almost time for a definite and united appeal to the members of the different churches and the charitable rich seriously to consider the harm which is being done by the cruelty of their kindness.

Other questions of machinery of the lesser importance are of interest. There is the failure of the Sunday Schools either to implant intelligible religious ideas or to foster a desire for spiritual communion and worship. There is the (as I think) deplorable theory that some special kind of popular "hall" is necessary for the development of the religion of "the poor"; that by massing these into huge aggregations you may encourage their reviving energies, save the expense of too lavish "plant," and use your single successful evangelist to the best advantage. But the essence of the problem resides in the spirit which lies behind the machinery and its influence on the religious life of London.

On the side of the working peoples this is certainly a period of unusual difficulty. The uprooting from the country and the transference to the town has caused a general confusion and disorder. Man has not yet clearly apprehended his position or appreciated its possibility. He has been "dumped" down in some casual street, unknown to his neighbours, unconnected with a corporate body or fellowship. He moves through time in a kind of confused twilight, dimly wondering what it all means. Material comfort and security is inevitably under these conditions his main interest. The memories of a life which is independent of the hard, visible boundaries become daily dimmer, as he clangs the hammer, or heaves merchandise, or manipulates continually hard, material things. I think we may safely affirm that this creation of a city race is in no small degree responsible for the present manifest failure of appeal of all spiritual creeds.

But the failure is none the less considerable from the side of the Churches. We come from outside with our gospel, aliens, with alien ideas. The Anglican Church represents the ideas of the upper classes, of the universities, of a vigorous life in which bodily strength, an appearance of knowledge, a sense of humour, occupy prominent places. The large Nonconformist bodies represent the ideals of the middle classes, the strenuous self-help and energy which have stamped their ideas upon the whole of Imperial Britain. Each lives in poor districts, in them, not of them. Each totally fails to apprehend a vision of life as reared in a mean street, and now confronting existence on a hazardous weekly wage from a block-dwelling or the half of a two-storied cottage. Our movements and inexplicable energies are received with a mixture of toleration and perplexity. We are recognised as meaning well, but our aims and ideals never become clearly intelligible. " What is he after ? " " What does he get ? " " What is behind it all ? "—are questions I have heard frequently asked as some church has bourgeoned out into fresh and ingenious enterprise. Sometimes we are interpreted as pursuing some deep game of party politics ; sometimes as a kind of unofficial policemen paid by the rates and taxes : more often perhaps as possessed of a kind of exuberant energy which must somehow find relief in religious services and mothers' meetings. Funds from outside raise churches and chapels ; funds from outside provide clubs and material relief. We appear and we vanish. After a few months of this perplexing enthusiasm the curate or minister is called to another sphere of work, and disappears from the universe of those who had just, perhaps, commenced to realise that he possesses some traits of ordinary humanity. If we could only apprehend how entirely baffling and irrational all this must appear to those who are looking out of, instead of into, the abyss, our surprise, I think, would be less at the vastness of our failure than at the magnitude even of our poor success.

Connected with this divergence we must recognise how scantily up to the present the Churches and missions have identified themselves with those demands of Labour, the deliberate attempts to strike at the roots of the ills and oppressions of the time, which the working man knows to be just. The battles of the past for social amelioration have been fought apart from, and often with the open opposition of, the larger religious organisations. "All the Churches are against me," Lord Shaftesbury notes in the course of his campaign for the redemption of the child-life of England. And the bitterest opposition to such social reformers as Charles Kingsley came from the official Christian communities. Are we better to-day than our fathers? Factory law, the right of combination, free trade, sanitary dwellings, a humane poor law—these were slowly and painfully accomplished without the assistance of the Churches. The needs are as insistent to-day. Decent housing and a home, shorter hours of labour, a living wage, opportunities of life, the development of common interests in the municipal community— where in such questions of fundamental justice as these are the united voices of the Christian community demanding the recognition of a universal responsibility in the name of the common fellowship? Undoubtedly it is because a certain section of the High Church party have fearlessly proclaimed this social gospel of a visible kingdom of God that they have earned, to a degree so perplexing to many who deplore their doctrines, the respect and friendship of the leaders of labour and the devotion of the poor. These clergymen have no monopoly of devoted work, nor do they give in charity more than the missions which endeavour to stem their influence. The working man has no affection for elaborate ritual. He accepts with resignation, as part of an inexplicable activity, the ornaments, the processions, and the ceremony. If they processioned round their churches standing on their heads, he would confront the performance with the same toleration. But they have gone down and lived amongst the people; they have proclaimed an intelligible gospel of Christian Socialism; demanding not "charity," but "justice." The campaign has brought upon them a storm of obloquy from the world of orthodox religion. It has earned them the affection of the poor. Such a life as that of Father Mackonoche, or Father Lowder, or, in recent times, Father Dolling, with his continual appeal for "a chance" for "my people," has struck the popular imagination and evoked a pathetic gratitude. I am aware that this social message is not the whole gospel, not perhaps the most important part of the Christian message. But it is far the hardest part to get uttered, and it is the message which the times imperatively demand. The cry for justice provokes a bitter indignation in quarters where the plea for charity evokes a ready response. It is not unnatural that many successful enterprises doing much good work should hesitate to alienate their supporters and subscribers with the revolutionary teachings of the New Testament. But I am entirely convinced that no message which does not contain as an integral and essential part of its proclamation this effort towards a visible social salvation will fall upon any but deaf ears amongst the working populations of our great cities.

Professing Christians, it has been a little cynically asserted, are the chief obstacles to the spread of Christianity in England. Those outside the Church are continually confronting the charters of our creed and the weekly profession of our intentions with the dull and uninspired acquiescence of our daily lives. Small wonder that they conclude on the whole that they cannot understand what we are after, and that what they can understand they don't admire. They see us as eager and tenacious of social and monetary success as those who make no profession of unworldliness. They note our great charities, but they note an equal if not greater charity in the unbeliever; in such a class as, for example, the players of a theatre, which many profess to despise. In many quarters the advice has been traditional amongst the workmen to avoid a "Christian" employer. They discern us kindling into occasional spasmodic violence, not at social wrong or the enormous suffering of the world, but when we are accusing some particular Church of attempting to over-reach the others in the distribution of public funds. They find us noisily advertising our own wares and proclaiming the shoddiness of our neighbours; devoting at least as much energy to the undermining of their efforts as to the establishment of our own. They note large numbers of actively professing Christians who manifest no obvious fruits of the spirit; who are querulous or exacting masters or mistresses, whose lives pass in a cold routine of self-centred business; alien altogether from that eager and passionate enthu-siasm of humanity to which St. Paul affixed the great name of charity. The verdict may be superficial—it neglects, and unfairly neglects, the other side of the picture; but that it is a verdict endorsed explicitly and implicitly by a vast proportion of the population of London, I have no doubt whatever.

Religion has rejoiced in the clear knowledge of God and forgotten the fellowship of man. And the punish-ment has been, not the overthrow of its outward prosperity, but the slow withdrawal of that revelation of which it seemed to possess so secure a certainty. So that now we walk for the most part blindly, in the twilight, with no clear vision of a spiritual world and an unseen Father. It may be that the way back to the unclouded height will be found through the humble and deliberate search after that fellowship which has been offended and denied. Confronted with records of the religion of ¸London in this time of tranquillity, I can imagine no more sensational discovery than the first message of the Christian teaching and its judgment of the life of the day. Teaching so familiar as to become meaningless may assume a new significance. The feast to which first are to be called the friendless and poor ; the " Inasmuch " with its triumph and its mysterious warning ; the strange and solitary revelation of future judgment for a rich man who lived happily with want and misery lying unnoticed at his doors ; the woes pronounced on the complacent orthodox religions, so entirely convinced that they are fulfilling every jot and tittle of the law ; these have a meaning for Christianity in England at the dawn of the twentieth century. Assuredly it is as well that the old gospel should be given a trial before we proclaim the necessity for a new.

Men need never despair of the future of religion. Humanity, as a great philosopher affirmed, is not destined permanently to inhabit ruins. A world which is forgetting God does not involve a God who is forgetting the world. The movement of new spiritual advance may arise from without, not from within the Church ; as so many of the great restorative movements of the past generation, whose divine origin and guidance were unrecognised by the members of the organised Christian community. We may be very confident that the time of frost and present cold will break up before the warmth of another spring. The Church by neglect of its election and high calling may prolong the misery and increase the confusion of time. But no human wilfulness or weakness can for ever delay the restitution of all things and the triumph of the end. A new dawn will one day illuminate the vastness and desolation of the city. Each solitary life of its millions, perishing, as it seems, unheeded and alone, is destined at last to find the purpose of its being in union with the Infinite, alike its origin and its goal.

IN PERIL OF CHANGE

"*The lights begin to twinkle from the rocks:*
The long day wanes: the slow moon climbs: the deep
Moans round with many voices."

—TENNYSON.

IN PERIL OF CHANGE

A WRITER once complained of Charles Kingsley, that he wrote as if always anticipating the happening of something tremendous about the middle of next week. The quotation is a judgment, less of the excitement of the author than of the insensibility of the critic. For, throughout the age in which Kingsley lived, something tremendous always did happen in the middle of next week. The spectator, astonished or indifferent, confronted one of the greatest of all historical upheavals of the foundations of the mind of man. The Victorian Age, which now, alike in its sobriety and its sanguine dreams, stands so remote in the background of the memory of those who are living in an alien time, will be stamped in the record of the future as an age of hurrying change. In many respects that change has resulted in a profounder transformation than had been effected by all the preceding centuries. The gulf is greater between the England of to-day and the England which, in its secure and tranquil life, accepted without emotion the death of the last of the Georgian Kings, than between that England and the spacious days of Elizabeth, or the coming of Augustine with a new faith from over the sea. Eighty years ago England was a quiet community, chiefly agriculturist, scattered over a little island. The traveller journeyed to Edinburgh or to Rome by the same methods of progress as those which had served the messengers of the Conqueror. The peasant flung his seed into the soil, and hoped for the direction of the forces of Nature, the rain and kindly sun, towards the attainment of the harvest, as at any day through all the centuries. The generations of the common people gathered for petition or praise, accepting the unchallenged announcement that the visible ruin of death was but a prelude to an awful judgment; when all the actual deeds done in the flesh would be brought to account; and the books set and the seals broken and the verdict proclaimed, which should decide the fate of the poor, pitiful human soul throughout unending time.

The age which has just gone by, with all its meannesses and heroisms, its periods of great passion and intervening tranquillities, has exhibited the passing of this earlier England. And now, those who anywhere attempt to penetrate beneath the surface, with all its humour and glitter and material opulence, realise that they are estimating forces and equilibriums in a new nation. In the earlier period such changes as were accomplished were visible and open; there were manifest tremors and violence in the world of politics and religion, controversies through the fabric of organic society. So Chartist Agitations, Oxford Movements, Anti-Corn Law Leagues, Liberal Aggressions, Evolution and "the New Reformation," with the noise of the fall of privilege and the songs of triumph of the victors, proclaimed to all men that great events were toward. But in the later time these portents of change had passed away. Men's minds turned towards other horizons: expansion "beyond the sky-line" and the harvesting of their rich fortune of prosperity. And the sound of the great storms of the nineteenth century died slowly into silence, as the rough seas subsided into the mere ground-swell of past disturbance, and this again to the quiet ripple of the waves along the shore. Content with the present, convinced that enough had been done, a little wearied with the tempests of reform, England settled down to sleep.

Yet to the sensitive eye this vanishing of visible upheaval has in no way checked or changed the processes of development and decay. The thirty years of reaction will appear to the future as fruitful in the seeds of transition as the previous thirty years of progress. For events in the world of thought and opinion—the only world which ultimately matters, which will inevitably now, or in the coming time, mould the world of material things in accordance with its claims—do not cease to march forward because men have become weary of the effort of adjustment. Throughout this passing time of order forces of creation and destruction have been playing upon the plastic material of the minds of men. Outwardly, things appear settled and unchanged. The ancient institutions of the realm, the Constitution, the feudal system, the Protestant faith, the Established Church, stand, it would seem, even more secure than in that restless past when the utility of all old things was being roughly called in question. Yet men need to remember—need again and again to remember—that a nation, no more than an individual, can bid time stand still, and proclaim the permanence of the summer days. There is an irony of judgment in the spectacle of all those past brief periods of peace, in which a people, on the verge of some vast disquietude, riddled with forces which are hastening the upheavals of the abyss, stands proud and satisfied, confident that at length it has attained the certainties of an afternoon, golden and unending. To-day, were we but as sensitive to disturbance in the world of man's profound convictions, as to the outward modifications of the forms of society in which those convictions are clothed, our ears might well be deafened by the noise of the crash of the elements, of growing and of dying worlds.

And, whether delayed by idleness or man's natural fears of the violence of an unknown future, and so postponed again and yet again by those whose first demand is peace at least in their time ; sooner or later, without any doubt at all, the outward fabric must respond to the realities of the inner life. Ruins must collapse and be cleared away, and new dwelling places be constructed adequate to man's desires. To the eye which can scan the larger stretches of time, and see the end in the beginning, the process has been already completed before a stone has been disturbed. The French Revolution was accomplished when society laughed with Voltaire, instead of lamenting, over the Church's immoralities ; and applauded Rousseau's proclamation, with lean, upraised claw, of the coming of an age of innocence and gold. And all the intervening time of troublous dreams, of financiers oppressed with a national bankruptcy, and bishops timidly essaying a reform of manners, and the coming of a new king and an age of enlightenment amid a universal rejoicing, were but the passing scenes in a drama whose fifth act had been already composed. A similar insight can be applied to the things of to-day. The passing of the first peasant, unchallenged, into the labyrinth of the city, his discovery there of independence and an adequate return for his labour, was the passing of the feudal system in England. The company which witnessed the admission of the first Dissenter into Parliament witnessed also, all unwittingly, the fall of the Established Church. And the perplexities of the author of " Colenso's Arithmetic " over the reconciliation of irreconcilable numbers in the estimates of the wanderings and the fightings of the children of Israel, marked the close of a particular type of Protestant civilisation which had been dominant in England for three centuries.

Here are three institutions built out of living forces into forms and systems congruous with a former energetic life, which now stand, to the impartial eye, undermined in their foundations. Each had been fiercely assailed during the time immediately passed; and each, while the springs of an inner life remained, stood secure against all the forces of reason and of hatred which fell upon them. In the mid-century, the fury of the middle classes and of manufacturing England threw itself against the old Landed System. Cobden, after the freeing of trade, was already joyfully proclaiming " the crash of feudalism " as the completion of his policy. The landed interests were tense with the consciousness of the coming of change, and banding themselves together for a final, desperate, and, as most would have confessed, hopeless resistance. Yet the fifty years have passed, and, with their passing, all the noise of conflict. The system remains, and in practice almost unchallenged. Little more than thirty years ago, the visible end of the Established Church appeared but a matter of days, The destruction in Ireland had seemed but a prelude to a greater destruction this side of the sea. In the records and memoirs of the 'seventies, while the forces of the Liberation Society and other assailants breathe the consciousness of victory, the records of the Church's leaders are full of mournful forebodings of an imminent and inevitable destruction. Yet the kaleidoscope has changed; and the noise and forecast of coming success have died into silence. And to-day the Liberation Society has become a negligeable force in politics, and all questions of reform or disestablishment of the national religion relegated to purely academic discussion. Little more than a generation back, again, the popular faith seemed tottering upon the verge of ruin. The adherents of the " New Reformation " were openly anticipating a renewal of the large upheavals of the sixteenth century. The astounding advance of the sciences, the examination by the new critical methods of the ancient Biblical narratives, the spread of education and a more humane culture would leave, it was held, the popular religion as a mere survival of absurd and forgotten things. Yet the days have gone, and the visible change has not hastened. Protestantism stands entrenched and secure; its temples increasing in number and in splendour; its adherents, it would seem, confident in themselves and in the triumph of their cause. It is the survivors of the crusaders of these earlier days who now, in some sadness, contemplate the walls they had set themselves to destroy, still high and inviolate; and who now wonder why all the efforts of their forces and of Time have thus forlornly failed.

So these questions have drifted out of the region of living politics. The reformer who enters upon his career with arguments concerning land reform or religious equality is likely to be roughly reminded that some time has elapsed since the death of Disraeli, or that he is not living in the days of the Prince

Consort. The word "Disestablishment" would produce, in the mind of the present-day statesman, the same bewildering effect as the word "delicacy" upon Matthew Arnold's friend. For the first time, those committed to the maintenance of the older order are prepared to relax their efforts, as they assure themselves that at length the danger is passed, and, for many generations, the victory assured.

Yet, while the outward signs of struggle have thus died away, hidden and unseen forces have been effecting a more fatal destruction. To-day, indeed, the end is far more clearly assured than in all the time of the conflict. While the leaves were green and the sap flowed freely in the branches, the tempest beat down in vain. The tree stands now in the security of a quiet air. But, if the vital forces are withdrawn, and within the wood has turned to a little dust, all the fair outward seeming may hold a delusive danger: a breath of summer wind may ensure a ruin which could not be accomplished before its time by all the storms of winter.

And such appears, to some at least, to be the condition to-day of ancient systems, whose stability at the present receives scarcely a passing challenge.

The first, and perhaps the most far-reaching of these, is the English Landed System : the feudal organisation, with all its implications of leadership and obedience, as embedded in the very heart of the old life of England. Here is one place in which the thirty years of silence have effected more momentous changes than all the hubbub of the former time. Rents were high in the early 'seventies, land increasingly valuable. The landed interest had attained supremacy in Parliament for the first time in a generation. The great uprising

of the agricultural labourer had been successfully overcome; and, with the breaking of the Union, the farmers
were rejoicing at the battening down of the hatches
upon the revolting slaves. The old tripartite division
of landlord, farmer, and landless labourer might have
appeared as something in the nature of a Providential
order, convenient to the genius and conditions of the
English race.

A statesman has well said, that if the great changes
which have fallen on the English landed interest during
the last few decades had been essayed by legislation and
human demands, instead of by blind and impersonal
forces, they could only have been accomplished through
revolution and civil war. An immense fall in prices
has resulted in a widespread destruction. Rents and
farmers' profits have alike diminished, in places below
any possible continuance of the old system. The persistence of feudalism under these circumstances could
only have been affected by two stringent provisions: the
one, the closing of the ports of England to foreign food;
the other, the barricading of the entrances of all the
cities to the agricultural labourer. With organisation
destroyed and all hope of improvement abandoned, the
labourer has quietly taken revenge on his masters.
With hatches battened down, the slave has crawled out
of the window. So that now an exodus of all the young
and able-bodied, all who possess energy and hope and
confidence in themselves, pours an ever-increasing flood
from the deserted fields into the streets of the towns.
Imagination has been struck by the dolorous case of
Ireland, a population, it would appear, vanishing from
its own land. Isolate rural England, and exactly the
same problem is revealed. It is the cities alone which
retain the influx, and keep the people of England, a

landless people, still within the borders of their own land. Wages rise steadily to attract the forlorn remnant, land passes from arable to pasture, from pasture to scanty sheep runs, or developes special cultivations, dependent upon nomadic labour lured outwards for a moment from the slums of the cities. But still the famine of men deepens ; and from east to west the cry goes up, that what is left is scarce worth retaining, that the departure of the present generation will witness the end of an age.

Here is the change at the silent basis, that assiduous and docile stratum of serf labour upon which the whole complex structure was reared. A change no less profound has been effected, meanwhile, around the summit. The structure is being replaced, piece by piece, by other material ; until, at the end, without visible collapse, the whole thing has become transformed. The old country gentleman, the type of the lesser landed aristocracy of England, is already becoming a thing of the past. On the one hand has come the blow of the fall in land values. On the other, an increasing comfort and extravagance of society has stimulated a more rapid squandering of fortune. He is vanishing from Parliament. His voice is no longer potent in the councils of his party. His place is being taken by the men of the new wealth—rich brewers, financiers, a Rutherfoord Harris or a Harry Marks. He is vanishing also from the land of his inheritance. One day his house and lands are sold to one of the new rich, desirous of establishing a position and founding a family ; and he has passed from the horizon of those who regretfully, or with bitter memories, are compelled to own allegiance to another master. The larger estates, indeed, still remain for the most part secure. The American marriages, the gold-fields of South Africa, the harvest of the increasing ground rents of the cities, have here prevented the crumbling of the whole concern into ruin. But although some kind of material prosperity is thus secured, and round the great houses a race of dependants can still be reared, and the occupations of game-preserving or gardening or the repairing of motors replace the direct cultivation of the soil, yet the spirit of the old cannot be transformed to the exotic life of the new. The country house, instead of being a centre of local interest, is now an appendage of the capital. A tiny piece of London is transferred in the late summer and autumn to a more salubrious air and the adjacency of the coverts. Rural England appears as slowly passing into gardens and shooting grounds, with intervening tracts of sparse grass-lands, committed to the rearing of cattle and of pheasants, rather than of men. Fifty years ago, one class of reformer could still, without absurdity, find the solution of social discontent in a revived feudalism. A Carlyle or a Ruskin would passionately plead with the gentlemen of England to take up the burden of government committed to a landed aristocracy. What observer of the England of to-day would have the hardihood to proclaim a similar message ? Frenzied efforts of sectional influences attempt to deal with the special hurt that grips them. The farmer demands Protection and such impossible follies. The landlord seeks grants-in-aid in relief of the rates. The country clergyman laments the vanishing of nearly half his income in a generation. The friends of the labourer desire more and better cottages, or a modified educational system, or the music-hall entertainment, as alone able to keep him contented in his position. They are one and all blind to the fact that they are confronting, not a series of special discontents, but a whole dying order. Changes, which they can neither comprehend nor control, are creating an England alien from the England which they have ever known.

The change could be accepted with tolerance, and even with some humour, but for the fact that the ruins and the playgrounds cumber the ground, and forbid the creation of the new order. The new millionaires might play at patronage, the model village be spread out for the delight of the town visitor, the farms and fields crumble into picturesque decay, were it not that the elimination of any free and healthy country-bred life means the loss of elements of stability and human well-being vital to the future of the race. The land available is limited : and the effort demanded for the creation either of a scientific agriculture on a large scale, or of a race of free yeomen or peasant farmers, finding economic security in co-operation, supplementing the work of the fields with home industries, is effectually damped by the opposition, on the one hand, of those who know not that their day is over, on the other of those entirely convinced that their day has come. So that there is no active effort to establish a system which everywhere abroad, from Brittany to Bulgaria, is alone proving adequate to the exigencies of the newer time. To the patriot the spectacle is one of desolation. He knows the necessity of a continual stream of vigorous life to replenish the furnace of the cities. He recognises that that stream is likely to vanish through the drainage of its sources of supply. He is convinced also that the restoration of the people to their land, in which at the present they move as aliens, is one of the insistent needs of social advance. He can examine in diverse districts of England, in

Dorset, and Hants, and Lincoln, and Worcester, solitary experiments which have shown conspicuous success. Yet he finds no interest in his schemes, no response to his appeal. He is beating the thin air in vain. Reformers like Mr. Rider Haggard are compelled to confess that the whole subject is regarded as caviare to the general, that the man who would determine to thrust it forward runs the risk of being branded as a bore.

Such of the land. What of the Church during the same tranquil time? With the active onslaught upon the Establishment dying away, there have here been changes equally noteworthy, equally suggestive of some future explosive action. Briefly, it may be said that these changes have developed two deep-flowing and diverse currents. While the clergy, as a whole, and the more militant laity, have been drifting towards a Catholic position, the great bulk of the laity, faithful and unfaithful, have remained Protestant or indifferent. This statement does not, indeed, imply an endorsement of the follies of those who see a vast "Romanising" conspiracy amongst the bishops and clergy, or who contemplate with wrathful impotence the announcement of a dogma, or the elaboration of a ritual, which they hold to be puerile, dangerous, or foreign. Extremists must always accompany any large movement of spiritual assertion, and always scandalise those who demand, first of all, sobriety and adherence to the orthodox ways. It is not a "Romanising" but a "Catholic" revival, which the student of religions will emphasise. The attempt is deliberate to emphasise the Catholic elements in the compromise of the sixteenth century, and all those particular conceptions of religious life which gather round the real existence of a visible Church. On the one side, now, are the Catholic assertions. The Church is seen as a definite organism with a divinely constituted ministry. The Sacraments appear as channels of a supernatural life. Symbolism is welcomed as the expression of a deliberate ritual of worship. There is insistence upon a disciplined life ; with the observance of seasons and times ; the setting forth of an austerity, a fervour of devotion, a humility, courses of self-examination, as the way towards the perfect life. On the other, is the opinion of the vast bulk of present public opinion ; to which the Church and its ministers are matters of very human construction, of no particular authority or veneration ; and the Sacraments at most pleasant memorial ceremonies ; and ritual is absurd ; and times of abstinence or special devotion entirely repugnant ; and the highest aim of religion the setting forth of a sober and not too exaggerated piety, sweetening the struggle of the life of the day. Here is an antinomy which no legislation can reconcile. The hope, still stoutly maintained by a few forlorn fighters, that it will be possible by special legislation, Church Discipline Bills and the like, either to purge the Church of England of all its Catholic elements, or to reduce these by threats and persecutions to a decent Protestantism, shows a pathetic ignorance of the actual possibilities of the future. Could some such shattering decision be obtained by law, or embodied in legislation, as that which has recently stripped half its endowments from the United Free Church of Scotland, and the Catholic position be declared untenable within the Establishment, without any doubt at all those thus dispossessed would go forth contentedly into the wilderness ; and the remnant would find itself in a position somewhat parallel to the " Wee

Kirk," with large endowments and no ministers to enjoy
them. No one can study the position of the movement
which its opponents delight to call "the Catholic reaction," without being conscious of the existence of a
vigorous life. Its congregations are large and enthu-
siastic. Its churches, many recently built in slum or
suburb, are erected and maintained largely by present-
day contributions. Most of the vital force of religion, as
at present manifest in the Church of England, the effort
towards social regeneration, the militant combat against
unbelief, has enrolled under its banners. Few sights
are at once more ludicrous and more pathetic, than the
efforts of the faithful ladies and laymen to stem the tide.
The appeals in bulky correspondence in the *Times*, the
description of enormities seen in some village church,
the money so freely expended upon "Protestant"
defence, the rich livings awaiting the skilled advocate
of the orthodox belief, all fail; because lacking in that
one element of spiritual ardour and enthusiasm and confidence in its cause, which neither indignation can
kindle nor money buy.

Beyond this fundamental and dangerous divergence,
time has brought other changes. The old position of
the Church as an accepted element of a social order, the
traditional attitude of the clergyman in the fabric of the
country life, is passing with that order's decline. The
clergy have lost heavily by the fall of the tithe and of
land values; and their poverty now presents a separate
and importunate problem. The layman offers a steady
and successful resistance to any suggestion that he shall
take upon himself the burden of their support. The
supply of clergy actually decreases, despite the enormous
increase of population. Attendance at the Church's
worship seems likewise to exhibit a steady decline.

Thought has driven far beyond the boundaries of the old formularies and historic creeds. To the men of the twentieth century the assertions and warnings of the mediæval age sound strangely remote and incongruous.

At the same time, the actual present relationship of the Church to the legislature of the nation is becoming more and more conspicuously impossible. It is tied with the bonds of a vanished past, unable either to reform itself or to obtain relief through legislation. In each specific instance, a Parliament, composed of men of all religions and of none, gravely or frivolously discusses the expediency of action, in debates which are at once unedifying and ridiculous. Those who have deliberately repudiated any connection or membership are the first to advocate the modifications of its theology or the tuning of its pulpits. The deadlock has extended even into the manipulations of its machinery. A tiny Bill for the authorisation of two new Bishoprics, for which the funds had been privately subscribed, was lengthily discussed, bitterly opposed, and only carried, after years of delay, by the definite determination of the Government to push it through at any cost. Nor is it possible to see how, without the fortunate accident of a Prime Minister unusually concerned with the Church's welfare, it would be possible for such a Bill to be ever carried again. No future Ministry, it will be safe to say, whether Protectionist or Radical, will be much concerned in occupying time or arousing resistance with minor measures of Church organisation. Beyond is the universal chaos of opinion amongst those who can at once appeal to, and refuse to be bound by, formularies stereotyped into uniformity three centuries ago. Each particular reformer sets forth his gospel, and challenges his opponents either themselves to fall back upon the position from which he has diverged, or to bring his orthodoxy to the test and judgment of the paralysed secular arm.

The situation has become, in these latter years, manifestly impossible. A movement has arisen within the boundaries of the Church, and obtained allegiance from all parties, towards the forwarding of an internal reform. But, in its actual progress, the movement seems drifting farther and farther away from an apprehension of the hard realities of the situation. The effort has been directed, and rightly, towards the formation of some kind of National Council, a union of reformed Convocations, or some specially constituted Synod, to which may be committed the maintenance of discipline and adjustment of formularies, and ultimately the control of material endowment. But the distrust of the various parties of the Church, each for the other, is so profound, that the preliminary difficulty has not yet been solved of the constitution of such a Council, and the qualification of the body which its members shall be authorised to represent. The States-General once called together, it is feared, movement must of necessity originate :—from Council to National Assembly, from Assembly to Convention, and an ecclesiastical Reign of Terror. The one party, therefore, more and more distrustful of the religion of the average complacent citizen, has demanded sometimes that the franchise shall be limited to those confirmed, who have the right to communicate; more frequently, perhaps, to those who actually communicate with some assiduity. The faith which believes that the State will ever again incorporate in statutory definition a body whose qualifications shall be that each " shall. communicate at the least three times in the year, of which Easter to be one," is only surpassed in its naïve simplicity by the faith that, to a body so constituted, will be handed over the goodwill and fabrics and endowments of the National Church of England. On the other side are those who desire for the suffrage merely the qualification of a ratepayer, accompanied by a refusal to "contract out," and deliberately to repudiate membership. Inheritors, though unknowingly, of the traditions of Hooker and of Arnold, these discern the Church as a reflection in another aspect, a more humane and spiritual aspect, of the activities of the State, the whole constituted people. They are prepared, in conformity with such an ideal, to carry through large modifications. They would subdue the defiant doctrines to the requirements of modern thought. They would modify the moral law of the Church—such as the law concerning divorce and marriage—into harmony with the slow moving changes of the main stream of the national morality. They would strive to include certainly all Christian, perhaps all theistic or ethical, bodies in this national body. They are impatient of subtle theological divisions which separate sect from sect, and set them thundering each against the other. They desire to work towards an "undenominational" religion of a cheerful and not too exacting character, which shall emphasise the more distinctively British virtues, provide the emotional satisfaction of a simple spiritual worship, conduct the work of charity, and maintain missions and the standard of morality and right reverence for the accepted order, amongst the working classes and the poor.

The one party emphasises the adjective—"National"; the other the substantive—"Church." The obstacle to the one change is the passive resistance of the laity; to the other, the active resistance of the clergy. Yet it seems difficult to see how movement can be long delayed, and how movement can proceed upon any except upon one of these two lines. Upon which of these the choice ultimately falls, depends the character of [that Church's future. The paths steadily diverge from the present point of junction. If the first prove triumphant, one can picture the Church of the future, a separated body in doctrine and discipline and, ultimately, undoubtedly in moral standard ; becoming more and more alien from the main stream of progressing opinion. With some endowment assured, and a great stimulus of ardour and enthusiasm amongst its members, it is safe to prophesy conspicuous activity and devotion, a rising standard of life and obligation. One can discern a body raising always a banner in open defiance of the newer changes in moral law, and gathering round it as a centre all the re-actions from the hurried progress of things, all picturesque rallies towards the worship of an older time, all to whom the lethargy of the decent and the ignobly decent, and the severe technical outlook of a scientific world, are remote and hostile. Ultimately, no doubt, though only perhaps after centuries and through change, both on the one side or the other, some kind of working union can be prophesied between this isolated Church on the one hand and the Church which at present centres in Rome on the other ; both fighting a battle for preservation in the midst of a civilisation entering upon that "positive" stage which is the hall-mark of old age and coming death. Such is the anticipation of that most courageous and in-dividual of all social prophets, Mr. H. G. Wells ; who sees in the "New Republio" the Catholic or Roman Catholic the sole form of Christianity surviving, gather-ing round it all the ardours and devotions which still maintain a condition of revolt against the furious energies and purposes of the new scientific creed.

There is, however, an equally probable alternative. "The nation looked at from the secular side is the State," wrote Bishop Creighton, "looked at from the religious side, it is the Church ; and separation between the two is impossible." Development upon these other lines would herald a process of adjustment of the Church's formularies and discipline, through violent and bitter change, to the common sense of the time. One can foresee the vanishing of much that appears outworn. Ancient prayers and articles would be thrown over as out of date. Creeds would be modified towards a studied vagueness. Petition would be adjusted towards conceptions of a reign of law in nature, and a time of security in society. Such changes might involve cataclysms. But there is no cataclysm (even to a clean sweep of the Bench of Bishops, or the driving out of a half or a third of the clergy from their livings) to which the Church's past history is unable to afford a parallel. It is possible to picture a Church of the future after the work of "adjustment" had been completed. It would be a Church in close touch with the stream of dominant opinion, with a flexible adaptation to changing conditions. It would still be playing a vital part in all "national" celebrations, with a chaplain for the prayers of Parliament and the pomp of Coronation for King or President. One sees a progress towards a comprehensive vagueness, with a diffused philanthropy and humanitarian sentiment, rather than any high spiritual ardour. It would be much occupied in distribution of alms, and communications from the nation of the wealthy to the differentiated nation of the poor. There would seem, under these conditions, no inherent obstacle to the fulfilment of the genial visions of James Mill : with a Church "without dogmas or ceremonies," and the clergy employed to give lectures on ethics, botany, political economy, and so forth, besides holding Sunday meetings, with decent dances, specially invented, and "social meals," with tea and coffee substituted for bread and wine. Nor would moral adjustments fail to follow the intellectual ; and the vision of " the sleeper " in the popular novel, waking in the days to come, and cheered by conversation with " one of the subsidiary wives of the Bishop of London," might not prove entirely a fantastic dream.

For if there is one thing manifest in the world of thought to-day in England, it is the steady if silent collapse of the foundations of the ancient national faith. The intellectual position once changed, it is but a matter of time for the actions and limitations to collapse also. The new morality is already commencing to regard as things trivial or tedious those survivals which have lost intelligible meaning, and are merely maintained by the inertia of the resistance of the average man to disturbance. Many years ago Matthew Arnold had excited a violent hatred by the candour of his diagnosis. "Its organisations," he asserted of the popular Protestantism, " strong and active as they look, are touched with the finger of death ; its fundamental ideas, sounding forth still every week from thousands of pulpits, have in them no sympathy and no power for the progressive thought of humanity." Ardent desire for its fulfilment doubtless had ante-dated the prophecy. The leisured and wealthy classes were to shed their conventional religion as a garment at one end of the scale. At the other, the great mass of the "populace" were to develop into aggressive and self-conscious life, without even having entered the universe of religious experience. But, between these, the successful and expanding middle classes were for many decades to dominate the national life and policy, and impart to that life their peculiar flavour and tone, and establish their definite type of Puritan civilisation; so that one extremity of society would grow ashamed of violation of its moral mandates, the other afraid. That great tradition of austerity and reticence which, alarmed at the demand for fuller existence and the large curiosity of the Elizabethan Age, had "entered the prison of Puritanism and had the key turned upon its spirit for two hundred years," emerged at last with the vigour of the stored-up energies of generations of clean living. It found its qualities triumphant in a commercial age. Never did the prospects of Protestantism look fairer than in the age in which Arnold was announcing its dissolution. It had torn its way into the Universities and public services, from which it had been excluded. It had re-entered, it had in a sense absorbed, the main current of the national life. It had woven into the very fabric of the national system of Education a religious teaching entirely acceptable to its desires.

But, in essentials, we can now see that Arnold was right. In the triumph lay the seeds of decay. The coming out into the open day had meant of necessity the exposure to the disintegrating forces of the rain and sun. The old religion, with its affirmations and denials, of Protestant and of Puritan England—the civilisation definitely dependent upon that particular outlook on the world—is to-day visibly dissolving. Within a generation its dominant doctrines have been quietly cast aside.

Predestination and Calvinism, in their unflinching forms, have practically gone. Even in Scotland, with its relentless logic, the true home of its birth, they are repudiated by the main stream of the Presbyterian tradition. In England they seek refuge in the remoter Christian sects. And the new Calvinism of the natural sciences, with its blind forces and destinies, more inexorable and terrible even than the ancient conception of an inflexible directing Will, has not yet entered into the schemes of any of the popular religions. Gone, also, is that doctrine of Everlasting Punishment in a lake of material fire, to which are immediately committed at the moment of death all those who have not accepted the scheme of salvation. A few years ago, the most typical figure of English Protestantism, Mr. Charles Spurgeon, could thus picture to his terrified audience the "Resurrection of the Dead":—

"When thou diest thy soul will be tormented alone: that will be a hell for it; but at the day of judgment thy body will join thy soul, and then thou wilt have twin-hells, thy soul sweating drops of blood and thy body suffused with agony. In fire exactly like that which we have on earth, thy body will lie asbestos-like, for ever unconsumed, all thy veins roads for the feet of pain to travel on, every nerve-string on which the devil shall for ever play his diabolical tune of hell's unutterable lament."

From what representative Nonconformist pulpit could a similar statement be put forth to-day? The change has come, and with a rush, within a lifetime.

And going or gone, also, before the labours of a persistent critical method, is that belief in a literal and verbal inspiration of the books of the Hebrew Scriptures, which invested with the glamour of a Divine origin every tangled genealogy ; and accepted esoteric meaning for every unedifying incident ; and discerned the Mosaic code as originating in the writings of the finger of God upon tables of stone, amid the thunders and lightnings of Mount Sinai.

With these recognised changes within the fold have gone larger changes amongst those outside, who never accepted with whole-hearted conviction the affirmations of the faithful. To these the abandonment of Calvinism has meant the practical repudiation of any directing will in human affairs. The repudiation of the fear of Hell has meant the fading of any conception of retribution for the sins done in the flesh—the future apprehended as an unending sleep, or the asphodel and lilies of a good-tempered God. And the work of criticism has meant the destruction of all authority in the Hebraic or Christian scheme of life, a rejection of all evidence of a special Divine revelation. The conception of sin has changed from that of "a monster to be mused on" into "an impotence to be got rid of"; and effort towards the increase of enjoyment, personal or general, is set forth as the foundation of the new ethical code.

These changes are being assisted by the natural development inherent in an age of security and triumphant material success. The menace of social upheavals, ruin, and the breaking up of laws, sounds faint and far away. In the life of the cities the forces which make for disturbance — the larger disquietudes, Nature and the wind that blows from the hills, the insistent presence of the Dead—are being effectively banished. To-day the older austerity is deliquescing into an increasing, if still half-timid, determination to throw off the ancient restraints. The insistence on the English Sunday of silence and spiritual exercises ; the whole-hearted condemnation of the theatre, dancing, card-playing, all literature and art unsteeped in reticence ; the hatred of the public-house, of betting and gambling ; the branding of the supreme viciousness of any violation of the monogamic order of society, or an union unblest by Church and State—all this belongs to a vanishing England. The march of change is not everywhere evident. There are occasional rallies, and fortresses which still present an unyielding front to a change branded as a National Apostasy. But each year and each day exhibit some subtle advance, as one man after another realises that the sanction has vanished for some particular restraint, and that nothing is keeping him from pursuing the desirable course but the forces of custom and routine.

This is not to say, indeed, that the whole fabric of the Protestant religion is immediately collapsing in England ; or that the great Nonconformist bodies, in which that Protestantism is most conspicuously vocal, are about to wither into nothingness. It is to say, on the one hand, that an increasing population is developing, to whom the doctrines of Protestantism are unbelievable, and the practical worship that is dependent upon these doctrines repugnant ; on the other, that, within those bodies themselves, there is fermenting a large process of change. There will be " Independents " and " Baptists " and " Methodists " at the close of the century. But the Methodism will not be that of Mr. Hugh Price Hughes, nor the Independence that of Dr. Binney, nor the Baptist's faith that of Mr. Charles Spurgeon. It would be foolish to assert that all is loss or all is gain in this momentous change. There is, indeed, a liberation from restraint, an advance towards freedom, combined with a wider culture and curiosity, and a general mellowing and humanising of individual life. But there is a loss also in the dying away of a contempt for pleasure, and a consciousness of purpose in the world, and of the infinite difference between good and evil, and the infinite value of the human soul. Mr. Burden, in Mr. Belloc's story, the sturdy ironmonger of Upper Norwood, has been the butt of all the sharp wits and satires of the age. He is at least a more reputable figure than his son, Cosmo, with his weak thirst for ineffectual pleasure, or Mr. Barnett and Lord Benthorpe and Mr. Harbury, with their cant of an expanding Empire and Imperial destinies, and their inner cheerlessness and greed.

Such are some of the things now in England in peril of change—the Landed System, the Established Church, the Popular Religion. There is opportunity for a statesman who would rightly apprehend the situation, and definitely interpret to the nation the danger of the collapse of ruins. Yet, confronting present affairs and the temper of the people, one can but emphasise something of the almost forlorn heroism of the enterprise. The land implicates a thousand vested interests, crying if assailed. The falling feudalism is backed by the wealth of the newer commerce. The increasing cities care nothing for the ruin of rural England. In the country, every day weakens the forces essential to reform. Twenty or fifteen years ago, those vanishing villages could still be kindled by some intelligible hope. The " Land for the People " was a popular watchword, influential, at least, at successive elections. To-day

another generation has fled the fields ; and written all
over the crumbling buildings and passionless people, is
the apathy which is content to wait for the end. From
what unimaginable crevasses of the city labyrinths—so
runs the obvious challenge—from what secluded hamlets
removed from all the past destruction, are you going to
lure forth the companies of stout peasants and yeomen
with energies adequate to the England of your dreams ?
Compared to this, the work in Ireland was child's play ;
yet in Ireland the transformation was effected only after
one of the fiercest fights in all history, an incredible
suffering, an incredible devotion of a whole nation prolonged through twenty years. What species of "Land
League " or united "Nationalist " party, fighting for
Agrarian Reform, is probable or possible in the England
of to-day ?

Nor is the question of the Establishment any more
hopeful. Here is an organisation to be torn up, whose
roots reach deep down into the basis of society. A
thousand hazardous questions immediately arise. What
of the future, of endowments, of fabrics, the care or
ownership of cathedrals and village churches ? From
what material, with what qualification, are you to
construct the living Church that is to remain after all
your efforts ? What again of the great Dissenting
bodies, and their claim to represent at least a vigorous
portion of the religious life of the nation ? What of
adjustment of formulas and obligations, of marriage
laws, Thirty-nine Articles, or the Apostles' or Athanasian
Creed ? Here is a task, compared to which the mere
denouncing of the Concordat in France appears but a
little thing; a task, indeed, which might appear only
possible in the white hot fires of revolution.

Yet in all these, as was said at another time in peril

of change—standing still is the one thing more impossible than going forward.

Ingenious efforts are often attempted to disentangle historical parallels to the present in the past, and from these to emphasise confidence or disquietude concerning the future. Writers have recounted the story of these latter days in England in the language of Gibbon concerning the dying Roman Empire. Here, also, can be found agriculture declining at home, and all the people crowding into the capital; fed from the corn ships of Alexandria or Argentina. Here, too, is the decay in the ancient austerities and pieties; the sudden and intoxicating consciousness of a supreme greatness, of an Imperialism exacting tribute from the four corners of the earth; and the breeding of a parasitic race of little street-bred people, demanding before all things food and pleasure :— free meals and professional games and vicarious " little wars." The menace is not lacking also, as in the famous forebodings of the Roman historian, in the rise of shadowy and inscrutable nations, the barbarians in the cold North. In the East are the yellow races awakening from slumber. In the West is the newest-born child of all the hardiest of the peoples. Each may be able, not only through the old methods of actual invasion, but in the new methods of trade competition, to strike a fatal blow at the heart of Empire.

Others have found a similarity between the commencement of the sixteenth and the commencement of the twentieth centuries in England. In the former as in the later day a Church, heavily weighted with the burden of the things of a dead past, is struggling towards internal reform. A new learning has suddenly rolled back the dim horizons and boundaries of thought, and opened limitless vistas. And in those days also, a moment's breathing space was given before the changes in the world of thought became translated into the world of action, and the new knowledge crashed into the chaos of the Reformation.

Others, again, have found much that the observer would do well to study in comparing the England of to-day with the France of the years immediately preceding the Revolution. An increasing burden of national expenditure, and the development of an absentee landlordism, there hastened the coming of change. A kind of general atrophy of governing power amongst the governing classes had ensured the failure of the forces of resistance. An improvement of economic condition in a momentary "Age of Gold" had brought hope to those dim and submerged classes among which hope rarely comes. And, indeed, one can realise that if only hope—hope, that most dangerous of all revolutionary forces—were once to penetrate among the poor of the cities of England, some explosion of elemental forces might boil up beneath the thin layer of the ordered society of to-day, and again amid the furnace flame reveal the "heights and depths which are still in man."

A deeper examination in each case will show the impossibility of thus interpreting the future from the lessons of the past. Never before has met together that particular combination of forces which in any particular age, in their contact and interaction, are creating a new world. The new world of the future we confront with as little knowledge of its possibilities as was possessed by any prophet of the past. In the time immediately before centuries of quiet men foretold the beginnings of a universal desolation, the coming of the twilight of the gods. On the verge of vast and shattering cataclysms men proclaimed that never was the sky more serene, the continuance of security more sure.

Examination of the actual present can but emphasise evidence of equilibrium disturbed. The study of the past can but guarantee that through rough courses or smooth, heedless of violence and pain, in methods unexpected and often through hazardous ways, equilibrium will be attained.

The substance of much of this book has appeared in the " Contemporary Review," the " Independent Review," the " Commonwealth," the " Speaker," the " Pilot," and the " Daily News." I am indebted to the courtesy of the editors for permission to make use of it in this volume.

UNWIN BROTHERS, LIMITED, THE GRESHAM PRESS, WOKING AND LONDON.

.

ImThe Story.com

Personalized Classic Books in many genre's

Unique gift for kids, partners, friends, colleagues

Customize:

- Character Names

- Upload your own front/back cover images (optional)

- Inscribe a personal message/dedication on the
  inside page (optional)

Customize many titles Including
- Alice in Wonderland
- Romeo and Juliet
- The Wizard of Oz
- A Christmas Carol
- Dracula
- Dr. Jekyll & Mr. Hyde
- And more...

CPSIA information can be obtained at www.ICGtesting.com
Printed in the USA
BVOW08s1145050813

327861BV00016B/238/P